JULIAN OF NORWICH,
THEOLOGIAN

JULIAN OF NORWICH, THEOLOGIAN

DENYS TURNER

Yale
UNIVERSITY PRESS
New Haven and London

Yale University Press books may be purchased in quantity for educational, business,
or promotional use. For information, please e-mail sales.press@yale.edu (U.S. office)
or sales@yaleup.co.uk (U.K. office).

Set in Fournier type by Duke & Company, Devon, Pennsylvania.
Printed in the United States of America.

The Library of Congress has cataloged the hardcover edition as follows:

Turner, Denys, 1942–
Julian of Norwich, theologian / Denys Turner.
p.   cm.
Includes bibliographical references and index.
ISBN 978-0-300-16391-9 (cloth : alk. paper) 1. Julian, of Norwich, b. 1343. Revelations
of divine love. 2. Sin—Christianity. 3. Salvation—Christianity. I. Title.
BV4832.3.J863T87 2011
230'.2092—dc22

2010049526

ISBN 978-0-300-19255-1 (pbk.)

A catalogue record for this book is available from the British Library.

10 9 8 7 6 5 4 3 2 1

This boke is begonne by Goddes gifte and his grace,
but it is not yet performed, as to my sight.
—Julian of Norwich, *A Revelation of Love*

CONTENTS

PREFACE

SOME OF MY ACADEMIC colleagues seem to know what they think before they talk. Others, among whom I count myself, need to talk in order to know what they think. As with speech, so with writing. Because I did not know what I really thought about the theology of Julian of Norwich's *A Revelation of Love*,[1] I decided to write a book to find out. At first I envisaged a short work. But as I wrote and came to better understand the complexity of her thought, I discovered that it was impossible to make any one thing clear to myself without attempting to get clear about many others, with the result that Julian's connections of ideas—intricate and subtle—began to spin out like a web. And so the manuscript grew, though I believed as I wrote, and still believe now, that it is of no greater prolixity than was due in justice to her thought. If anything, it is still too short.

I have been reading Julian for many years, but have not until now tried to write about her at any length, because I felt sure of two things: first, that her *Revelation* offers a complex, rich, and also coherent vision that falls into the shape of a genuinely "systematic" theology; and second, that I had not got the hang of how it does so. I read what few books and papers there are that attempt a thorough treatment of that theology, and was not convinced that they fully succeeded where I knew I had so far failed entirely. There was only one thing to do—attempt to write myself into an understanding of how that theology works, of what drives it, and how it resolves. This book is the result. I doubt that it succeeds any better than the others do. But if it fails, it will do so of a somewhat different purpose.

Julian's work in the form of the Short Text is the first writing in the English vernacular of which we can be sure that its author was female, and I am convinced that the Long Text, written twenty or more years later, is one of the great works of medieval theology in any language by an author of either gender. It is time, in my view, to assess that theology, contained in but two versions of a short monograph and limited as it is in range, by the most demanding standards of comparison with her medieval peers—Anselm, Bernard of Clairvaux, Bonaventure, Thomas Aquinas. Of course, in quantity of output and comprehensiveness of theological range, Julian does not rank with these great masters. But, in that what she writes is truly theology in some sense (or, as we will see, senses) that all four would have recognized, she surely does.

However, even on the score of theological character and quality, such a grand comparison is not easily made, if only for the reason that *A Revelation of Love* did not fit comfortably within standard taxonomies of theological genre in her own times, let alone does it do so in ours, insofar as those taxonomies are limited to categories of monastic styles of biblical theology, scholastic styles of systematic theology, and otherwise to the "mystical." As I shall explain in the first chapter, Julian does not exactly invent a new form of theological writing unfamiliar to readers of her age, for others write in similar ways.[2] Nonetheless, hers is distinctive.[3] Unlike the typical monastic theologian, whose starting point and method of procedure are typically and explicitly scriptural, or the school theologian, who sets out theologically from a carefully formulated statement of a problem or *quaestio*, Julian's theological reflections are elicited through a process of progressive intensification and complex elaboration of particular and personal experience. Hers is not a theology derived deductively, inferentially extruded from some set of general theological principles, nor one derived directly from an intensive exploration of explicitly cited scriptural sources. Situated in time in precisely recorded detail (Julian tells us the date and circumstance—she is, so far as she knows, dying), the raw material of her theology consists in a set of sixteen "shewings" revealed to her in person: sometimes in visual image, sometimes in the form of words spoken to her directly by the Lord, sometimes in the form of "understandings" given to her, some bidden, some unbidden. All three forms of showing are but starting points for Julian's interrogation of them for their mutual consistency and degree of correspondence with the teaching of the Church or her own experience concerning one key issue, the problem of sin (the core issue addressed by this book). For prima facie, she sees conflict rather than concordance between the two. The style of her elaborations is often that of one puzzled by her theological data and is consequently of a problem-solving character. But more generally, her style is much like that of the variation movements of classical sonata form. Having announced her first shewing, each of the succeeding fifteen is, she says, in one form or another, a variation on the first, and, in the end, all fifteen return to it. Moreover, in each of them Julian is to be found testing, exploring, expanding, and releasing the potentialities of the basic thematic material, often modulating away from it into distant and apparently unrelated keys, or transforming the tiniest melodic features of each shewing into major thematic developments of theology. In fact, so impressed was I by the force of this musical analogy for Julian's theological strategies that at one time I thought of giving this monograph the title *Variations on a Theme of Julian*.

For I thought then, and by and large still do, that I should do nothing in this book but continue in the style of the theological reflections of her *Revelation* by writing some further variations on a theme of Julian, with the justification in so doing that at the end of her Long Text Julian tells us that her "boke is not yet performed." It isn't only this concluding remark that invites a complexity of further response; everything about her writing demands one. Julian, as I shall explain at many points in what follows, systematically refuses to finish, because she intends theological incompleteness. And she intends theological incompleteness on grounds that are themselves theological, or at least meta-theological, that is to say, because she knows that what alone completes the theological is also what transcends its powers, namely, the beatific vision. The theologian, in short, is forced to raise more questions than she can answer, for the questions that perforce arise within the limits of theology of necessity can be answered for now only inaccessibly beyond it. Of theological necessity, then, is her "boke not yet performed."

Not that it follows from this conception of the theological that there is a defined point at which theology throws in the towel and surrenders. Not, at any rate, for Julian. Her work ends at chapter 86 of the Long Text, but not because she has reached a defined theological ne plus ul-tra and hands over the rest to the "mystical," as if crossing a river on the theological frontier. There is no more intelligibility to the notion of a fixed boundary at the end of the theological than there is to there being one at the edge of space. If there is in any sense a boundary line dividing the theological from the ultimate vision of God, then, at every point, Julian's *Revelation* straddles it. Indeed, its character as theology consists in its precarious positioning on the cusp formed by theological knowing and mystical unknowing, and so it is in its entirety mystical theology. In the meantime, then, no theology is "yet performed"; and from that necessary, systematic incompleteness arises the demand placed on her readers to revisit Julian herself, to reimagine her theological pre-dicaments, to rethink her solutions, to renew and to be renewed in that same faith and hope that is hers, and to do all of these things within the knowledge that "love was his mening." For that is all there is. "Holde the[e] therin, thou shalt wit more in the same. But thou shalt never wit therin other withouten ende."[4] Julian's *Revelation* does not finish at some point where theology is supposed to end. The unending begins where all theology starts: with the divine love. That is mystery enough for her, and it is the whole of her theology.

I suppose, then, I could say that this is less a book about Julian's *Revelation* and more a set of reflections occasioned by it, a set of variations on a theme of Julian. But the theme is less melodic than harmonic—it is a dissonance contained in a series of simple "bodily sightes," visions of an innocent man judicially tortured and executed, witnessed at the point of his death by a woman who, she tells us, also seemed to be dying[5] and had sometime beforehand prayed for "mind of the passion."[6] This woman—Julian—got more than she bargained for, as those commonly do who unwittingly pray for what is beyond their powers of coping. Perhaps when Julian prayed for "mind of the passion" she thought her request to embody no more than the desire for an increase in that devotional empathy with the suffering Christ that was so much the goal of late medieval meditation practice.[7] But what she got in answer to her prayer was more a theological predicament than a mere intensification of devotion. For in these visions was contained nothing but paradox, a cacophonous discordance, that both demanded and resisted harmonic resolution. For Julian saw therein at once a revelation of an omnipotent and utterly reckless love and its apparent defeat by sin. In Christ on the Cross she saw hope, rational and theological, apparently in ruins. On the one hand, then, the Cross is her predicament. On the other, she is told that all the answer to her predicament, the only one she is to be given, is contained in that same bodily sight—the solution is in the problem. There are no further resources for an explanation, there is no place else to go other than where the problem is, in the Cross of Christ.

The answer to Julian's prayer, therefore, paints her into an exceedingly tight theological corner with respect to her central problem, which is, put at its simplest, "Why sin?" Julian, to say the least, allows nothing in her statement of that problem that would ease her way to its solution. As we will see, she rules out, on the part of human creatures, all such accounts of human freedom as would entail that necessarily human beings sin. Hence, on the side of God, a sinless world of free beings is certainly conceivable and within the divine power to create, she says. So why, if God is nothing but almighty love and could have done it, did he not do it? And so it is that the answer to a pious woman's conventional prayer for a greater devotion to the Passion of Christ thrusts upon her the demand that she should do some theology for herself, since that "mind of the passion" turns out to be no matter of a simple pious empathy, but rather draws her into an intellectual and sensual engagement with a dialectical problem that Julian cannot ignore. She accepts that there are indeed mind-defeating mysteries, but what she will not allow is the confusion of mystery with plain self-contradictory nonsense. And so she embarks on a theological inquiry in quest of adequate theological solutions where there are solutions to be found, for only there, where solutions come to an end, may appeal to mystery be allowed. Haltingly in the Short Text, more confidently in the Long, she composes a "boke" that cannot in this life be "performed" *because* it is theological. And because it is theological, it is also mystical.

It is true that, for my part, much of what follows in my own reflections on Julian and her theological predicaments is devoted to tracing her moves out of that tight corner. But I must say that, as a philosophically trained reader of her work, I did at first resist the strictness of the limits she imposes upon the properly theological conduct of her task, for the stock-in-trade of the philosopher is explanation. And in the way that philosophers expect to be able to provide such explanations, Julian refuses them all—or at least shows no inclination to entertain them. But soon enough, as I worked through Julian's moves out of her tight corner, I came to see that in fact there are good philosophical reasons for her rejection of philosophical explanations. Those philosophical reasons convinced me that there are no general rational grounds on which to "justifie the wayes of God to men," as Milton has it,[8] and that no theodicy is possible such as would formally and conclusively demonstrate the consistency of the omnipotent goodness of God with the stark facts of human sin and evil. And even if those philosophical grounds for resistance to philosophical explanations are not to be found as such in Julian's texts, Short or Long, still, as underpinnings to her theological instincts, they can be supplied. And so it is that, departing from the close exegesis of Julian's own text, in the first part of the book I attempt to sketch the outlines (no more) of those philosophical grounds for resistance.

I should perhaps offer some apology for stepping so far aside from Julian's text in the first part of this book. Even if Julian can be defended along the lines that since there are not, and cannot be, any philosophical grounds for positively explaining away the existence of sin in a world created by an omnipotently loving God (and so she ought not be faulted for not having provided them) we, her readers, do have a right to insist upon some defense of her position against charges of plain *in*consistency. In chapter 2, therefore, I depart from the strategy of simply extending her reflections and explicitly take up general and conceptual issues of their consistency. I am sure that it will be said that my discussion of them falls between two camps. For I neither deal with those issues in the full-blown conceptual manner that the philosophers would expect and to the extent that the complexity of the issues requires, nor do I confine myself to the letter of Julian's own reflections on them. Not the first, because that would have involved writing another and very different book, and not the second, because, in fact, Julian herself has virtually nothing to say about those issues in the general, philosophical form in which I raise them.

On the other hand, I make no apology for my discussion's falling in consequence between places where others have placed their stakes, for their stakes are not mine. My discussion of these issues in the first part is designed for the purposes of a book about Julian's theology, not as an analysis of the general problem of evil, nor even of the particular problem of sin. What is relevant to my purposes is a question of whether Julian's theology meets a minimum condition for qualifying as systematic, the minimum condition for which being that it is at least not formally inconsistent. Clearly, Julian's theology of sin and divine providence is simply indefensible if the conflict between those two propositions, in the variety of forms in which they arise, is that of a straightforward contradiction. If to say that God does everything in principle entails denying that sin is real; or if to say that it is we who do the sinning entails that God does not do everything; or if to say that no action of ours can be sinful unless it is a free action entails that necessarily God does not cause it; or if to say that the reality of sin entails that there could not be an all-loving, omnipotent God, then Julian's theology is riddled with self-contradictions. For insofar as I understand Julian, it seems to me that she maintains all the antecedents of those propositions and denies all their supposed entailments, which means that she is at odds with assumptions commonly maintained in contemporary philosophical theologies, for which those inferences yield valid and sound entailments. Julian, however, maintains both that God does everything and that sin is real; both that it is we, not God, who sin, and that God indeed does everything; both that our sinful actions are free and that God causes them; both that sins are real events and that an all-loving, omnipotent God caused the world that contains just those sins. If indeed all these conjunctions are internally inconsistent, then no end of appeal to the paradox of the Cross, to the mystery of the Trinity, to the inadequacy of language, or to the limited capacity of human intelligence in defense of Julian's conjunctions could be of avail. Mystery is not to be claimed where there is nothing but incoherent mystification.

After all, the Cross may be defensible as paradox, but a plain bit of nonsense is quite another thing. And since contradictions have only the appearance of utterance, but in fact say nothing, no such appeals could achieve more than a vacuously optimistic rhetoric, nor could appeals to paradox and high mystery amount to anything better than low mystification. As I will argue, it is possible to show from her text that Julian maintains all those antecedents consistently with denying the supposed consequents, even though nowhere does she offer any explicit, formal refutation of the entailments, which, if sound, would show her theological positions to be self-contradictory and so unsustainable. It is therefore the purpose of the first part of this book to show that there are ways of so construing the relationships among sin, human freedom, and divine causality as to be free of internal inconsistency on the one hand and, on the other, so as to match up with what Julian herself says, in practice, of their relationships. In short, the purpose of this first part is entirely negative: to make the case that Julian's theology is at least not formally inconsistent in seeking a way between two possibilities of error, as it would seem to her—that of the atheist, who gives up on God altogether in face of the facts of evil and sin, and that of the "free-will defenders," who can defend God against the charge of complicity in our human sinning only by denying that God is the cause of the free acts by which we do so. Both the atheist and the free-will defender, of course, have no such problems of consistency as has Julian, for they have explanations. But then, I guess, Julian's response would be to say that of course explanation is easy if, with grand conceptual gestures, you simply sweep away half the data of belief and experience with which theology must work.

As for the complaint that in ranging this far from Julian's text I have left her behind, my response is that I do, and I do not—and again, I make no apology for either. Of course, in one sense, I do leave Julian behind, for I cannot, in those chapters, document my expansion of her theology with references to her own text in the same detail as is possible in the second, more theological, part of this essay: I have to rely on that reading of what she does say that implies my expansion of it. I do not apologize for that, because in going so far beyond her text, I have, as I say, envisaged this whole essay of mine in the spirit of Julian's own invitation to take her thought forward in the same way that the Long Text was extruded out of the Short. For such elaborations contain no intrinsic principle of finality and can be endlessly continued. In that sense, in this work of mine, I am doing no more than Julian does in her Long Text, though it goes without saying that mine is a secondary business of interpretation compared with her primary and constructive theological achievement.

In any case, there are things we can do that Julian could not. We can situate her theology in the space it occupies among her medieval comparators and more than that, in the space it occupies within our own times. In this book I do both, and so I range far from what we know for certain of her own theological sources, for I engage her theology in a series of running dialogues with a number of medieval theologians—with Augustine especially, but also with Dante, Bonaventure, Thomas Aquinas, and Duns Scotus, when and where their theologies and hers would seem to illuminate one another. And although we cannot know for certain that she had read any of these authors directly, and can know for certain that she had not read some of them, why should I not thus engage her regardless? Julian addresses her theology to her "evencristen," and I am one such. And for those of us who are her fellow Christians, Julian is a common theological source, and her theological struggles with paradox require to be thought through again and again, for they frame our experience neither more nor less than they frame hers.

This book is not, of course, intended as a comprehensive introduction to the theology of Julian of Norwich. It is too incomplete thematically thus to qualify, for I have confined my discussion to a few central and particularly problematic issues raised by her Long Text, including providence, the love of God, sin, and salvation, while leaving aside a number of major themes that would loom large in any comprehensive survey of her theology. On the other hand, if thematic comprehensiveness has not been an aim, another has. I have tried to situate this book, and Julian's theology, at that hermeneutical point at which, in my experience as a teacher, I find many students: they have made their way through the Long Text at least once and are strongly drawn to Julian's sympathetic mind, but are as puzzled by her theologically as they are attracted to her spiritually. I share their problem. For when I too first read *A Revelation of Love* I found it as conceptually difficult as it is personally engaging—and, honestly, I still do. It is to students, with me thus puzzled, that I have addressed this book, hoping to have done little more for them than to remove some obstacles, mainly conceptual, in the way of their entering for themselves and on their own terms into a medieval text that is one of the most exhilarating, moving, disturbing, and inspiring works of theology in any age.

ACKNOWLEDGMENTS

I HAD SOME PARTICULAR READERS especially in mind when I wrote this book. They are the students I have taught over my few years, since 2005, at the Yale Divinity School and its Department of Religious Studies, especially in my survey course on medieval theology. I owe them much, and wished to give them something in return, for they put up with a teacher who abused their enthusiasm and goodwill and exploited equally their critical energy and their patience to his own end of working through to some clarity of mind about, among many other medieval theologians, Julian of Norwich. But I am even more indebted to some who took the trouble within heavy schedules of their own work to read drafts of chapters and offer criticisms and suggestions for improvement, all of which I have taken into consideration in the course of revision. In particular, I owe a debt of gratitude to Kelly Van Andel, Katherine Reinhard, and Danielle Tumminio, some of whose comments, though unacknowledged in the endnotes, had an important influence on the earliest drafts of this book. Laura Miles, PhD student in the English department at Yale, taught me anything worthwhile to be found in this book about the spirit and mentality of the anchoritic life in late medieval England, and Vittorio Montemaggi, formerly of Cambridge University, now professor at Notre Dame, was the first to convince me of the importance of Dante as a theological poet and has inspired me with his vision of that theological significance ever since. I could not resist drawing Vittorio's Dante into conversation with my Julian, for they are "evencristens" to one another, as they are to us all.

Otherwise, in the final stages of the revision of the manuscript I was able to benefit from some especially helpful advice, both in detail and on more general matters of structure, from Jennifer Banks, the acquiring editor for religion at Yale University Press. In the best traditions of such editors, Jennifer seems able to combine a publisher's editorial responsibilities with sensitivity to an author's intentions, a combination that is as valuable as it is rare in the world of academic publishing. I am deeply grateful to her, as I am for the same reasons to my copy editor, Robin DuBlanc. There is an art of selfless reading of another's work almost entirely lost on all but the very best teachers and copy editors. This teacher, however, had many more occasions than one to bow to the authority of Robin's superior reading and compositional skills, much to the improvement of this work.

More even than these, I am as grateful as I am indebted to two research assistants who worked in turn on successive drafts: one is Katie Bugyis, who took in hand a very raw manuscript and shook out of it many an unclear or ill-expressed attempt to get Julian's theology straight and succeeded in coaxing from me some initial clarity of purpose relative to those often quite different purposes served by other works of Julian scholarship. Above all, I am indebted to Courtney Palmbush, without whose energy, concern for detail—whether of textual reference or of semantic nuance—and insightful understanding of what I was trying to say and patient evincing of a clearer statement of it, this book would now be little better than the shoddily written and ill-organized mess that it still was when I presented it to her in later draft form. I forbear to excuse either Katie or Courtney of all the defects that remain: for so closely have they worked with me on this essay that even if the final responsibility remains principally mine, they must take their share of it. That being so, to the same degree they share the credit for any merits this book may have. There was a time when I had a right to think of myself as their teacher. Now is the time for me to acknowledge that it is I who has learned from their help and advice.

A work such as this is in its published form the one-eleventh of an iceberg that appears above the surface of the ocean. An invisible ten-elevenths of an iceberg's mass support that visible one-eleventh. Thus divided is the debt of responsibility for this book's production: perhaps one-eleventh is owing to me as its author. But for sure ten-elevenths are owed to my wife, Marie, and to Ruth, John, and Brendan, our children. I could never have been the person who writes had I not been the lucky husband and father to such a family.

Finally, it is to the dean of the Yale Divinity School, Professor Harry Attridge, that I dedicate this book. His support for the highest standards of theological and pastoral work at the Yale Divinity School is as unfailingly generous as it is understated in manner. He was a principal agent in getting me to Yale. For me, that is reason enough for more gratitude by far than a mere book dedication.

A NOTE ON JULIAN'S TEXT

SINCE I HAVE WRITTEN this essay with a student readership principally in mind, I have throughout cited what is now easily the best study edition of Julian's work, containing both the Short and Long texts, outstanding introductions, detailed notes, appendixes, and bibliographies: *A Revelation of Love: The Writings of Julian of Norwich*, ed. Nicholas Watson and Jacqueline Jenkins (University Park: Pennsylvania State University Press, 2006). References in the notes are almost invariably to the Long Text (LT) followed by chapter and page numbers in the Watson and Jenkins edition. The few references to the Short Text (ST) give section and page number in the same volume. There are only two complete manuscript sources of the Long Text, the Paris (Bibliothèque nationale MS Fonds anglais 40) of the late sixteenth or early seventeenth century and the mid-seventeenth-century Sloane (British Library Sloane 2499). Otherwise, there is but one, fortunately complete, manuscript of the Short Text, copied sometime after 1435 from an exemplar dated 1413 (British Library Additional MS 37790), and excerpts from the Long Text compiled circa 1500 together with others from the writings of Walter Hilton (London, Westminster Cathedral Treasury MS 4, fols.

72v–112v). It should be noted that the Watson and Jenkins edition is a mildly orthographically modernized hybrid, combining the best readings of all manuscripts, but noting all the variants of the manuscript sources.

PART ONE

Providence and Sin

CHAPTER ONE

Julian the Theologian

Julian's Theology as Systematic: Scholastic and Monastic Models

IN THIS CHAPTER I set out little in detail of Julian's substantive theology, attempting but to assemble some preliminary suggestions about what kind of theologian she is. I read her in what follows as always being a systematic theologian, sometimes more explicitly than others an anchoritic theologian, often a vernacular (or, perhaps better) demotic theologian,[1] an apophatic, and, more problematically, a mystical theologian.[2] Each of these terms of theological taxonomy requires some elucidation with reference to Julian, and I must begin with a word or two in explanation of what I mean in describing her theology as systematic. It is not until later (it awaits the whole book) that I attempt any demonstration that hers does indeed, in the sense established, meet the condition required.

For some, the word "systematic" will say something very different from what they want to hear about Julian, whose style is far from the word's common associations today. Even in her own late medieval context the description might seem less than appropriate, since the word calls to mind—perhaps especially in connection with university or school styles of theology—the detached, sequentially organized, dialectical arrangements of theological *quaestiones* typical of the *Sentences* commentary or of the textbook *summae*. In fact, given the associations conjured by the words "systematic" and "theology" today, it could seem that to represent Julian as a systematic theologian is precisely to miss the point and value of her theology. And given those resonances of the word, the conclusion is justified. On the school model of theology Julian's work is inevitably devalued. Compared with the sharply defined criteria governing the method of, for example, Thomas Aquinas, Henry of Ghent, or Duns Scotus, with their analytical distinctions of terms and topics, their goal of dialectical lucidity, and their comprehensive coverage of the field, Julian's *Revelation* will no doubt seem rambling, repetitive, diffuse. Its strengths are other than those of the theological masters of Paris or Oxford. Nor ought its differences from them be judged defects.

The Pseudo-Denys once said that theology moves in three ways: on a straight line, in a circle, and in a combination of both—that is, in a spiral.[3] The straight line and the circle have two dimensions; the spiral has three. Whereas the straight line allows for two directions of flow, back and forth, one after the other, and likewise the circle, round and back again, the spiral combines both directions of movement at once, forward along a line, backward along a line, and either way, roundabout. Julian's theology is distinctly spiral: it moves forward, as one does along a straight line. It constantly returns to the same point, as one does around a circle. The repetition is therefore never identical, for it has always moved on—it has a progressive trajectory, up or down, into higher reaches or greater depth. If the force of the word "systematic" in connection with school theology is typically inferential and linear, forward from premises to conclusion, backward from conclusions to their presuppositions, this is only a half-truth with Julian, for her theology is both linear and circular, and so spiral: hence, it is not the less inferential and linear for being also circular.

The problem of how properly to describe Julian's theology is not, in my view, with the descriptions of her *Revelation* as systematic or as theology, but with an excessively linear, school-based understanding of those terms. The summae of the schools of the twelfth and later centuries were, unsurprisingly, schoolbooks, texts. *Sentences* commentaries were, roughly, PhD dissertations, and disputed questions were devices of teaching and learning. Why should they have been otherwise? After all, they were devoted to a conception of theology as a subject to be taught and examined in a university degree course—according, therefore, to a curriculum—in institutions offering training within a fixed period of years to qualify students for entry into the higher ranks of a professionalized clerisy, or to recycle them through an academic career, or, sometimes, both. Medieval universities taught theology primarily as a portable set of skills to be used by the priesthood in the pastoral and homiletic service of the Church. It is little wonder that it was the friars who took most enthusiastically to university styles of theological learning, as the schools offered exactly the transferable theological skill that the preaching orders needed for their distinctively mobile and urban ministries. The nature of those summae as systematic is principally due to their pedagogical purposes; they are systematic at least in part because their intention is curricular organization, as any reader of, for example, the general preface to Thomas Aquinas's *Summa theologiae* will readily observe.[4] The conception of theology as systematic insofar as it is embodied in those university texts is therefore specific to a very particular purpose for theology itself: that is, to a conception of theology as teachable, portable, and transferable, and of a university course in theology as training, whether for preaching or pastoral missions, or as a step on the way to ecclesiastical preferment.

Perhaps because most theology is still done within the successor academic institutions of those medieval universities, even today it takes some historical imagination to grasp fully how revolutionary was the change that shifted the theological center of gravity into the new universities of Europe in the twelfth and thirteenth centuries, bringing with it the radically new conception of theology as a teachable subject. In medieval terms, this is a very late development. And we have learned in the last four or five decades to be cautious of models (whether of theology or of the systematic) too dominated by the styles of the late medieval university, if only because of Jean Leclerq's masterly *The Love of Learning and the Desire for God*,[5] which told us of a more ancient, and distinctively monastic, theology. For the medieval monks, theology is not a subject in which courses are taken so as to acquire professional qualifications. It is their contemplative way of life. Nor do monks take their theology anywhere, as they are vowed to stability of place. Theology for the monks is closer in spirit to the contemplative *theoria* of the Greek fathers of the Church, and is a complex of lifelong activities, which moreover extend out beyond this life into the next, into the beatific vision. For the monks saw their contemplative lives pre-mortem as continuous with the next, in contrast to the active life, which begins and ends this side of death.[6]

In what sense could monastic styles of theology be described as systematic? Certainly not as the schoolmen envisaged theirs. Though by no means all (Anselm of Canterbury and Hugh of St. Victor are obvious exceptions), many twelfth-century monks reacted with suspicion, if not overt hostility, to what eventually became university-style practices in which the whole range of theological topics was divided systematically into linked series of quaestiones put up for dialectical debate. And some were suspicious of the very idea of a theological quaestio, as if the act of entertaining questions in itself invited and encouraged an attitude of skepticism about faith. Bernard of Clairvaux and his friend William of St. Thierry thought it was with Abelard that the rot set in,[7] and they were scandalized by his demonstration that even the scriptures themselves, and all the more the traditions of their interpretation, could not always be harmonized, implying that those traditions contained not just one resource speaking with a single authoritative voice but also contentious dissensions.[8] For many monks seemed to think that once you envisaged the possibility of theological questions, you incurred the necessity of allowing more than one possible answer, both a *sic* and a *non*. And of course as a matter of logic they were right. You do not have a genuine question unless it allows for at least two possible answers. As Thomas Aquinas was to say in the next century, theology is intrinsically *argumentativa*,[9] or, as we might say, problem based, and if not rationally demonstrable (because you cannot prove the articles of faith), then at least rationally defensible (because you can by argument rout the opposition). For Thomas, every theological topic is introduced by an *utrum*—"Whether it is the case that . . ." But for just that reason, systematized, professionalized theology as taught in the schools could appear to some to trivialize the techniques of the discipline reductively into a dialectical art that, as Thomas again was to say, could be exercised in the schools even by men of unworthy personal life.[10] School theology seemed to reduce to a skepticism-inducing technique that which for the monks was essentially a contemplative way of life, a way of holiness.[11]

Yet in a very different sense from that of the schoolmen, monastic theology was rule governed by their rule of life as monks. The monks' theology is indeed organized, but its organization is not dictated by a curriculum to be studied over a fixed term. It is conceived of as a contemplation that threads through the daily *horarium* of a lifelong ascetical-spiritual regime structured (as the metaphor of the twelfth-century Carthusian Guigo II has it) as a *scala claustralium*, a "ladder of monks."[12] This ladder, Guigo said, has four rungs—reading, meditation, prayer, and contemplation. The cloistered religious, monks and nuns, could distinguish these practices, but they had no desire to separate them. They read incessantly, mainly (though of course not exclusively) the Bible and the fathers, and when they were not reading these works privately they were singing the Psalter. The slow pace of the singing of the daily hours of the Office or the recitation of the *lectio divina* led spontaneously into meditative reflection on the text read or sung, which in turn led to aspirational or intercessory prayer[13] and thereon to contemplation. And if school theology is organized to serve an ideal of teaching, then the monastic theological styles are rooted in contemplative *reading* of the scriptures, a practice of reading and reflection that developed into a practice of writing in that most distinctive of monastic theological genres, the continuous scriptural commentary. The monks' scriptural commentaries read like written-out meditations, because often enough that is exactly what they are.

One can go further. At a consciously methodological level, monastic reading was regulated by some sense of formal method, by an explicit hermeneutical strategy, a four-step "ladder" of monastic reading, that distinguished and articulated the relations between the literal, allegorical, tropological, and anagogical layers of meaning that all scriptural texts might contain.[14] Although, of course, this formal schema of "four senses" of biblical interpretation found its way into scholastic practice, within monastic practice it was incorporated more explicitly and more comfortably into the monks' vocational lifestyle. The technique was simultaneously a hermeneutical and spiritual strategy that mapped onto the spiritual "ladder of monks" in structure and purpose, for it required the continual, endless search for the hidden anagogical—or, as they also called it, mystical—sense of the scriptural texts lying within and below the literal surface. It was this mystical sense that pointed eschatologically beyond this life to the next and promised personal engagement with that which was the goal of all their vocation, the goal of the contemplative life itself. Thus, biblical text and monastic reader are similarly "placed"—eschatologically on the contemplative cusp at which time and eternity intersect. In the twelfth century Alain of Lille even connected this monastic eschatological impulse with his own monastic habitation. There is theological significance, he thought, in a Latin pun: the monk lived for the time being in a *cella,* which was next door to his final dwelling place, his home, in *caelo.*[15] It was in his cell that the way was to be found to the celestial. In that way were the contemplative life and the theological task more or less identified one with the other.

Julian as Systematic Theologian

In what sense, then, may Julian's theology by comparison be described as systematic? It is insufficient, but no harm as far as it goes, to concede that she owes something to the styles of both the school and the monastery. Later I will take up Oliver Davies's suggestion[16] that Julian's style of continuous theological elaboration, both within each of the two versions of her work, the Short and the Long texts, and even more evidently in the massive expansion of the first that is found in the second, shows marked similarities with the monastic meditative practice of lectio divina and its expansion into spiritual/mystical commentary on scripture. Moreover, though the date of composition of neither text is certain, we do know that at least twenty years elapsed between the composition of the Long and the Short texts, twenty years of reflection and continual deepening of insight into the meaning of those initial revelations, a deepening that has no natural end point: one gets the feeling that Julian is also one who must keep writing in order to work out what she thinks. There is, after all, no course one can complete in the deepening of prayerful insights into mysteries. And just as the monks were rarely exercised to finish their scriptural commentaries—they were not writing monographs—so the Long Text extends but does not complete the unfinished business of the Short Text.[17] Julian's epigraphic statement at the end of the Long Text, that even after a lifetime of revision and expansion, her "boke is not yet performed, as to my sight," is monastic in instinct.[18] Of course her book is unfinished. But here may I venture a brief comment about the word "unfinished" as it pertains to theological texts in the Middle Ages.

In the Middle Ages there was a variety of ways of failing to finish a text. There is Thomas Aquinas's way, as in the *Summa theologiae* and in his *Compendium theologiae*. Both summae stop short of their intended conclusions, for Thomas simply gave up writing them, either, as the legend has it, because an overwhelming vision in December 1273 caused him to account his massive output as "nothing but straw,"[19] or because he suffered a nervous breakdown from overwork, which seems just as likely—I calculate that Thomas's output equaled an average of several Agatha Christie novels per month between 1270 and the end of 1273. But unfinished texts as they are, they were finishable because they adhered to a clear and complete outline, and in the case of the *Summa theologiae* disciples completed the work by compiling extracts from his earlier *Sentences* commentary and his *Disputed Questions*. Another way of not finishing is Bernard of Clairvaux's, who wrote eighty-six sermons on the *Song of Songs*—and got only as far as the first verse of chapter 3 out of the eight chapters of the biblical text. Again, you could "complete" the cycle, and again, in fact, a disciple did. But to do so does not compel so much as does completing a work like Thomas's *Summa*, for Bernard had pretty much said all that he wanted to say in the eighty-six sermons he had composed, and was content to let the matter rest there. The third method of incompleteness, however, is different from both previous, because unlike them it is theologically strategic. Julian's Short and Long versions, unlike Bernard's, are both complete as texts. But both texts, unlike Thomas's, contain business that is inherently unfinishable, and this is because, as we will see, what they are about determines the theological method. You cannot complete a theological text that is about the uncompletability of theology. And this is a different motivation for incompleteness, being more like the way the monk's trajectory from lectio divina to contemplation is never ending, never ended, until the beatific vision itself.

But that said, there remains a perfectly good sense—and a monastic one—in which Julian's theology may be said to be systematic. Julian's work is remarkably self-conscious methodologically. In particular Julian is clearly familiar with the medieval theory and practice of scriptural hermeneutics. Her distinction between those elements of her revelations that consist in "bodily sights" and their "spiritual meanings," her probing of the first so as to extract the second, aided on occasions by direct hermeneutical instructions from "the Lord"—these all map neatly onto the classic patristic and medieval distinction between "literal" and "spiritual" senses found in Origen,[20] later taken up into the Latin traditions by Gregory the Great[21] from Cassian,[22] and on into Julian's own time through the monastic practice of lectio. Whether or not Julian was ever a Benedictine nun of the community at Carrow,[23] she shows familiarity with monastic hermeneutical practice and makes systematic use of it within her own reflections, and not only in her employment of the semitechnical schema of the "four senses." For above all, she closely follows Augustine's hermeneutical teaching in her reading of her shewings, as did the monks: if in doubt, Augustine said, as to how to read a difficult passage of scripture, the question was to be settled in favor of that meaning that was most conducive to the achievement of *caritas* in the Church.[24] The whole meaning, Julian tells us, of all her shewings is "love." In these connections at least, Julian's *Revelation* is much indebted to the styles of the monastic traditions of theology.

Yet if a problem-based dialectical style characterizes the school theologies, then Julian can be said to owe at least as much to that style as to the monastic, if not more. Her *Revelation* is riddled with sic et non, with theological tensions. It is no exaggeration to say that a major part of the Long Text consists of a single enormously extended "utrum," a vast, loosely composed, *quaeſtio disputata*. Restless inquiry dominates the rhetoric of her work—assertion is repeatedly followed by objection, indicating a refusal to be intellectually satisfied.[25] Even her revelations themselves, consoling as she often finds them at first, give her little lasting peace, because she cannot easily square what they tell her of the divine love and compassion with either the Church's teaching about, or her own experience of, sin and its punishment. And though in the end she knows, and insists, that there is nothing shown to her in her revelations that is not contained in the teachings of the Church and vice versa, she admits that she cannot "see" the one in the other or the other in the one: they at least appear to conflict.[26] Hence, if they appear to conflict, but could not possibly do so, there is necessarily dialectical work to be done. And even if, like the monk, the goal of her revelations is the discovery of the mystical sense, in the meantime she strongly resists appeals to mystery while there is still any prospect of solving her theological predicaments dialectically.

Julian, then, is often as much puzzled as pacified by her revelations. Her reflections traverse the whole range of theological data—that is, the shewings themselves taken together with the scriptures, the Church's teaching, and what her own experience tells her. She knows that she cannot discount any element in that complex of theological sources just because in conjunction they appear to her to conflict. Of course that conflict provokes in her a demand for conceptual reconciliation—although, as we will see, in the end she rates that demand as impossible to satisfy—but only in the end. At all events, the seeming conflict at the heart of her faith demands of her and evokes a complexity of response that has every right to be regarded as theological, indeed systematic, in senses of those terms recognizably scholastic.

Julian as Anchoritic Theologian

It is right, therefore, to acknowledge that as to theological genre, Julian's *Revelation* owes debts both to monastic and to scholastic styles. It is right, but inadequate, because she is doing something in a number of ways different from what monks and schoolmen did. Julian was an anchoress for a good part of her life, and in fact she may have already been vowed as a woman enclosed in an anchorhold in Norwich for at least some of the time during which she composed the Long Text, and very probably for all of it.[27] There is little enough study of how the circumstances of anchoritic women in the late Middle Ages may have influenced their spiritual and theological writings,[28] if only for the reason that few anchoresses wrote at all.[29] But at least some things of a negative kind can be said with certainty to follow from her condition as an anchoress, and others of a more positive kind may fairly be the subject of speculation. An anchoress is a woman, and so for sure Julian had no formal training in the university schools of theology—no medieval woman did. Nor is an anchoress a cenobite; Julian lives indeed according to a rule,[30] but not in a rule-governed community, for she is a solitary. She takes vows, as nuns, monks, and friars do, but though like the Benedictine nun or monk she is vowed to stability of place, those vows are taken as an individual before her local bishop, not before an abbess and a community of sisters. Technically, then (that is, by canon law), she is a common lay parishioner, attached to a parish church. But yet, in practical, pastoral reality, she is positioned at the margins of the ways of life of her fellow Christians, being neither religious nor secular, neither clerical nor yet an ordinary laywoman, professed but not a nun; she is canonically marginal just as the physical positioning of her cell is attached to, but remains outside, the main body of her parish church. Physically, as well as theologically, an anchoress lives, to employ a phrase of Bernard's, *in regione dissimilitudinis*, in a "land of unlikeness," a place of "exile."[31]

Julian as Demotic Theologian

One is bound to predict that the writings of a woman in those circumstances, particularly a woman of such outstanding intelligence and sharpness of mind, would be characterized by just what we find in Julian's *Revelation:* stylistic freedom, aware of but uninhibited by formulaic methodology, a style essentially exploratory, reflective, meditative, and above all, vernacular. Nor by that last description do I refer only to the fact that she writes in her local Middle English (ME) dialect.[32] I mean also that she writes vernacular theology—theology, as she puts it, for her "evencristen,"[33] and for that reason the term more appropriately descriptive of Julian's literary and theological openness is, as Alastair Minnis has suggested to me, "demotic." Julian the anchoress may be walled up in a tiny confined space apart, but for that very reason she can write for no specialized community of readers, and must address all her readers as if she were indifferent to their particular canonical standing within the Church.[34] Indeed, she writes for the common Church—for the baptized, not for the ordained or consecrated alone. And this fact is itself remarkable: for in the history of the Western Church, a theological treatise (as distinct from series of *sermones ad status*) explicitly addressed to any and all Christians is not the norm, at any rate not since the time when Latin was itself the vernacular. Even physically, if hers is a space apart, it is a space located centrally in a commercially vibrant city. Her theology is correspondingly urban, correspondingly lay. A monastic community can seem theologically sufficient unto itself, as also may a community of academics. An author of both kinds has access to a readily available readership: monks most commonly write for other monks, academics write in the patois of their scholarly community. In contrast with both, an anchorhold embodies a paradox. Its very smallness of scale and poverty of theological resources deprives its occupant of the advantages both of an intellectually self-sufficient community and of a given readership, and so demands openness to other spaces than its own: an "inside" so confined demands a relationship with its "outside." In this sense an anchorhold is liminal space, space outside boundaries and between them. If negatively an anchoress has to negotiate her own space in distinction from the regular spaces of medieval Christian readerships, positively she is also capable of mediating, from the space she negotiates, free and independent relationships with those many other spaces.[35] And while no one should want to go so far as to say that her circumstances as an anchoress determine the distinctive features of Julian's theological writing (and certainly not I), nonetheless I do venture to say that at the very least there is a closeness of fit between her theological style as vernacular and demotic and her condition of life as anchoress in that cell in Norwich, situated in multiple senses "between": between distinct theological genres, between a Latinate theological formality and a vibrant orality of style, between canonical "spaces" in the Church, and between standard visionary texts (common enough among women of her time) and hardheaded dialectical styles of theology, from the formal pursuit of which, by gender, she is excluded.

And if all this seems too speculative, there is one concrete historical circumstance that may more securely link her condition as an anchoress with the liminal vernacularity of her theological and literary style. Julian sets the scene for her revelations by telling us that, in answer to her prayer, she became so ill as to be near to death, but not to the point of actually dying.[36] Julian therefore enters her revelations from a deathbed on which she will not die. Accordingly, she enters the anchorhold in which she will live consecrated by the ritual of the burial service (the rite of initiation of an anchoress declares that her anchorhold is a tomb, in which she is buried with Christ).[37] And as the anchorhold is situated liturgically and symbolically between life and death, so also are Julian's revelations situated theologically between time and eternity, between ecstatic vision and quotidian experience, between the uniqueness of her shewings themselves and the common responsibilities of her evencristen. And so it is unsurprising that her theology is poised in a space uncircumscribed by the boundaries of the open, ruminative styles of monastic biblicism and the closed, inferential styles of scholastic dialectics, exploratory of that space while respectful of, and indebted to, those theologies whose boundaries it transgresses.

Julian's "unlettered" womanhood, her condition as an anchoress, the exceptional character of her shewings—all these forms of marginality contribute to a freedom of vocabulary and image, an expansiveness of thought, and a singularity of theological emphasis that set her apart from mainstream styles of medieval theology. In fact, it is fair to say that although Julian's *Revelation* is one of a handful of works of medieval theology that is genuinely popular in our times, being widely read within the English-speaking Christian churches today for its intrinsic contemporary value, it is, in fact, so singular that it is as unprecedented as it is unrepeatable. It generates no successors in theological type, and it neither belongs to nor creates any theological genre, whether in its own late medieval times or in ours. Nor is this only because few theologians these days see visions, or even any longer dream dreams.

Not that Julian's *Revelation* is in every way exceptional. After all, there is a type of women's theological writing in the Middle Ages that is visionary in the same way hers is. But few such writings combine with that reliance on the authority of her shewings the dialectical toughness and rigor with which Julian interrogates them, Hildegard of Bingen being the obvious exception. Julian is not content merely to "behold" her shewings. Beholding them in contemplative rest in their "meaning" is, she says, a grace from God that she might or might not be given. But "seeking" their meaning—that we can all do. Indeed, she says, the Church tells us we ought to do it—and it is that seeking that seems to come the more naturally to Julian. Julian refuses to suppress the questions that her searching mind spontaneously provokes. Of course, too, in this respect her work has parallels with Marguerite Porete's *Le mirouer des simples ames aneanties*.[38] As Rebecca Stephens has argued, Porete's early fourteenth-century work plays probingly with theological issues of liminality in a manner similar to Julian's, and it does so from a similarly liminal standpoint beyond the boundaries of theological authority, distinctively possessing Julian's same powerful sense of intellectual freedom.[39] But in two ways Marguerite's *Mirouer* differs from Julian's *Revelation*. Marguerite has no interest in shewings, being rather dismissive of their significance.[40] And as to the nature of her liminality—Marguerite consciously probes the margins of doctrinal orthodoxy, while Julian, on the contrary, sets her questioning of her revelations firmly within what by medieval standards are orthodox limits—though I am aware that others are less sure of that than I am.[41] It is less in matters of theological and doctrinal substance, and more in matters of intellectual disposition, metaphoric range, literary and linguistic style, and sheer fresh energy of thought, that the singularity of Julian's work is to be found. There is a kind of radical theological naïveté in *Revelation*—sometimes even a *fausse naïveté*—that speaks across the centuries to our own times. And therein lies a paradox. This work is in so many ways a one-off. Yet somehow it is the work's relative independence from all models of theological writing, whether of her own times or of ours, that has made it so accessible to us today—more so, it seems, than at any other time in the history of its reception.[42] Though perhaps, on reflection, this wider circulation in our times is not so surprising, since ours is a culture in which all theology is inevitably written from the margins—from the standpoint of their relationship to the wider culture, no theologies are today authoritative in the way the subject was in the Middle Ages.[43]

Julian and the "Incompleteness" of Theology

Not that, for all its demotic character, Julian's is in any way a popular work. Taken as a whole, her theology is unquestionably difficult, morally demanding, intellectually complex, and resistant of simplistic solutions to dauntingly intractable theological problems. Hard teaching is softened by the bowdlerization visited upon her text by some highly selective anthologies of "spiritual reading" that fragment her thought into pious pericopes. Thereby are slackened, when not cut, the tensed sinews of a complex theological anatomy. In consequence, that which characterizes her work as theology—the delicately poised structures held in place by the interplay of such tensions—collapses into a sentimental morass of beautiful phrases and images. "Alle maner of thinge shalle be wel"[44] is all very fine and upbeat. But it has been made a hackneyed platitude because it has become detached from its origin in a tough doctrine of providence as well as from Julian's frightened and frightening sense of the reality of sin and evil that, as she sees, challenges all but the hardest-won hope: "and stonding [understanding] alle this, methought it was unpossible that alle maner of thing shuld be wele, as oure lorde shewde in this time."[45] And a distilled extract of hazelnuts and the divine love,[46] beloved as a reading at church services (and why not? it *is* beautiful), loses half its power when detached from Julian's difficult and problematic doctrine of Creation and of the relation between our human "substance" and our "sensuality." The charmingly archaic Julian is at best harmlessly decorative, at worst naïvely optimistic, and either way, of little significance in the history of theology. I discovered, however, when struggling to put together for this book a more comprehensive picture of her systematic theology, that Julian the theologian in all her complexity is not after all quite so "charming."

Things could be worse. It would be just as easy, and just as misleading, to anthologize Julian in such a way as to reduce her popularity ratings at a stroke. One would need only to compile a counter-anthology of passages in which (so it would appear) Julian turns out to be a harsh "double-predestinationist,"[47] an anti-Semitic sectarian Christian,[48] and so gruesomely sadistic in her descriptions of Christ's Passion (some might think) as to relegate Mel Gibson's film *The Passion of the Christ* to the minor league of snuff movies.[49] Some aficionados of *Revelation* will no doubt take umbrage at this catalogue of a charmless Julian as a one-sided and unhistorical caricature, as it is well that they should. Because if they do, they might just take the point that the Julian of the quotable bon mot is no less a caricature, is no less unrepresentative of the subtle, delicately poised and complex thought of Julian the theologian. What makes Julian the particular theologian that she is resides precisely in her exploration of the tensions generated by the two equally irresistible, but apparently opposed, convictions that dominate her work. On the one hand, she is acutely aware that the appallingly irrational cruelties of sin that the world contains deserve just and due punishment, as the Church teaches. On the other, and no more nor less unshakeably, she is convinced that just *that* world containing just that quantity of sin and evil was created by a Love who is absolute, and absolutely invincible, who does not, and cannot, condemn. Her text is authentically theology because of the manner of its response to that fundamental predicament.

Nor is this predicament merely a dialectical problem generated by the internal pressures of an academic theology. It is imposed upon each and every evencristen as an irreducible fact not only for theology but also for the practice of living. Taking the word "experience" in its broadest reference to include both her special revelations and her ordinary Christian perceptions of sin, Julian's experience is as fraught emotionally as it is intellectually. For her, the harsh and morbid stanzas of the *Dies irae* sound as many true emotional notes as the hopeful verses of the *Nunc dimittis*, and she has no idea how these two hymns can be sung by the same voice: the problem is as much emotional and experiential as it is conceptual. Her shewings afford her no conclusive answers. Never is she shown any one compendious vision containing both truths in harmonious conjunction. When she pleads for an explanation, all that the Lord will tell her is that what is "unpossible to the[e] is not unpossible to me,"[50] upon being told which Julian is not fazed, as one might have expected. On the contrary, that impossibility drives her theologically forward, and it becomes the fundamental principle both of her theological epistemology and of her spiritual practice to eschew simplistic explanations, indeed, to eschew all desire for them: "For I saw sothly [truly] in oure lordes meming, the more we besy us to know his prevites [secrets] in that or in any other thing, the furthermore shalle we be from the knowing."⁵¹

For Julian is certain that any theology that purports to know how the divine love and omnipotence and the existence of a world of sin might be reconciled must be wrong one way or the other, either about sin's reality or about the reality of the divine love. Those realities appear to her to be so starkly opposed as to crush between them all possible space within which an explanatory narrative could be told. On one score, therefore, she is resolute: there is no possible story that is within our power completely to tell, there is available to us no solution to the conflict between sin and love, no explanations—not even the famous example of the Lord and the Servant recounted in chapter 51 of the Long Text provides resolution. For that example, as we will see in chapter 4 below, is a mere narrative fragment that declares nothing new in terms of a solution; it serves only to refocus her theology upon the significance of a fragment of another story about which the Church preaches and which figures largely in the earlier, more overtly bodily episodes of her *Revelation*—the story of defeat on the Cross.

This solution, the Cross, is itself a riddle. Yet for all its irreducibly paradoxical character, it is the only story that to Julian could be credible. It is paradoxical that the Cross's demolition of the intellectually mediating space that explanations seek to occupy is exactly where our salvation is to be found. There are only two realities for Julian: sin and God's love. Nothing mediates between these realities except sin's defeat of love, that is, the Cross. When she is tempted to look beyond the Cross to heaven, she resists, because she wants no other focus of explanation than the crucified Christ.⁵² Notably, there is no concluding Resurrection narrative in Julian, no further episode of dénouement, no upbeat reversal of the fortunes of the Cross. That is not the Gospel. That is Hollywood's role for the Marine Corps, an entirely secular form of optimism, and a merely

Pelagian story that tells of the hope that may be placed in superior force. No such narrative is possible, because the conflict between sin and love is the final conflict, and the Cross is the final outcome of that conflict. It is perhaps Julian's central theological insight that sin wages war against love because sin is of its own nature violent, but love wages no wars at all, not even against sin, for love is absolute vulnerability. Love knows no other strategy than that vulnerability. For that reason, then, neither is any subsequent reversal of the Cross's violent defeat necessary, for it is precisely in that victory of sin over love that sin is defeated. In its victory over love sin defeats itself. Sin's failure to engage perfect love in a contest on sin's terms of violence and power *is* sin's defeat, its power being exhausted by its very success. For killing is the best strategy that sin can come up with; it is sin's last resort. The Resurrection, then, is the meaning of the Cross, the meaning that the vulnerability of love, its refusal of the sword, is stronger than sin's power to kill. That is all we know. That is all we can know. The meaning of the Cross neither allows for a fairy-tale ending nor needs one.[53]

Julian as Negative Theologian of the Trinity

If, therefore, there is something distinctively demotic about Julian's theology, a theological vernacularity that seems to connect with the strategic "betweenness" of her condition as an anchoress, then it is shown most explicitly in her resistance to easy answers. For what everyone knows—with the exception, perhaps, of some philosophers—is that there is only bogus consolation in such solutions to the problem of sin and evil as purport to demonstrate their consistency with the omnipotent love of the Creator, and Julian's theological instinct of resistance to solutions, easy or difficult, seems well judged by the measure of common experience. What is more, it seems right to link this character of anchoritic betweenness with the particular form of her theological apophaticism, caught as she is epistemologically and practically between the conflicting pressures of her twofold experience: of sin and of love. Hence it seems right to connect all three—the demotic, her theological betweenness, and her apophaticism—with one another. And what connects all three is the Cross. The Cross for Julian is no mere topos of her *Revelation*. It is not even as little as its most important topos. It is the embodiment of her theological epistemology as such; for Julian theological knowledge itself is cruciform, and the tensions between love and death that meet in the Cross are exactly replicated in the conflicted experience of her evencristen. It is Julian's experience as a whole—her shewings, the Church's teaching, and her own human perceptions of how things are—that is internally conflicted in a complex, dialectical way. She knows by faith that those conflicts can be—indeed, that they already are—resolved: "how *shoulde* any thing be amisse?" she exclaims.[54] But if they are resolved as to her faith, they are not resolved, they are not performed, she says, as to her sight.[55] Julian's theology, then, is written, thought, lived, as by one suspended in that epistemological space between the darkness of faith and the light of seeing, as her Christ is suspended on the Cross in the space between life and death, in faith praying to his Father for a why that explains, but dying without an answer. The Cross, then, is Julian's topos: but the topos is the method, and the method is the topos.

As I will argue in subsequent chapters, Julian's central propositions about sin in its relation to the providential love of God are that "sinne is behovely"; that sense can be made of that notion of the "behovely" only in connection with a providential narrative; that we would be able to make sense of sin, therefore, only if we were in possession of the whole providential narrative, that is, a completed salvation history; and that we are not in possession of any such narrative, but only of a fragment of it, namely, the Cross. The mystery of the Cross reveals to Julian what we can know of the Trinitarian nature of God, and it is in that connection between the Cross and the Trinity alone that the theological unity of

Julian's work is to be found. If it is in that narrative fragment, in that broken, paradoxical story of the Cross, that anything is shown to her about the nature of sin and about why sin exists, it is shown insofar as the Cross reveals the Trinity to her, and reveals the Trinity to be nothing but love, compassion, and pity. Somehow it is within the purposes of Creation, somehow it is behovely, that a love unlimited by any finite ends, goals, or interests should create just this world of sin. We can know that this must be so, but we cannot know how; we cannot provide any explanation. To possess the knowledge that explains how that conflict is resolved we would have to be in possession of the divine self-knowledge, to know by means of the Trinity's own self-knowledge, and to love by means of the Trinity's own love, and that knowledge and that love are the Trinity's very being. And so they are infinitely beyond us. By grace in this life we can enter into some participation in that selfsame life of the Trinity, for the Trinitarian life in us—grace—*is* the Christian life. But to live the Trinitarian life within history is to live by means of a mystery, it is to live the divine self-knowledge in the form of faith, and it is to live by means of the divine love in the form of vulnerability, suffering, and defeat. This, then, is the Trinitarian shape of the Christian life: the Cross. And that, one supposes, is why it is that when some Christians wish to invoke the Trinity in prayer they make the sign of the Cross. To be sure, the sign of the Cross is the epitome of the theological unity of Julian's *Revelation*.

These theological connections startlingly place the mystery of sin at the very heart of the Trinitarian life. The very love that is the Trinity willed to reveal itself in a world in which there is sin—that is, the mutual love of the Father and the Son that is the Holy Spirit is revealed uniquely through just this world, and not through any other of all the possible worlds. That this should be so defeats the mind's power of explanation, for the conjunction is incomprehensible, on the contrary appearing to us, and to Julian, as disjunction. In consequence, for all the affirmative wealth and positive vibrancy of Julian's Trinitarian vocabulary—it is a riot of dense coloration and shadings—and for all its striking homeliness and human familiarity,[56] one should not be misled into the lazy characterization of her theology as cataphatic, as if in contrary distinction from the apophaticism of the starker and more astringently negative metaphors of, for example, her contemporary, the author of the *Cloud of Unknowing.* The "darkness of God" is every bit as deep for Julian as for that nameless Carthusian monk. Julian's darkness of God is a darkness at the heart of the divine providential will, at the heart of the Trinitarian love.

It is of course true to say that Julian is not in the same way apophatically unnerved as the *Cloud* author seems to be, who writes as if the apophatic recognition that God is beyond speech required him to watch his language at every point lest he get God wrong: hence, out of apophatic caution, his advice is that the closer the soul comes to God in prayer the more limited human speech ought to, and does, become.[57] Julian, by contrast, seems unperplexed, albeit by an equally apophatic conviction. For her, the more one penetrates into the mystery of the Trinity, the more the repertoire of imagery expands. She speaks confidently of "Father," "Son," and "Holy Spirit," and plays with a variety of triadic variations of Trinitarian vocabulary, each serving via its resonances with our human experience to evoke some different experience of God. The Trinity is "fader," "moder," and "spouse";[58] "moder," "broder," and "savior";[59] "almighty," "all wisdom," and "all goodness";[60] "fader," "moder," and "lorde";[61] "oure fader [who] willeth," "oure mother [who] werketh," and "oure good lorde [who] confirmeth";[62] "in the furst we have oure being, and in the seconde we have oure encresing, and in the thirde we have oure fulfilling";[63] and more enigmatically, "I may," "I can," and "I wille."[64] And yet for all the affirmative richness of her theological vocabulary, hers is a linguistic strategy every bit as apophatic as that of the *Cloud* author or Meister Eckhart. That Julian has no problem with deploying such a huge range of affirmative metaphors about God is because, as I have argued elsewhere,[65] her cataphatic confidence is in itself an apophatic strategy, as if it is by means of, not despite, the proliferations of Trinitarian vocabulary that she achieves the goal of placing God beyond all possible words.[66] That is, Julian gets to the same apophatic place as does the *Cloud* author by the opposite literary strategy, precisely by an excess of affirmation that, as it were, collapses under the weight of that very excessiveness. Theological vocabulary for Julian is not a particular discourse, a "religious language," a restricted range of "properly" theological talk, bound by its object's range. God is not an object of a particular kind of talk in the way that a number is the object of mathematical discourse, for God is not an object. And since all talk is about objects, all language fails of God. So you can either just stop "prattling about God" altogether, as Eckhart advises,[67] or else do the opposite and make sure that you do *not* cull back the variety of talk about God to some restricted, pious, or "appropriate" domain. It is the same apophaticism either way, for if by way of speech nothing goes, everything does: in the matter of talk about God, if every word fails, every word should be tried. Julian, therefore, does not have to watch her language about God as if some words were good words in which to talk about God and some bad: all talk about God is possibly good, and no talk about God succeeds in comprehending God's reality. And Julian's way with this double-sided nature of theological language is, as it were, to garrulously talk her way into the silence of God's mystery, to achieve the apophatic by means of a surplus of the cataphatic.

Julian's strategy of free-spirited proliferation of Trinitarian vocabulary is, then, perfectly consistent with a fundamentally apophatic sensitivity, and even if it is not Julian's style to articulate a formal theological epistemology in the manner of the scholastically trained theologian of the schools (you will find in her no explicit statement of a *theologia negativa* such as one finds in Thomas Aquinas, Henry of Ghent, or Denys the

Carthusian), she maintains a balance, nuanced and uncannily precise, between the deployment of a maximum range of metaphor about God with a sense that none of it, and not even all of it, does anything more than draw us into unspeakable mystery. The style of her apophaticism is nearer to that of Bonaventure's *Itinerarium mentis in Deum* (*Journey of the Mind into God*) in more respects than one, but specifically in this respect, that his apophaticism is nearer to being a *theologia crucis* than a *theologia negativa*, or rather, is a *theologia negativa* constructed in the shape of the Cross of Christ.[68] For, as Bonaventure says, when the natural world, the inner life of the soul, the highest conceptions available to the human mind—those of being and goodness—have all had their say and have spoken of their Creator, when all the capacities of Creation have been resumed in the human nature of Christ, wherein they speak with a perfect voice undistorted by sin, it is still not thus that the Father is revealed to us in Christ, but only in the collapse of all that symbolic capacity into meaninglessness and defeat on the Cross. That "passing through"[69] the waters of death is the *transitus* that leads to the *Deus absconditus*, the hidden Father, whose love for the Son is the Holy Spirit.[70] For Bonaventure, then, as for Julian, the shape of the Trinity is cruciform, and the mystery of the Trinity is the mystery of the Cross, which is the mystery of divine love. And as that transitus through death is the theological heart of Julian's *Revelation*, so, as we have seen, is it the ascetical and spiritual meaning of her anchoritic way of life. Moreover, it is only in virtue of that inner connection between the Cross and the Trinity that her *Revelation* is appropriately called *A Revelation of Love* at all: the meaning of that love which is the Trinity, insofar as it is made present within history, is contained in the mystery of the Cross.

And that mystery of the Cross is all Julian is ever told about the meaning of sin. If sin's being behovely is made sense of by the narrative within which it occurs, and if the only narrative we are given within which the existence of sin makes sense is the Cross, then it follows that in one sense nothing is resolved: for the Cross is on the one hand the "great deed" that the Trinity does, the deed that finally defeats sin;[71] but on the other hand, the Cross is paradox—it is but a narrative fragment. That narrative fragment contains the whole meaning of the Godhead, the whole meaning of Creation, the whole meaning of the Fall and of Redemption, wrapped up in a single paradoxical historically dated event, the meaning of which is beyond us. For if that event is the Trinity's great deed of love, Julian tells us, the "*last* great deed" that the Trinity will perform will show us why: *why* it is that an omnipotent love, who could have created a world without sin, nonetheless created just this world with just the amount of sin and evil that it contains, and with the consequent suffering of innocent and guilty alike; *why* it is that that omnipotent love, which could have revealed its nature and infinite extent to us in any other way she chose, did so by way of the extrajudicial execution of an wholly innocent man; and *how* it is that only that violent death reveals the meaning of sin to us. Then, when that last great deed is "performed," we will *see*—then we will possess vision.[72] For now we may live, and Julian may write, only a text that "is not yet performed": we may live, and she may write, only as Jesus died, without a why. The apophatic theology in her *Revelation* is also the apophatic theology of its composition.

Julian as Mystical Theologian

What, finally, are we to say about Julian and mysticism? More than once in what follows I insist that Julian is no mystic, which is less perverse than it might sound, given the egregiously anachronistic meaning that the word possesses in our modern times. For in that modern sense Julian plainly is no "mystic," even if, as many scholars of the patristic and medieval traditions, including myself, have argued,[73] in a sense of the word "mystic" more appropriate to her times, Julian just as plainly is

one. Consequently, in view of the greater popularity of that anachronistically modern meaning of the word, it is still today safer not to count
on the success of these arguments in dissuading even some parts of the
scholarly world (which ought to know better) of imposing on the interpretation of patristic and medieval theologians notions of the mystical
that are more indebted to late modern anthropology and comparative
religion than to any such conceptions of the word as could have been
familiar to those theologians themselves. It is less misleading to say with
McGinn that "no [medieval theologian] practiced mysticism"[74] than to
risk major misinterpretation of their theologies by calling either their
writing or their practice by that name.

And so it is with Julian. To put it simply, Julian makes no claims
to any kind of union with God through Jamesian "ineffable experience."[75] But the hold that the Jamesian account of the mystical retains
on the scholarly mind is shown by the impressive case that Kevin Magill
makes for reading Julian as a "visionary" rather than as a mystic, on
very good grounds with which I entirely agree, that insofar as mysticism is defined in the Jamesian terms of ineffable experiences, Julian's
Revelation is entirely misrepresented by that term.[76] Of course it is true
that Julian does appeal to experiences, and of two kinds: those special
experiences, uniquely her own, given to her directly by the Lord in her
sixteen shewings, and those given to her in her common practice as a
member of the Christian Church. But in neither case are her experiences "ineffable." In fact, as Magill most ably shows, they are in both
cases distinctly communicable, and it is a principal purpose of his book
to demonstrate the importance to Julian of her role as communicator of
her experiences to the Church as a teacher. Not ineffable are her shewings, because these come to her mainly through bodily images of a quite
conventional medieval kind, and, where they do not, the Lord commu-
nicates to her in verbal responses to her troubled questions—what in
a later terminology came to be known as "locutions"—both of which

Julian can communicate to us in plain Middle English. And neither are the experiences that she receives in common Christian practice ineffable; Julian's strongly marked personal sense of sin and of guilt, and her fear of punishment for sin, are mediated to her through the teaching, and no doubt also the preaching, of the Church. As for some mystical notion of "union with God," she tells us that it is not in any case her shewings that achieve this, for these shewings are but particular graces granted to her and by no means because of any merit of her own, and they do not of themselves draw her into any exceptional closeness to God.[77] As I make clear in chapter 6, it is in and through the Incarnation alone that we are reunited in our "sensuality" to our "substance," that is held, free of sin, in an infrangible oneness with God. Sin splits our sensual—that is, human, time-bound—experience away from the place within us where that continuity with God remains unbroken. Sin fractures our being and our perception into discontinuity, with the result that we misperceive both God and ourselves and set them—God and our free agency—disjunctively in opposition. It is in the perfect unity of the divine and the human in Christ that our substance and our sensuality are reunited, and that restoration of human experience to unity is mediated to us through the Church and through the common means that the Church provides to its evencristens, prayer, ascetical practice, and the sacraments. There is nothing mystical about any of this that is not in any case the mystery of the sacramental life of the Church. Truly, then, Julian is not a Jamesian mystic.

But if in that anachronistically inappropriate sense of the word Julian is no mystic, then neither is she well represented, as by Magill, as a visionary in contrast to a mystic. Magill's terms of contrast are misleading. Julian may be no Jamesian mystic, but to force a contrast between the mystical and the visionary on the strength of a Jamesian account of the mystical is in itself to concede too much to that Jamesian account. In any case, it is very much the heart of my reading of Julian's teaching that her visions—better is her own word, "shewings"—should not be taken on their own, that is, independently of the complex dialectical interplay that they engage in with her own experience and the common teaching of the Church. My case in this essay is that Julian is a mystical theologian in a sense of which I tried to give an account some years ago in my book *The Darkness of God*. To imply any sort of disjunction between the mystical and the theological *and therefore* between the visionary and the mystical is, in Julian's case, taxonomically unhelpful.

If, therefore, Julian is a mystical theologian, this is simply because she *is* a theologian, a believing Christian constrained by the conflicts she experiences between the conjunctions that she must hold on to, that is, to both the unconditional sovereignty of the divine love and the undeniability of sin and evil in the world that love has created. Inclusion—both love and evil are real—is threatened by exclusion—they seem mutually incompatible. And Julian will not affirm the claims of either at the expense of the other. If Julian's theology is distinctive by virtue of its commitment to inclusiveness, to a spirit of "both/and" as distinct from a spirit of "either/or"—and it is—the point is easily misunderstood. For if we are to get the dialectical nature of her theology right—if we are to understand how that theology does justice both to the human tragedy of sin and to the overwhelming power of the love of God, that is, to our experience of the conflict between them; and if we are with any degree of adequacy to construe that theology in its nature as a mysticism—then we will have to grasp how they all consist not in her affirming an untroubled "both/and" *as against* a troubling "either/or" (for that at a second-order level is but to affirm the primacy of the disjunctive "either/or" over the conjunctive "both/and") as if you could not have both. Rather, Julian's theology is distinctive in its organization around the conjunction of *both* "either/or" *and* "both/and."[78] For it is by virtue of the forces generated by that *aporia*, it is in the medium of the tensions that her shewings, the Church's teaching, and her ordinary

Christian experience set up for her, that Julian conducts her theological *meditatio*. And it is by virtue of those tensions that her theology achieves its character at once of the mystical, of the experiential, and of the dialectical, and so in the conjunction of all three, of the systematic. That is a conception of theology, as it seemed to me, worth writing a book about with a view to understanding it.

CHAPTER TWO

Clearing the Conceptual Space

WHEN IN GENESIS 1 God is said to have looked upon his Creation and seen that it was good, we are perhaps inclined to think, in view of the sorry events recounted in Genesis 3, that the divine optimism was a trifle premature. And to some it seems disturbingly so, theologically speaking. For if we had to say that God, the Creator of all things visible and invisible, was as responsible for the sinful choice of Adam and Eve or for the existence of the serpent who tempted them as he is for the birds and the bees, then we would be in deep trouble with our theology of Creation. For birds and bees are indeed delightful things, but they make no choices. When it comes to the choices of Creation's free agents, however, the record is bleaker—for as often as not, free agents choose to sin.

And so it is that some of those who worry on this account devise a theological strategy known as the "free-will defense," which involves saying—broadly speaking, for versions differ—that when God created man and woman, he created a space for them from which his creative causality had to be absent, a space called our freedom. This space, being empty of God, could be safely occupied by sinful choices without compromising the goodness of whatever else that God *can* be said to have created. The point being, it seems, that it is in the nature of the case that a space occupied by God's causality could not be space occupied simultaneously by our free, moral agency. Hence, the freedom to sin comes from God. But the sin we freely do does not.[1]

This solution might seem attractive to Christians and other believers insofar as it lets God off the hook, so as not to be held at least directly responsible for the evil that humans freely do. But the price of exempting God from blame for a sinful world along such lines of defense can seem unacceptably high on the score of the doctrine of God itself. As Herbert McCabe often used to say, the free-will defense would appear to presuppose a quite idolatrous notion of God, since it would seem to rely upon a notion of the divine causality as necessarily standing in relation to human free acts in much the same way as a created cause would—that is to say, as excluding them.[2] It is of course true that I could not consistently say of a human action both that I caused it as a free agent and that some created cause other than I caused it. But God cannot be construed as thus acting upon my freedom to its exclusion except on some idolatrous reduction of the divine causality to that of a created cause.[3] God's causality stands altogether otherwise than created causes do to human free acts, as later in this chapter we will see. Just as unhappily, the free-will defense would seem to join forces with a quite Pelagian account of human agency, since it would appear to suppose that I *could* act freely independently of the divine causality. And that does not seem to be right, at any rate as Christians profess to believe, for according to their creed, all that is, "visible and invisible," is caused by God, and "all that is" includes, one must suppose, free human acts.

In view of which, we should begin by noting just how far the theology of Julian of Norwich departs from that of the free-will defense and also how, though she does allow her conviction of the divine goodness and power to be challenged by the existence of sin, she resolutely refuses to qualify her conviction of the universal sway of divine providence, or of the intimacy of the involvement of the divine causality with each and every free act, in the light of it. She would seem to prefer no solution, a sort of constructive agnosticism, to any that would purport to show conclusively how her certainty concerning the omnipotence of the divine love might be formally reconciled with the challenge of sin. Her position seems to be this: we know that God is almighty love. We know that God creates and sustains all things, including our free, sinful actions. We know that there are truly sinful actions. And we know that God cannot sin. What we cannot do is occupy the standpoint from which we could see the consistency of these propositions. Her position seems to be the theological equivalent of Gödel's incompleteness theorem concerning number theory—or perhaps both are special cases of a general restriction on the completability of any fundamental theoretical system. Given that a theoretical system is consistent, *nothing*—or at least nothing we can know within that system—could demonstrate its consistency.[4] In the absence of such a demonstration, the best the theologian can hope for is the rebuttal of claims to show their inconsistency. And if Julian herself engages in no such formal rebuttals, she appears to entertain no doubts that such can be supplied.

In any event, one thing is for sure: what we know today as the free-will defense seems to have no place in Julian's theology, which proceeds from wholly different assumptions about the relation between the divine causality and human agency. The free-will defense would seem to her to be a wholly misconceived solution to the problem of sin, principally because it sees sin as a problem in a way that she does not. Julian does not say that sin is a scandal of inconsistency that we need, and potentially have, a theodicy to remove, if by a "theodicy" we mean a comprehensive manner of explaining away God's responsibility for sin or, more generally, evil. Sin is, of course, a scandal for Julian. Sin shocks her. But disturbed as she is by sin, she believes it to be both theologically necessary and logically consistent to say also that "sinne is behovely."[5]

Now that proposition lies at the heart of Julian's theology as a whole, it is central to her doctrines of Creation, Fall and Redemption. If that proposition cannot be defended against charges of internal inconsistency, then her theology as a whole collapses into incoherence.

Hence, if we are to avoid the conclusion that Julian's theology is no more than a medieval case of what Jeremy Bentham described as "nonsense upon stilts,"[6] we need some ground for defending her conviction that sin is behovely against that suspicion of basic incoherence.

While we may have no need on Julian's theological terms for some theodicy that purports to show how and why it is that, sin being behovely, "alle maner of thinge shalle be wel,"[7]—for knowledge of the how and the why of sin is simply unavailable to us[8]—what we do need are theological grounds for saying that "alle maner of thinge shalle be wel," and in consequence, without any explanation of how it could be so, that sin is behovely. But before venturing an account of how Julian holds all these elements together within a coherent theology, since it is in the first instance not entirely clear what she means by behovely, it is necessary in this chapter to set out a few points, first by way of clarification as to what she means by that word, and second by way of clearing conceptual space for a substantive account of her theology of sin in later chapters. It will become progressively clearer as the argument proceeds that Julian's theology of sin, providence, and salvation (within which her belief that "sin is behovely" gets its sense and its justification) rests on implicit assumptions in philosophical theology, importantly different from, and in equally important respects at odds with, the explicit assumptions of the mass of today's philosophical literature in that field. Clearing space for Julian's theology is what I have in mind in this chapter. I have no purpose of full-blown philosophical defense of those assumptions, which in any case, as I say, are implicit, rather than explicitly articulated, even in her much expanded Long Text.

The Behovely *and the* Conveniens

I begin with a lexical point. It is impossible to be certain what theological sources Julian read, so one will not get very far with hard fact as to what theologies might have influenced hers. Famously, she describes herself as "a simple creature unletterde."[9] Certainly this means that she had no formal theological training, and in that light it seems hard to credit the picture of the academically learned theologian that Colledge and Walsh envisage.[10] But it is not entirely profitless to speculate as to what theological resources she may have known. I once supervised a research student who gained much understanding of the late medieval character of Julian's theology from the purely counterfactual exercise of annotating the text of the *Revelation* with references to Latin theological authorities, especially Augustine, Bernard of Clairvaux, William of St. Thierry, and Bonaventure, as if, were it not all but certain that she had not read them in their original texts, she had explicitly drawn upon them as a theologian of the schools might have. This exercise yielded, albeit only hypothetically, much the same view of her theological literacy as Colledge and Walsh more categorically describe. And certainly, she writes as impressively as might a fourteenth-century theologian who did know these sources.

Less hypothetical than the scholar of Colledge and Walsh's Julian is the case Elisabeth Dutton makes that she could have been familiar with vernacular compilations of theological materials extracted from a variety of theological sources, ancient and contemporary.[11] This is much more likely, and such compilations would have drawn Julian into a theological milieu in something akin to the way in which a student of our day is drawn by acquaintance with equivalent compilations in the form of undergraduate course packages of excerpted primary sources in translation—that is, with a range of standard topoi and received solutions to major issues. But, speculation apart, and apart from the certainty that Julian lacked formal (that is, university theological) quali-fications—which goes without saying for a woman of her times—her being "unletterde" might mean almost anything and virtually nothing. It probably meant that she was unable to read Latin off a page unaided.

But that does not mean that she knew no Latin and could not understand it if someone read it to her.[12] It is likely that "unletterde" means that it was only Latin she could not read or write, implying that she could read English for herself, and no scholar today doubts that Julian was formally literate—as Colledge and Walsh say, "Whatever 'unlettered' may mean here, it cannot be 'illiterate.'"[13] And it may certainly be said that, as Watson and Jenkins note, Julian's style has a distinctly oral character to it, for she writes, *if* it is she who writes, very much as one speaking out loud, or even dictating.[14] As to the meaning that Colledge and Walsh attach to Julian's description of herself as unlettered, namely, "lacking in literary skills," maybe they are right about what she meant. Paradoxically, of course, that is the one clear sense of unlettered that cannot apply to her *Revelation*. Hers is a beautifully composed text.

The fact is, then, that we have no certain idea what Julian could read, did read, or had read to her. On the other hand, if the safest and most conservative view concerning Julian's theological sources is that she probably had not read standard theological treatises in any systematic way, that only goes to show the relative unimportance of formal Latin literacy in the late Middle Ages in terms of the transmission of theological traditions. If, in a narrow sense, Julian does not know these theological authorities as a formally trained medieval theologian would have, there is a range of broader senses in which Julian could have known the medieval theological traditions well. Theologically she comes from the same place that they do.

All of this is by way of protecting my flank in view of the lexical point I want to make regarding Julian's use of "behovely." This lexical point, which, given our uncertainty about her sources, I can state with the modesty due of a speculation, is that we can understand much of the logical, epistemological, and theological force of Julian's Middle English word if we take it to bear the meanings of the Latin word *conveniens*, which Julian would have understood had she been literate in the Latin authorities of her time. In short, behovely means to Julian much the same as what conveniens means to theologians of the high medieval schools. When, therefore, Julian says that "sinne is behovely," what she means is that sin is conveniens, and she means it in the sense that Anselm, Hugh of St. Victor, Thomas Aquinas, and Bonaventure would have understood it, which is, as I shall explain, roughly this—that it "fits," it is "just so," and that there is something with which it fits. And that is the lexical point quickly and painlessly done with, though not of course uncontroversially.

Convenientia, *Contingency, and Necessity in Logic*

Next, we turn to a point in logic. It is true that some modern versions of Julian's text translate her behovely simply and straightforwardly as "necessary." "Sin is necessary," then, as Clifton Wolters has it in his older paraphrase for Penguin Classics,[15] as do Colledge and Walsh.[16] But this oversimplifies and distorts the complex logic of the word. Spearing has "sin is befitting,"[17] which is better, as is Glasscoe's glossary listing of "expedient" or "appropriate."[18] For what is described as behovely in Middle English, and as conveniens in medieval Latin, does indeed have some character of the necessary about it, or, with somewhat lesser force, we can say that what is so described is in some sense as it "should be," or that it meets with some prior expectations of it. At the very least, you say of what is conveniens that it is not arbitrary. But what character of necessity is implied, and what force there is to the "should be," is likely to be incomprehensible to us today, since too many philosophers in our post-empiricist times have constrained themselves to work with a comparatively impoverished logic of modal terms. For the medieval thinker, conveniens appears to bear meanings that fall between our notions of the necessary and its correlative term of contrast, the contingent, as they are construed in much contemporary philosophy.

This is especially so with one of the "two dogmas of empiricism," as Quine called them,[19] namely, the view that all necessity is *de dicto* and analytic, or, in other words, that all necessity is the necessity of a proposition—a proposition being necessary, if its being true or false is determined by the meaning of the words alone. "No bachelor is married" is, in this sense, a paradigmatically necessary proposition, because "bachelor" *means* "unmarried male." You know that no bachelors are married not because you have conducted exhaustive research into the evidence, but simply because you know what "bachelor" and "married" mean, and "unmarried male" does no more than spell out those meanings. But the trouble with the restrictive confinement of all necessity to analyticity—as is evidenced by the trivial example given—is that as the necessity converges upon the tautological, so it is bought at the price of factual vacuity. Since no information about the actual world, about actual bachelors or males, is needed to know its truth, none is conveyed by such necessary propositions. Hence, if all necessity is analytic, then it follows for this empiricist dogma that there are no *de re* necessities. No proposition about the world can affirm more than a contingent fact, a state of affairs that could have been otherwise. There are not, and cannot be, any necessary "matters of fact," no "natural" necessities.

Noting how poorly theological purposes are served by such empiricist assumptions, some Christian theologians have turned with surprising enthusiasm to more Platonist alternatives, or at least to readings of medieval theologies as importantly indebted to them. But Platonist alternatives serve our purpose of extracting a meaning for Julian's behovely every bit as ill as do those of the empiricists. For Platonism seems no less drastically committed to such complete disjunctions between the necessary and the contingent than does empiricism, appearing to do little more than present like disjunctions from the reverse side of the ontological options. "What there is" for the empiricist is the contingent. "What there is" for the Platonist is the necessary, the universal Forms or Ideas.

But this conclusion is derived, it would seem, by a manifestly invalid inference from the premise "Necessarily, what is known is true" (which is no more than a definition of "to know") to the substantive conclusion that only the necessarily true is known. Invalid as the inference is, from it Plato generates the further conclusion that of the contingent—that which merely happens to be so and could be otherwise—there cannot be knowledge (*episteme*) but only opinion (*doxa*).

Now if in that way you bind knowledge in with the necessary on the one hand, and on the other deny all character of necessity to the particular, then, for reasons that will be discussed later in this chapter, the medieval conception of the conveniens gets swallowed up in the vortex between the disjunctions, whether they are of the empiricist or of the Platonist persuasion. Not many today, one surmises, buy into the Platonic theory of Forms. But as a very general philosophical mentality inherited by many more than those who subscribe to that theory, the Platonic complete and exclusive disjunction between knowledge—which is only of necessary Forms, and opinion, which is only of contingent particulars—allows no more room than does empiricism for knowledge in the strict sense of the conjunction of qualified necessity plus qualified contingency out of which the medieval notion of *convenientia* is built.

Doctrines of either the empiricist or the Platonist kind, therefore, stand in the way of comprehending Julian's sense of behovely, and if we are to get a grip on this sense, we will have, by contrast, to concede rather more epistemologically to a medieval theological instinct for a category of the conveniens than to either empiricist or Platonist philosophies. And this medieval convenientia is a category that fits somewhere within whole hierarchies of differentiated grades of necessity and contingency, de dicto and de re, in logic and in nature. Historically it was theological exigency that set the epistemological and logical pace here. Since the time of Anselm at least, the much-debated medieval question "Cur Deus homo?" ("Why did God become man?") raised another meta-question, "Was God's becoming man—for whatever reason—necessary, or was it contingent?" And to the meta-question, the answer was seen to be "neither." It was *conveniens* that it should be so. The Incarnation was neither a necessity imposed upon God, nor just a divine whim. It was meet and just, *conveniens*[20]—or, had you been writing in Julian's Middle English, behovely.

On which account, then, we have to allow to a medieval mentality a conception of "more or less" when it comes to necessity and contingency. For there are varying extents to which things that are thus and so might have been otherwise; hence, there are variable limits imposed by varying degrees of necessity on how far they could not have been otherwise.[21] Therefore, beyond the necessities and contingencies of logic and the natural order, there are looser forms of both, and those that seem most relevant to understanding Julian's behovely include some that are tied up less with either logic or natural fact than with matters of individual identity and particular story. As we might put it, they are *narratival* necessities and contingencies.

Narratival Necessities and Contingencies

Elsewhere I have argued along the following lines for such forms of flexibility in our conceptions of necessity and contingency.[22] It is plain that there is a continuum of varying necessities and contingencies that link events into a meaningful, narratival sequence about a particular individual. It is thus that we connect up episodes of a person's life into a biographical narration of that person's individual identity, and in doing so we string together sequences of *particulars* meaningfully. It is thus that we combine, in ways that Platonists have difficulty in explaining, the two elements of uniqueness and meaningfulness. Though there may, for all I know, be many other human beings called "Denys Turner," the author of this essay (you will be glad to hear) is unrepeatable. There *cannot* be two of us. The narrative of the author of this essay's existence is likewise unrepeatable, and one might say (to put the point in Platonist terms) that Turner's existence is pushing toward the edge of maximum contingency. And yet, howsoever particular that narrative may be, that sequence of particulars can bear meaning, can amount to a "story." In fact, the only way of "knowing" Denys Turner is by acquaintance with his story, with how it adds up—or doesn't—and with how the events of his life fit within it—some in greater, some in lesser degrees of necessity.

As thus: my being a member of the human race is not at all a contingent feature of my story, for there being a meaningful narrative of me entirely depends upon my being human. Again, with iron necessity logic rules out my being my sister, because there cannot be just one story of me and my sister, and were I my sister I would be my sister, not I. But perhaps there are important episodes of my story that do not depend quite so crucially, for example, on my being male as all of them do on my being human or not my sister; perhaps more easily still one could envisage my story being told in a way that is recognizably the story of me were I gay rather than heterosexual; and as for my nationality, as it happens, very little difference would be made to my story were I to have been Irish rather than English, and even less were I to be 5 feet 7 inches tall rather than 5 feet 8 1/2 inches. Which facts about the particular individual named "Denys Turner" are connected with necessity and which with contingency—such that a narrative is a biography of *just* Denys Turner—is a question that the particularities of that biography must themselves determine.[23] Of course that story is itself contingent, in that there might never have been any Denys Turner in the first place, for there is no necessity attached to my having ever existed. But I did come to exist, and within that sequence of particulars of which the story of Denys Turner is told, some facts and events are more, and some less, necessary.

Nor is that all. Though, reluctantly, I have to concede that my existence as such is utterly contingent, I am under no compulsion to conclude therefrom that my existence is arbitrary, that I "just so happen" to exist. I rather fancy that my existence is behovely, or, as you might say, my existence is God's gift to the human race. But if that is true it is only because every human being is in the same way a gift, a new episode in a larger meaningful story. For the representation of each human being's existence as neither necessary nor arbitrarily contingent, and so as behovely, as much depends upon there being a providential story within which the existence of each human being "fits" as do the events within Turner's individual story that "fit," or have a place only within, and gain their meaning only from, that story. Either way, whether as belonging within the narrative that is mine, or as my narrative belonging within a larger, providential narrative, the behovely gets its meaning only from within a narrative. The logic of the behovely is narratival.[24]

And narratives are always particular, individuated. If, as Julian believes, sin can be seen to be behovely, then this can only be because there is a narrative of everything whatever, because the sum total of things adds up to a story, to just *this* story of just *this* sequence of events, including those sins. For there is just one sum total of events that is human history, and what is behovely is what fits within the particular narrative of just *this* world. We could say that the world we inhabit, and the history we have made, are, in respect of this character of singularity, very much like a work of art—unique; and that Julian's notion of what "fits" is, in consequence, more of an aesthetic kind than a logical one.

One might think of it this way. The conveniens, that which is behovely, possesses not a law-like intelligibility of the kind that one provides when explaining something against the background of the causal mechanisms and sequences that generate it; the "just so" of the behovely is not that of the scientific prediction that is borne out by events. What generates the expectation that the conveniens meets and fulfils is a particular story, the exigencies of a plot that just happens to have turned out in this way or that thus far and, so far as it has got, makes sense of what happens next. Nor is this narratival way of "making sense" of what follows anything like the way in which the conclusion of an entailment is made sense of by the premises that entail it; again, it is more like the right way something happens in a story. For even if everything in a narrative could have, logically, been otherwise, when we say of what does happen that its happening was behovely, it is because it was just right that it should happen so, and not otherwise, as if with a kind of narratival necessity. It fits. There is a plot to it. Its contingency is not that of the arbitrary. It just "so happens"—it is not necessary. But also, its happening is "just so"—it is not contingent. In short it is conveniens, behovely.

And the same conclusion shows up in the way in which the relations of prediction to retrodiction differ between the two cases of scientific and narratival explanations—or, more generally, between any universal, rule-bound, explanation and that of any essentially time-bound trajectory of particular events. For the power of natural laws to explain natural phenomena lies in the predictions they license. And what a natural law allows or requires you to predict, it also allows you to retrodict. That is to say, if, given certain initial conditions, a natural law allows you to predict that such and such will occur in the future, then just because of that it allows you to retrodict that given the occurrence of those same initial conditions in the past, the same outcome will have occurred then. Whereas the case is different with a narrative, for within a narratival trajectory prediction and retrodiction are, as the philosophers say, "asymmetrical": narratives generate very little predictive power of any kind, and then, at best, a negative one—as the narrative progresses, the possible further outcomes reduce, though they never dwindle to the point of excluding the possibility of utterly surprising events that transform one's expectations of what may happen next.[25] Correspondingly, some very straightforward narratives may allow you to retrodict with cumulative grounds for doing so, as the story goes on. In such stories, the point of what has happened gets progressively clearer so that you increasingly see why earlier events make sense—*within* the narrative. Few stories, however, are so straightforward. In most, the narratival trajectory is strewn with surprises, and so, on the contrary, it gets increasingly obscure, and the possibilities of achieving retrodictive intelligibility are reduced, hindsight being postponed to the end—as in many a detective novel. In such cases it is only in the end that you understand. It is only then, in the end, that you see that what happened was not at all as you thought it was at the time, but that how what happened "fits."

It is perhaps easiest to see this in music, for its arrow of time is, like history's, unidirectional. A PhD student of mine to whom I had been waxing on about Mozart complained that Mozart's music is just too "predictable." This is exactly wrong. Everything in Mozart's music is supremely *un*predictable; but also, everything in Mozart's music is supremely *retro*dictable, so transparently retrodictable as to create an illusion of utter predictability and obviousness. When a cadence or a modulation is completed in an unexpected way, you are *both* surprised *and* know immediately why it had to be just so, and how its being just so reveals anew everything that precedes it.[26] Stories and music—perhaps especially music of the classical period—in the end make the surprising turn of events to be obvious, as if after the event we can see how we might have predicted it, even though, before the event, in no wise could we have done so. But the theological case is a special case of narratival incompleteness akin to that of Mozart's setting of the "Et incarnatus est" of his C minor mass. It is one of the most beautiful arias that Mozart ever wrote. And partial sense is made of it by its contrast with the thunderous clamor of the Credo setting that precedes it. But still, it hangs loose to the whole of the Credo, because Mozart never completed his setting of the full text, and there is no way of predicting, none of hearing, how that aria would have sounded had it found the place intended for it within a setting of the whole Credo. The case is just the same theologically.

Narratival completeness can rarely be anticipated, and the full meaning of any individual episode can never be known except *post factum* within the completed story.[27] Even if you have reason to be confident *that* a particular event within the narrative is behovely, you may not be able to see how it is so until the end. But in the theological case, there is no standpoint at the end. For at the end is not theology, but the beatific vision. And there is theology only because we are *not* at the end.

The Particularity of Narrative

It is of crucial importance for the understanding of Julian's behovely that it gets its sense from the particularity of the narrative it belongs to: it is in just *this* world, exactly as it is, that Julian can say that sin is behovely. Failure to advert to this leads to the line of criticism that Julian's theology of providence places itself invulnerably beyond any sort of counterevidence, especially the counterevidence of sin and evil, by the simple device of escaping into tautology. It might be thought that if for Julian God is the cause of absolutely everything without exception that happens, and, that being so, absolutely everything is part of the plot, then the notion of there being a plot—that what happens is a story in which all turns out to be and to have been well[28]—is thereby made absolutely vacuous; indeed, it becomes a tautology to say of anything that, if it could happen, then it would be behovely.

It is, of course, a general truth about narratives that the grander they are and the more inclusive, the more nearly tautological they become—or at any rate, the closer they edge to the logical status of general, and so necessary, and so vacuous, truths, and as such cease to be narratives. For, as I have insisted, narratives are particular. Now what Julian appears to have in mind is a narrative that is, logically, the grandest possible: it amounts to the claim that everything that has happened and ever will happen—whatever the outcomes—will fit with everything's being "wel." Hence, the objection runs, it becomes absolutely tautological to say of any particular event that it is behovely, because it would seem to mean that in describing an event as behovely you are saying nothing about it other than that it happened. Such was the objection put by one critic[29] when I rehearsed this reading of Julian at an academic seminar.

To which I reply, not so. For what Julian says is that whatever does happen is behovely. She does not say that whatever could happen would be behovely. And not everything that could have happened has happened; nor is everything going to happen that could happen. Hence, from the fact that anything that has happened was behovely, and that anything that is going to happen will be behovely it does not follow that anything else that has not happened would have been just as behovely as what did happen, or that anything whatever that could happen in the future (but will not) would be just as behovely as that which will happen. There is, therefore, a particularity and a contingency to the actual events of all time—that is to say, they form a particular history such that, logically, it is possible to entertain describable counterfactuals. Such counterfactuals are real but unfulfilled possibilities, and it is possible to envisage the state of affairs that would have obtained had things happened otherwise than they have. Logically, there are events that could happen such that, were they to happen, they would count against Julian's faith that all will be well, in the same way as it makes sense to consider what events we would have to remove from the record of history such that, had they not occurred, the French Revolution would not have broken out with the storming of the Bastille in 1789.[30] And even if the variables in either case are immensely hard to marshal into a meaningful retrodiction, the proposition that whatever is going to happen, "alle shalle be wele" in our world, created as it is by an unconquerable love, is not reducible to the vacuous generalization that in *any* describable state of affairs all would be well. Hence, to say that everything that happens also forms a story of all being well is a substantive theological belief-claim about just *this* world, about what actually has happened and actually is going to happen. Julian's proposition is not the tautology that anything at all might have happened and anything at all might be going to happen, and all will be well notwithstanding. Hers is a substantive truth-claim about actual events, and it is a truth-claim we could not have known we are entitled to make short of its being revealed, whether canonically in scripture, or to Julian personally in her shewings. Moreover, it is a truth-claim that, as Julian only too freely concedes, is manifestly contestable on evidence that would appear to be considerably weighted against it. Tautologies, on the other hand, are invulnerable to all such contestation.

There is, moreover, a further respect in which the particularity of the world we have got is crucial to Julian's theology. For among the counterfactuals Julian claims that she can envisage is that there might have been no sin. If sin is behovely, it is certainly not necessary. It is here that the departure of her theology from the assumptions of the free-will defense is most radical. For free-will defenders it is impossible that there should be a world of free human beings in which God has guaranteed that there is no sin. As Plantinga says, "It was beyond the power of God himself to create a world containing moral good but no moral evil."[31] Julian does not accept this. There seems to be nothing at all in Julian's *Revelation* to indicate her thinking that it would be incoherent—that is, contradictory nonsense and an impossibility—to envisage a world in which God brought it about that everyone freely chose nothing but the good. J. L. Mackie, an atheist of our times, agrees, drawing the conclusion that since God did not bring about such a world, though he might have, "his failure to avail himself of this possibility is inconsistent with his being both omnipotent and wholly good."[32] Julian's initial instinct is the same as Mackie's, not Plantinga's. She tells us that her first anxiety about sin—her first theological scruple—was to "often" wonder why

God had not prevented sin in the first place, since of course he could have "prevented" it: "And I saw that nothing letted me [held me back] but sinne. And so I behelde generally in us all, and methought: 'If sinne had not be, we shulde alle have beclene and like to oure lorde as he made us.' And thus in my foly before this time, often I wondred why, by the grete forseeing wisdom of God, the beginning of sinne was not letted [prevented]. For then thought me that all shulde have be wele."[33]

Immediately she admits to realizing that this was a foolish anxiety—"This stering was mekille [much] to be forsaken"[34]—but it is interesting to note that what she realizes was foolish about this scruple was not her having mistakenly thought that God could have created a sinless world and did not, for she admits that he could have done so. Her mistake had been in her supposing that "alle maner of thinge [could] be wel" only had God created a sinless world, and so in thinking that he should have done so. So she had wanted to know—*this*, she admits, was foolish—why he had not. In consequence, once Julian has got past her "foolishly" mistaken inference, the position would seem to stand thus in relation to Plantinga and Mackie. Plantinga denies the premise that Mackie and Julian affirm—that God could have created a sinless world. Julian denies the conclusion that Mackie thinks follows from that premise—that God should have created it—because she thinks the inference is invalid either way. Julian's is the more complex, and logically subtler, position.

That God could have created a sinless world appears not for Julian to be in doubt. Why should she have doubted it, since she, along with all medieval Christians, believed that God had in fact done so? For God made heaven, where some number of human agents that have inhabited this world in which there is sin go on to inhabit a world in which it is guaranteed that all of them—in complete freedom and for all eternity—will choose nothing but the good. Nor does her conviction of this possibility involve any incoherence. For what is meant by the divine omnipotence is that God can bring about anything that can without contradiction be described, and Julian seems to assume this understanding of the divine power. It is possible without contradiction to describe a state of affairs in which human agents, being confronted with the options of good and evil actions, always in fact freely choose good actions. Consequently, it cannot be incoherent or contradictory to envisage God's bringing about just that world. And of course it is easy to see how one might be tempted into thinking that necessarily "alle maner of thinge" would have been well only in a sinless world. But we should know better than to yield to that temptation. Of course, we know that in the sinless state of affairs that is heaven "alle maner of thinge" is well; but in the world we actually inhabit, where sin is possible, we cannot know whether each and every outcome would have been better, still less that total outcomes taken overall would have been better, had there actually been no sin in it, than, taken as a whole, everything is in this one in which sin is part of the picture.

Julian, at any rate, is unconvinced. As we will see in chapter 7, she believes that there are significant respects in which we are better off inhabiting the sinful world we have got than we would have been in a world altogether without sin. And as to whether this actual world is or is not the *best possible* world, Julian's answer has to be, not so. This world is not the best possible world. But this is not because there is a conceivable world that answers to the description "best possible," compared to which this world falls short. This is not the best possible world simply because nothing *could* answer to that description. The description "best possible" makes as much sense of worlds as it does of any work of art: that is so say, none. There cannot be a fourteen-line poem that answers to the description "best possible sonnet," no best possible symphony, no best possible novel. Neither, then, of worlds. At least in this connection Plato is right: no individual instance of any kind can be the ideally best of that kind.[35]

And so it is that the foolishness for which the Lord chides Julian is her having failed to see that in whatever world God had created, "alle maner of thinge [would] be wel"; consequently, in this world that God has in fact created and in which there is sin—*because* it is a fallen world sin is inevitable,[36] even if its being fallen is not—all can be well, too, and sin's inevitability is part of the picture, part of that plot, of all manner of thing being well because sin's necessity has the character of the conveniens.[37] And that, in the end, is the theological meaning of behovely and of conveniens: that sin is behovely means that sin is needed as part of the plot—or, if you like, that the plot needs sin in the way that plots do—contingently indeed, but all the same just so.

Objeccions

There are, then, no universal, formal, and abstract criteria for what is to count as the behovely, but only the particularities of a contingent narrative, of an actual history of unrepeatable sequences of events, the particular narrative of just this sinful world. And it is within that actual historical sequence, constituted by the divine providential governance as salvation history, that Julian's notion of the behovely derives its sense. Now to speak of "salvation history" is not to speak of some activity called "salvation" as apart from the whole of history, but to speak of all of history's having the character of salvation. And this is to say that the particular time- and space-bound trajectory of events, that is, all that has actually happened in all time and space, including—indeed, including *especially*—human free actions has a plot: what has happened was meant to happen in just that way. And this, finally, seems to be Julian's meaning. The Lord tells her: "See. I am God. See I am in all thing. See I do all thing. See, I never lefte my handes of my workes ne ever shalle without ende. See, I lede everything toward the end that I ordaine it to, fro without beginning, by the same might, wisdom, and love that I made it with. How shoulde any thing be amisse?"[38] And that being so, we should have reason for saying that even sin is *conveniens*, or as Julian says, behovely, if only we could identify the narrative, or at least be sure that there is one with which the existence of sin fits. For there being a divine plot within which sin also fits is just what is meant by "salvation history." And here we can see what at least the main elements of Julian's theology of history must be if, in the sense in which I have been trying to explain the word, she can describe in the first instance the existence of any sin at all, and in the second, the occurrence of just the amount of sin that there is, as behovely.

It should be noted, of course, that nothing that I have so far offered by way of explanation of the meaning of Julian's behovely gets us even close to Julian's grounds for her substantive theological claim that sin is behovely. For thus far I have but attempted to sketch some account of the *logic* of that term, its formal character of "fittingness" within the particularities of a narrative. The discussion of Julian's case for her *substantive* claim that sin is behovely, the claim that the narrative within which sin fits is a good one, a narrative of love and compassion within human history, forms the agenda of subsequent chapters. In this chapter, as I have explained, my agenda is limited to a sort of conceptual space-clearing for that subsequent exposition and explanation, and thus far, that task of space-clearing has been confined to extracting a *meaning* for that term that will do duty for Julian's positive doctrines of providence and salvation. Before concluding this chapter, however, it seems necessary to take one further step into new territory: into the consideration, if only a cursory one, of some major objections in principle—and, within the assumptions of much philosophical theology of our times, obvious ones—to that substantive conclusion of Julian's theology.

In fact, obstacles of the severest kind stand in the way of giving her theology even an initial hearing. Julian, we said, maintains that God could have created a world without sin but did not, and must therefore, it seems, bear responsibility in general for the sinful condition of a world he need not have created. But she maintains also that God is involved in every act and event of the world's history, causing it all—for he has not simply given human beings the gift of freedom and can do nothing consistent with having given it to them that would prevent them running moral riot in consequence. "Ther is no doer," Julian insists, "but he." Putting these two propositions together, then, do they not yield the conjunction that because God causes the very free acts by which we sin, necessarily he must cause the sins that we freely enact? In which case a second objection arises, since the first would seem to entail on the human side some form of quietistic response to the evils of our world: if God has preordained the world exactly as it is, why should we even contemplate resisting those evils, since the divine preordination of them guarantees their happening whatever we do? And a third question arises, prior to these two: is it not in any case simply inconsistent to say of any human act both that God causes it and that it is free?

Does God Cause Our Free Actions?

As to the third question, it would rend apart the unities of Julian's theology as a whole were we to seek a way out of the problem of the relationship between God's causal sway over each and every free act and her soteriology, of such kind as to attribute to God a salvific role in regard to history as a whole but no causal agency in regard to those human free acts. If Julian's theology can be defended against accusations of formal incoherence, it will be only if it is not inconsistent to say that God brings about the salvation of the human race by means of his causing the free actions of the human beings that are to be saved. Julian's theology is wholly resistant to that picture of the divine providence and governance of human affairs according to which God causes the overall drama of human history, as it were macromanaging the general lines of the salvific plot, leaving human agents to exercise their freedom of action within the plot, but free only insofar as they are free *from* the providential causality. For it would amount to little more than paganism to maintain that the providential outcome of salvation history is a post-factum business of God's making the best of what happens—as if maintaining a sort of herding cats notion of providence wherein God has no causal role in the making of human choices but awaits their outcome, and then herds them as best he can. It is certainly not Julian's belief. She tells us that she "saw truly that God doth alle thing, be it never so litile. And I saw truly that nothing is done by happe [chance], but alle by the foreseeing wisdom of God. If it be hap or aventure [accident] in the sight of man, our blindhede and our unforsight is the cause."[39] The logic of Julian's position is clear, and its problems stark. If God does not cause our free actions, then God cannot be the cause of our salvation. Yet how can they be free if God causes them?

Julian's theology of providence seems broadly in line with that of Thomas Aquinas. In terms equivalent to hers, Thomas says that the regime of divine governance is supreme over every particular event that happens and is the immediate master of all—"etiam . . . minima particularium."[40] For Thomas, God is the universal cause, nothing excluded. In his divine providence, God knows everything that will happen—and not, indeed, as if God were a mere spectator in possession of all the evidence needed to predict all future outcomes, including our free actions. For if that were how God knows what I will freely do at 11:00 a.m. tomorrow, then my doing it at just that time could not be a free act, being determined by the antecedent conditions on the ground of his knowledge of which God knows that I will perform just that action, just then. Moreover, what is true of God is true of any knower, divine or human. Insofar as we can *know* what will happen in the future, this is to the extent that we know the antecedent conditions that determine those outcomes. But an action cannot be both free and determined by antecedent conditions. Therefore, insofar as any knower, divine or human, can know anything that will happen in the future on the evidence of antecedent conditions, that future event cannot be a free action.

Thomas concludes that if God does know what free actions I will perform tomorrow—and God knows this—such knowledge is consistent with those actions being free only if God knows what I will do in the same manner as I know them when I perform them. For my knowledge of what I am doing differs in kind from your knowledge of what I am doing. I know that I am waving good-bye to someone not, as you might, on the *evidence* of the movement of my arm, but because that is what *I* am doing, because I am that action's cause. It is only if I am the cause of my action that it is free. And it is precisely as that action's free agent that I know what I am doing, that is, directly, not on the evidence.[41] And, for Thomas, it is in exactly the same way that God knows what I am doing, that is to say, *as its cause*. Indeed, for Thomas, that is the *only* way in which God could know what I am doing consistently with what I am doing being freely done.

In that sense, at least, God's relationship with the free actions of humans is a special case of God's causal relationship with everything. So far as concerns the general case, Thomas by no means supposes that because everything whatever falls within the sway of the divine governance that everything does so in the same way. God's sovereign providence maintains its sway over everything, but it does so thereby achieving the perfection of each creature according to what it is created to be, according, that is, to its own nature. Thomas the teacher explains: better than a professor's doing no more than teaching his or her students what they are to know, is if he or she can also teach them how to pass on their knowledge in their turn by teaching others. For the knowledge that enables one to teach others what one knows is a better form of knowledge than that which one simply possesses for oneself. And so God has created a world in which not only does each thing achieve its own good—as it were, for itself—for with some things their good consists in their sharing in the divine governance itself. Thus, Thomas says, "God governs the world in such a way as to establish certain causes for the governance of other things,"[42] so that the immediacy of the divine providence does not exclude God's bringing about this created effect by means of that created cause.[43] In fact, it is perfectly obvious to Thomas that if the whole universe of natural causes is caused by God immediately, it is nonetheless a system caused by God to operate by means of its own natural laws, being, as it were, a democracy of natural causation. Of course everything whatever is immediately dependent on God's causality for its existence, for everything is created *ex nihilo*, and nothing that now exists could do so otherwise than by virtue of God's creative act. Indeed, for Thomas, for a creature to exist at all *is* for it to be "created out of nothing."[44] But what there is in the world—that, for example, there are giraffes—God brings about through the natural processes of evolution over billions of years of, as most today would agree, random mutations thrown up by the interaction of multiple chains of causality. That there are giraffes, therefore, is the result of the world's natural processes effecting what those natural processes were created to effect. In that sense, then, God can bring one thing about by means of another thing that God has brought about, and so indirectly, the immediate dependence of each and every thing upon God's creating causality notwithstanding. For God is the total cause of all causalities, and so of evolution's having randomly given rise to giraffes, because that is just what God brought about those evolutionary processes, among other things, to do.[45]

But, as I said, for Thomas human freedom is a special case. God brings about the history of salvation by means of the free acts of human beings. But by contrast with God's having brought about my existence indirectly by means of my parents—granted the whole causality of which process is dependent upon God's creating it ex nihilo—nothing at all mediates God's relationship to those free acts: God creates ex nihilo each and every free act, with nothing in between.[46] If one wants to speak of freedom needing "space" in which to be freedom, as the free-will defenders do, then it is right to conceive of that space as being unoccupied by natural created causes. Even God cannot cause a free act of mine by means of any created cause other than my own choices. But this is no restriction on the divine power, for God's power is not restricted by the impossibility of creating what it is a contradiction to describe. Contradictions describe nothing. So they describe nothing God cannot do. But just for the reason that no created cause can mediate between God and my freedom, it is entirely wrong to conceive of that freedom as a space unoccupied by the divine causality. On the contrary, rather than excluding God's causality from our free actions, we have to say that our free acts are where God's causality is most evident, most immediate—most, we might in fact say, revealingly divine. For it is within our freedom that the divine causality, as creating all things "out of nothing," is wholly undisguised by the mediation of any natural, secondary cause. If anything, then, my freedom reveals God more in the way that miracles do than as the natural world does, for the whole effect that is a free action directly reveals God precisely insofar as it is free. God's causality lies within my freedom, sustaining it, not outside it, not canceling it. It is within my freedom, therefore, that God is, as Augustine says, "interior intimo meo," "more within me than I am."[47]

If such are the reasons why we cannot avoid concluding that God is the immediate cause of our free actions, they are also the reasons why that conclusion is not, after all, so paradoxical. It would seem paradoxical to say that God causes my free actions by his immediate creative causality, as if this were the same as to say that God dangles human puppets on the strings of his governance, only were we to suppose that God's providential causality is to be understood in the terms of created natural causes. If no created cause can cause a free action other than I mine, this, as Thomas says, is because no created cause can create.[48] My free actions cannot be caused by anything other than God and myself: otherwise than as effected by my agency, a free act can only be created, out of nothing.

God's causing my free actions ex nihilo is therefore precisely what makes them free. A created cause can cause an effect only against a background of necessary conditions on which that causality depends. Parents can cause children, but only on given conditions that they do not cause with regard to gender and sexuality. A heavy object dropped falls to the ground only in a universe governed by gravitational principles. I can cause you to be irritated only on certain conditions of human psychology. No created cause can cause the *whole* reality of anything. But God can *only* cause the whole reality of my free action, that is to say, both that it is this action rather than that, and that it is this free action: as a view of divine governance the priorities on Thomas's account are exactly the reverse of those of free-will defenders, and, as we will see in our discussion of Julian on petitionary prayer in chapter 5, so are Julian's. For both, it is precisely by means of the free acts that God brings about that God brings about the whole picture, the work of our Redemption. Both what humans will freely do and how their free choices write the story of God's love are from all eternity known, and as known willed, and as willed infallibly they happen—freely. For God wills the lot—my action, its being freely chosen, and its place within the universal meaning of Creation, which is love. God wills the lot, and thus we act freely. For that is the meaning of ex nihilo, and ex nihilo is the meaning of freedom. As Julian says, he is the only doer. But then, so it follows, are we.

Is Julian's Theology Quietiſtic?

From which follows the response to the second objection. It could all too plausibly seem that Julian's conclusion about sin's being behovely only insofar as it "fits" within a providential story willed by God from all eternity must be fatalistic, or at least deterministic, and her practical attitude toward dealing with evil inevitably quietistic and excessively passive. It might seem that if there is "no doer" but God and in consequence all is well, because even sin is part of the plot of divine providence, and so behovely, then the Panglossian conclusion follows that nothing is to be done because nothing could be better than it is—or, at any rate, it would seem that there is no reason why we should strive that anything should be better than it is, for things are intended to be exactly as they are and are exactly as they are intended to be. So it might seem to follow, though it is clear that Julian herself is far from supposing that some such quietistic appeasement of sin follows from its being behovely. On the contrary, Julian anticipates the objection and resists the misinterpretation of her position that gives rise to it: "But now because of alle this gostly comfort that is before saide, if any man or woman be stered [provoked] by foly to sey or to thinke, 'If this be soth [true], than were it good for to sinne to have the more mede [forgiveness],' or else to charge the lesse to sinne, beware of this stering. For sothly, if it come, it is untrue and of the enemy. For the same tru love that techeth us alle this comfort, the same blessed love techeth us that we shalle hate sin only for love . . . for sinne is so vile and so mekille [much] for to hate that it may be liconned [likened] to no paine which paine is not sinne. And to me was shewed none harder helle than sinne."[49]

Moreover, not only is there no trace of quietism in Julian's theology of sin, or any implied by it, neither is Julian's apparent optimism based on some refusal to see sin and its evil in the stark light in which, on account of the catastrophically evil events of our own times, we feel we must do so today, for she, as we do, acknowledges that "ther be many dedes evil done in oure sight and so gret harmes take that it semeth to us that it were unpossible that ever it shuld come to a good end."[50] Nor again does her conviction that, in the outcome, "alle shalle be wele" reduce in any measure the freedom of the acts with which we resist or submit to evil as the case may be, as we have seen. For Julian, everything that you would say were there no God at all about sin, evil, and human agency—that every sin is freely done and freely avoidable—and about the conflict between good and evil into which human agents are inserted—that it is ineradicable—and about the need to struggle against evil and injustice—which is imperative with or without God—still needs to be said about them knowing, as by faith we do, that all of it is brought about by a God who in doing so devises a "plot" whose sole meaning is "love."[51] It is true, of course, that for Julian God's love trumps the lot, whether our sinful actions freely done or our freely chosen acts of resistance to sin: for those free actions of ours, including our sinful actions, bear a meaning that no free choice of ours could ever give them. But that proposition notwithstanding, Julian experiences no pressure to conclude that the human response to that love, whether to accept it or reject it, is in any way the less free for that. On the contrary, Julian's theology is entirely based on the assumption not merely that there is no contradiction between the divine providence and the freedom of the human will, but that, more positively, our human freedom is made possible only within the creative causality of God.

Does God Cause Sin?

Finally, then, the credibility and consistency of Julian's theology—if indeed I have got it right—is threatened at the point where now, it would seem, is its Achilles' heel. For this very intimacy with which God is said to be causally involved in our free actions, indeed, in their *being* free actions, would seem to exacerbate the problem of the first kind distinguished above: for is it not an implication entailed by this strong doctrine of divine governance, in a way that the free-will defense manages to avoid, that if God is the cause of all my free actions, then God is the cause of the sinfulness of my free, sinful actions? Of course, Julian firmly rejects the implication. But how consistently? Moreover, the problem of formal consistency is intensified precisely because of Julian's insistence that sin is behovely. For as we have seen, Julian says that whenever she asked, "What is sin?" she asked it as one who acknowledges that God did not so act, as he could have, to create a sinless world. What God has created is a world in which there is the quantity and intensity of sin that there is, so that even if it could be shown that God cannot properly be said to have brought about my sin, God may properly be said to have brought about this world in which I sin, including the free choices with which I do so. That being so, Julian has to conclude that because there is not a single thing that happens, howsoever little, that God cannot be said to have done or to do, to permit or to have permitted,[52] the amount and intensity of sin in the world is exactly right, exactly as it should be: none of it necessary, all of it freely done, and all of it part of the plot, all of it part of what was intended, *conveniens*, behovely. And that conclusion seems to be so scandalously offensive as all by itself to cast the gravest doubt upon the theological premises from which it follows.

The problem deserves to be faced squarely. Here we have a great theologian of the Christian Church telling us that sin is behovely. She tells us this not because she is cheerfully naïve about the world's evil, but because knowing the world's evil for what it is, she believes that it follows from core Christian beliefs about the divine love and power, that evil so "fits" with the divine plan that nothing can be "amisse." Behovely, then, not "amisse," was the bureaucratic, cold efficiency with which the murder of 6 million Jews was planned and executed; behovely, the ideologically motivated mass exterminations of the Pol Pot regime; behovely, the frenzied pogroms of Rwanda and the mass rapes of Bosnia; behovely, the betrayals of every adulterous spouse; behovely, every lie told in breach of trust; behovely, every sexual abuse of a child; behovely, every rich person's denial of food to the hungry. Thus, incredibly, for Julian, none of it is "amisse."

Incredible these conclusions are, and yet they do follow—specifically in consequence of Julian's line of defense as regards the freedom of the will. For must it not be said that if Julian will have no truck with the free-will defense, then her own solution is nothing better than an inverted form of what is wrong with it? If the free-will defense affirms the reality of sin at the expense of God's involvement in human freedom, would it not seem that Julian's solution can with consistency affirm the involvement of an omnipotently good God in our free acts only at the price of denying sin's reality? Of course Julian firmly denies that God in any way causes sin. And yet she insists that God does everything— "ther is no doer but he." So is my free sinful act not "something done?"

It is not surprising that, faced with this familiar problem, Julian is drawn into an ontological alliance with a familiar response to it, in her time associated especially with Augustine and Thomas Aquinas, according to which sin is nothing positive, but only privation: therefore, as regards sin, there is nothing for God to do. And to be sure we find such statements in the Long Text, as emphatic as they are (to many today) counterintuitive: that "sinne is no dede,"[53] and "it hath no maner of substance, ne no part of being";[54] in the Short Text, the message is blunter still: "sinne is nought."[55] Julian's meaning, so far as such descriptions go, seems unambiguous. And just as plainly, it seems at odds with the common experience of sin, not least with her own. For this line of defense would appear to deny the reality of sin—and yet as we will see in the next chapter, Julian's experience of sin is as of something all too real. In that next chapter we will in consequence be provoked to ask whether Julian's ontology of sin—her formal account of the nature of evil—and her phenomenology of it—her account of how sin is experienced—are not at odds with one another in a manner that challenges the consistency of her theology as a whole.

As I will suggest in that next chapter, it does not seem right in general to understand the Augustinian-Thomas description of evil as privation to entail that sin is unreal, nor in particular that Julian concludes from her own account of sin as having "no part of being" to any such effect. In any case, perfunctory as it is, what Julian has to say about the ontological character of sin is not set within any generalized metaphysics, and is no more than tactical, intended to allow for an important distinction relevant to her own immediate concerns: God causes my sinful actions in that they are actions, because God causes everything that there is. But God is not and could not be the cause of my actions in that they are sinful, because as there is nothing but failure in the nature of sin, it is only failure that can cause it.

To some, of course, this distinction between the cause of an action and the cause of its being sinful seems specious. But in principle it seems no more implausible to say that while God must be the cause of my action he cannot be the cause of its sinfulness than to say that, mechanically inept as I am, it was not *qua* skilled that my changing the brake pads caused my brakes to fail, but qua my lacking in skill that I did so. It was, of course, my actions of tinkering that caused the poor condition of the brakes. There were real things that I did, and they had real effects. But my actions were deficient in skill. And it was as such that they failed, and it was as failure that they caused a privation, none the less "real" for being a failure. And in the same way that I cannot qua mechanically skilled cause the failure of the brakes, so for Julian it is impossible that God who, qua Creator, causes my free act, can, qua Creator, cause its sinfulness. It is I alone in my deficiency who cause that action's deficiency in which consists its nature as sin.

Nor should we suppose that—as if in some raw, pre-moral, omni-potence—God *could* cause sin, but that he is restrained from doing so by some supervenient moral inhibition. God does not have the power to cause sin, and that is because sin is not something that any *power* could cause. And it is here that Julian's reliance on the Augustinian-Thomist ontology of evil as privation is explicit. When Julian describes sin as being without "substance," she means that sin is always failure. And it goes together with that conception of sin that it is not power, but only failure of power, that is the cause of sin. Really, then, it is my failure that causes the sinfulness of what I do, just as it is my mechanical ineptitude that really causes the failure of my brakes. But God cannot fail, not because God lacks the power to cause sin, but because it is only *lack* of power that can cause sin, and there is no power that God lacks.[56] Neither do I, who sin, possess some power to do so that God lacks: I cause my sins because I lack a power that only I, and not God, *can* lack. So, after all, it does seem at least consistent to say that God does everything except sin because, as Julian says, "sinne is no dede."

Is, then, the distinction speciously drawn between God's causing our sinful acts—insofar as they are free—and his not causing their sinfulness—because sin is deficiency, "lacking in substance"? It is not. Moreover, that distinction lies at the heart of Julian's answer to her question: "What is sinne?"[57] Above all, for Julian sin is self-defeatingly ironic. It is, as Julian says, laughably impotent.[58] Within one and the same sinful act there is intrinsic conflict, a conflicted reality. God creates ex nihilo the very freedom with which we sin, that freedom which, in itself, is an unmediated, direct disclosure of the divine love "living and working," as Julian says, at the deepest degree of intimacy within us, there where in our freedom is our identity. And yet, when we sin we are attempting to use the freedom thus created in us as if to establish an identity, a selfhood, independently of the divine action that made possible our freedom to do so. Sin is the attempt to block out, to obscure, the very condition of that freedom with which we sin, that is, the divine love that causes it. To sin, therefore, is to attempt to write the story of an ontological impossibility. It is the attempt to make a meaning independently of God, a meaning for ourselves. And such an attempt necessarily fails, because the very freedom with which we make that attempt is itself made by God, ours only because God made it in us. To sin, therefore, is to attempt to make a strategy of action and an alternative narrative out of a contradiction. Sin, as we will see that Dante tells us, has no coherent narrative. Sin's stories are empty. Necessarily sin is failure. Sin has failure written into its very nature *as* sin.

Obscuring as sin is of the divine love that makes it possible, the pervasiveness of the sin of the world, McCabe says, is not "a map of a bad God," of a God who makes sin. It is, rather, I who make sin, and so in that defeat of my freedom that is my sin I make myself into "a bad map of God."[59]

Conclusion

All which being said, it is worth noting that for Julian it is not to be counted an objection to her theology that we are in no position to make sense of *how* God's causing my free actions is compatible with their being free, or of how God's causing my free actions is compatible with some of them being sinful, or of how God's causing those free but sinful actions is consistent with God's goodness, and so with all things being well. For that we can make no sense of these things Julian not only admits but gives a good deal of emphasis to insisting upon. As she puts it, to know *how* it could be that sin is behovely would require our knowing now things that we could not now know, for they are, for the time being, secrets held within the mind of the Trinity itself and withheld from us until the final Judgment. For Julian, it is essential to know that we could not know, for any one sin, how it is behovely, still less how for the sum total of sin it is so. For we are not yet in possession of the whole narrative that will tell how. We ourselves are *within* that narrative. We are, as it were, in the course of being told by it too, and in the same way that we will be able to see how an unexpected, and possibly jarring, modulation in a symphony is made sense of by the piece as a whole, so one day, that is, in the beatific vision, we will be able to retrodict that which we could never have anticipated, the character of sin as behovely. But *only* then. In consequence, any explanation we may think we now possess in which it would appear to make sense to say this must, *eo ipso*, be mistaken about something. Julian does not deny that we should *seek* such explanations of sin and evil as are available to us. It is true, she says, that "it is Goddes wille that we have grete regard to alle the dedes that he hath done. For he wille therby we know, trust, and beleve all that he shalle do." Nonetheless, no complete explanation could be available to us, for "evermore us nedeth leve the beholding what the dede shalle be, and desyer we to be like our bretherne which be the saintes in heven, that wille right nought but Goddes will. . . . For I saw sothly in our lordes meaning, the more we besy us to know his prevites [secrets] in that or in any other thing, the furthermore shalle we be from the knowing."[60] Being *un*able to make final sense of it, therefore, is a test of the validity of our response to sin.

But to say that we can make no sense of it is not the same thing as saying that there is only nonsense to be made of it—which is what we would have to say if we knew her theology to be but a bundle of mutually contradictory propositions. Her general position concerning sin seems, in summary, to be the following: there is what we have to say about it, namely, first that it is behovely, that it is part of the plot, necessary if the true story of the divine love of Creation is to be told; and yet, second, each sin is freely done and might not have been, so that the existence of sin is a contingent fact. But how we are able to say both with consistency, *that* we cannot see, for we cannot in this life achieve the standpoint from within which their consistency can be comprehended, because we do not and could not know the sense the plot makes of it until the story is over. In principle there is nothing particularly mysterious about that. It is in the nature of stories in general that we do not know what they add up to until the end. And what is true of stories seems to be, after all, as good a definition as any of the predicament of theology itself, as of all good Christian practice too: theology shows where the mysteries lie, and if mysteries are demonstrably not nonsense, still it is no business of theology to try to reductively crack them. For Julian, as for the best in the medieval theological traditions, the business of theology is to know what we can know in the light of what we know we cannot know, and to do what we can do without fully comprehending its meaning. For its meaning is something that only God, and not ourselves, can give it.

CHAPTER THREE

Two Stories of Sin

Conflict between Julian's Sources

THE PURPOSE OF THE previous chapter was merely to clear the way for
the exploration of what are, at the very least, tensions internal to Julian's
theology, tensions to which she herself admits. But before exploring those
tensions in the form in which she addresses them within her own text,
it seemed necessary first to confront formally the objection that rather
than being theologically constructive inducements to deeper reflection,
they amount to obstructive inconsistencies and incoherent dead ends
such as would subvert any possible case for the systematic character of
her theology, or even any value to her work on any terms at all. Creative
tensions, after all, are not to be confused with plain self-contradictory
nonsense. Even supposing, then, that my attempts to rebut those claims
of formal incoherence are successful (admittedly they are all too cursory), they have in no way succeeded in eliminating a central source of
tension within Julian's *Revelation*, a tension to which she herself formally
adverts, and explicitly responds, at length. In this chapter, then, we
move forward to the examination of how those tensions are perceived by
Julian herself. Here, at least, we can work directly from her text.

Principally that tension takes the form of a troubling anxiety caused
by the conjunction of the two principal sources on which her theology relies: for here too there is conflict. On the one hand, there is the

authority of her shewings themselves, which might seem to support an ontological commitment to the unreality of evil and sin—for, she says, if we creatures most certainly do know of sin's reality, God, who creates everything, does not notice sin; sin is *"nought" to him*. On the other hand, there is the authority of the Church, whose support seems to fall on the side of her own quotidian experience of sin as something all too real. In her shewings, she sees that sin is nothing to God; in the Church's teaching, however, sin and punishment are central preoccupations.

Julian knows that her shewings thus beset her with theological difficulty. In those shewings she could see neither blame[1] nor anger in God,[2] and, more startlingly, she could see no forgiveness in God, because for God, sin being nothing, there can be nothing to forgive—"For this was an hye marveyl to the soule," she says, "which was continuantly shewed in all and with gret diligence beholden: that oure lorde God as aneynst [regards] himselfe, may not forgeve, for he may not be wroth. It were unpossible."[3] But with no less ambiguity, the Church and her own experience teach her that there is sin, that there is punishment for sin, that there is hell, and that "many creatures shall be dampned . . . dampned to helle without ende, as holy church techeth me to beleve."[4] It is as clear as anything is in *Revelation* that while she sees the one in her shewings and is taught the other by the Church, the seeing appears to exclude the teaching, and the teaching the seeing. For she does not see in her shewings what the Church teaches about the damnation of sinners, and the Church does not teach what she sees in her shewings about the Lord's not condemning them. Nonetheless, she insists that the seeing and the teaching are of equal authority,[5] and that the conjunction of authorities of equal standing rules out resort to any such easy solution to their apparent incompatibility as would attach greater weight to one or the other. To which, then, is she to turn? The conflict baffles her.

In fact, that bafflement is her *starting* point theologically. For, if sin ought to be "nought," as her shewings tell her it is, nonetheless the

Church also seems right in teaching that sin is "something." She knows for herself that sin has real causes, trajectories, and effects, which shape and form our world and its history. Every personal instinct of Julian's own supports this Church teaching. But if what the Church teaches is never absent from Julian's mind, it is simply absent from her shewings. Hence, if she is faced on the one hand with the reality of sin, of which the Church and her own experience tell her, and with the omnipotent love of God on the other, within the vision of which there appears to be no place for sin's reality nor any place for blame or punishment, then the solution to the conflict between them is going to have to be found in some sort of meaning for the assertion that sin "is no dede," has "no maner of being," and in an explanation of the place of guilt and punishment within a larger picture containing all that her theological sources teach her. In short, Julian is going to have to do some theology for herself. She is going to have to engage dialectically with her sources. As I put it in chapter 1, herein is a dauntingly problematic utrum, an agonized "How so?" And it is pretty clear that it was the necessity with which that quaestio is forced upon her that compelled Julian to compose that greatly expanded account of her revelation that we now know as the Long Text.

Julian's Shewings and the Church's Teaching

Julian sets out that conflict in the plainest terms as obtaining between theological sources, the authority of neither of which is she willing to challenge:

> Goode lorde, I see that thou arte very truth, and I know sothly [truly] that we sin grievously all day and be mekille [much] blameworthy. And I may neither leve the knowing of this sooth [truth], nor I se not the shewing to us no manner of blame. How can this be? For I knew be the comen teching of holy church and by my

owne feling that the blame of oure sinnes continually hangeth upon us, fro the furst man into the time that we come uppe into heven. Then was this my merveyle, that I saw oure lorde God shewing to us no more blame then if we were as clene and as holy as angelis be in heven. And between theyse two contraries, my reson was gretly traveyled by my blindhede and culde have no rest, for drede that his blessed presens shulde passe fro my sight, and to be lefte in unknowing how he beholde us in oure sinne. For either me behoved to se in God that sinne were alle done awey, or els me behoved to se in God how he seeth it, wherby I might truly know how it longeth to me to see sinne and the manner of oure blame.[6]

If the severity of the aporia, as Julian formulates it, ought not to be underestimated, then it is as readily misconstrued in its nature as it can be unappreciated in its intensity. The time is long past when Julian was regularly misinterpreted—very grossly—as having set up the conflict between the authority of her shewings and that of the Church's "techings," only so as in the last resort to have thrown down the latter in favor of the former—as did Clifton Wolters in an egregiously insensitive reading of Julian.[7] Nonetheless, even in some of the most sensitive readings the issue is construed (in my view, still misleadingly) as a conflict between two epistemologically independent theological sources, that of Julian's personal (and being personal therefore private) revelations, and that of the public, common teaching of the Church.[8] From either side of any such supposed epistemological disjunction, such a reading must be unsatisfactory.

As to the authority of her shewings, Julian makes it quite clear that there is nothing in them, because there could not be anything in them, that is not to be known already in the Church's teaching, even if, as she insists, she cannot see the one in the other. She is emphatic: no disjunction is warranted, none is required by her shewings, between what the

Lord reveals to her and the teaching of the Church: for Christ *is* the Church.[9] She insists that everything that is needed for our salvation— and hers—is contained in what the Church teaches, that our Christian life "is grounded" not on revelations and visions but "in faith, with hope and cherite."[10] Not otherwise than for every Christian is her own life grounded, because "Alle that I say of me, I mene in the person of alle my evencristen,"[11] and in any case, "For the shewing I am not good but if I love God the better. . . . For sothly [truly] it was not shewde to me that God loveth me better than the lest soule that is in grace. For I am seker [sure] ther be meny that never had shewing ne sight but of the comen [common] teching of holy church that love God better than I."[12] And to that "comen teching" her shewings add nothing at all: "And thus, by the shewing: it is none other than the faith, ne lesse ne more, as it may be seene by oure lordes mening in the same matter, by than it come to the last ende."[13] Julian claims no epistemological privilege on account of her revelations, nor any of personal holiness, and there is, moreover, no reason whatever to read such emphatic and careful formulas as some sort of merely conventional "humility topos," still less as some defensive strategy designed to forestall the ministrations of fourteenth-century inquisitors—as one might have anticipated, given that Julian was com- piling the Long Text in a period of English history peculiarly sensitive to accusations of heresy.[14] Julian's style is far from defensive or nervous. It is positive and confident. In any case, to construe the relationship between her shewings and the common teaching of the Church in such terms as these is very drastically to misunderstand how Julian herself conceives of the theological status of those shewings themselves. What Julian receives *in propria persona* as sixteen revelations have for her, I venture to say, nothing in the nature of independent, self-standing theological sources, no authority of their own. Rather, they have the character of "charisms," in a Pauline sense of that word.

One of the principal shifts in theological emphasis between the Long and the Short texts, resulting from twenty years or more of reflection upon the significance of her shewings, consists in a growing awareness of the readership for which they are intended, exemplified by the quotations given above. The Long Text reflects her realization that nothing Julian is shown is for her alone, and it is this realization that causes her to insist that they were not given her for her own spiritual advancement, still less was it on account of any spiritual achievement of her own that she was their recipient. Hence nearly every occurrence in the Short Text of the first-person singular pronoun "I" is replaced by the plural "we" of the Long Text to designate the recipient of those shewings. They are meant for her "evencristen": for the Church, not for Julian.

And this shift from an individual to a collective awareness of her own role is the result of her having reflected for years not only on the significance of the sixteen shewings taken singly or in conjunction, but also upon the nature of the "boke" in which she recounts and theologically expands them. The Long Text is no personal diary of her musings upon the shewings. There is no trace in the Long Text, whether in substance or in style, of the autobiographical. Her reflections upon the revelations in the Long Text reveal that she sees them as teachings of an essentially prophetic, charismatic character, meant for the Church. In fact, insofar as it is right to think of Julian as a theologian, we should perhaps say that she sees that ecclesial function as Thomas Aquinas also saw it: theology is teaching as prophecy.[15] And that characterization of her Long Text means that its intended recipients are none other than those of the shewings themselves—her evencristen.[16]

In the technical theological language of the medieval schoolmen, then, Julian's special shewings are *gratiae gratis datae,* "gifts freely given," unmerited, or, in the language of Paul's letter to the Corinthians, they are charisms, gifts of the Spirit to the Church, on which gifts no recipient through whom they are communicated can make any claim of their own. Julian's language here matches Paul's precisely. As Paul says, "He who prophesies speaks to men for their upbuilding and encouragement and consolation . . . he who prophesies edifies the church" (1 Corinthians 14:3–4), adding, as we well know, that it is only charity, and certainly not prophecy, that makes us of any worth before God. For herself, Julian says in connection with her first shewing (the résumé of all the rest): "In alle this I was mekille [much] sterede in cherite to mine evencristen, that they might alle see and know the same that I sawe; for I wolde that it were comfort to them. For alle this sight was shewde in generalle [to all and sundry]. . . . Alle that I say of me, I mene in the person of alle my evencristen, for I am lerned in the gostly shewing of our lord God that he meneth so.[17] . . . For the shewing I am not good but if I love God the better."[18] And, as if to emphasize that the target of the shewings is not her but her readers, Julian addresses them, for the first and only time in the whole extent of the Long Text, in the direct second-person plural: "and in as much as ye love God the better it is more to you than to me."[19] It is clear that what matters to Julian personally is what matters to Paul—not her shewings as such, but what through her they teach, namely, what Paul calls the "more excellent way," the way of charity (1 Corinthians 12:31). Julian's text itself enacts what it is about: it is addressed as a form of solidarity in love to her evencristen just as it is *about* that solidarity in love.

Understood in these terms as charismatic interventions of the Spirit into the life of the Church, then, Julian's shewings are, as Paul further insists (if no more emphatically than Julian herself), subordinate not only to the greater rule of charity, but also to the Christian community's discretion of spirits, an activity of discernment in which Julian herself engages to the extent of the eighty-six chapters of the Long Text, in all of which she is guided, she says, by the rule of the Church's faith. For "above the faith is no goodnesse kept in this life, as to my sight, and beneth the faith is no helth of soule. But in the faith: there will oure lorde we kepe us."[20] Whichever way one takes her shewings, that is, whether one considers them from the point of view of the readership for which they are intended—namely, her evencristen—or as measured against the rule of last hermeneutical resort—namely, charity—or as measured by the Church's responsibility for doctrinal discernment, it is clear that for Julian there are no grounds at all for any form of independent appeal to those shewings, as if they could draw either on any authority or even on any significance except within an ecclesial role. Christian charisms are no Promethean fire stolen from the gods by heroic individuals. They are gifts of the Spirit given through the Church, to the Church, and for it, and thus, as Julian likes to put it, they are communications by an "evencristen" to her "evencristens" within their shared reality as the Church of Christ: "And he wille that we take us mightly to the faith of holy church, and find there our derworthy mother in solas and trew understanding with all the blessed common. For one singular person may oftentimes be broken, as it semeth to selfe, but the hole body of holy church was never broken, nor never shall be without ende. And therefore a seker [certain] thing it is, a good and a gracious, to wille mekly and mightly be fastened and oned to our moder holy church, that is, Crist Jhesu."[21]

The "Internality" of the Conflict of Sources

It is at this juncture, where Julian's witness to her shewings meets with her witness as a common Christian, that the assignation to those shewings of a mystical character has the greatest capacity to mislead commentators. Julian is indeed frequently read as a "mystic," which would be no harm at all could we be confident of not carrying over with the word all sorts of meanings that owe nothing to Julian's conceptions of herself or to the epistemic character of her shewings. As I explained in chapter 1, our meanings of the mystical owe little to any medieval meaning, and rather more to those of a modern, anthropological interest, one of which is inherited largely from the influence of William James and his *The Varieties of Religious Experience*.[22] Unfortunately, we cannot be confident of avoiding such anachronistic readings of medieval mysticism. The empiricist epistemology that informs James's account of the mystical shows up most prominently—and most misleadingly in relation to the reading of Julian—precisely in its privileging of experience over interpretation, resulting in a sort of theological positivism that pervades much literature about the mystical today, most especially in the field of comparative religion. For if comparativists are to make anything of the notion of religion as a common category of experience uniting the great variety of its forms—even as uniting under a common conception all the great world religions, and each of these in their multiple varieties—then clearly that common ground cannot reside in the features of doctrine, ritual, social organization, or metaphoric repertoire in which those religious traditions articulate themselves. For it is in just those articulations that they most differ, perhaps even incommensurably. If on this sort of account there is to be a common core by their possession of which these complexes of belief and practice fall within the category of religion,[23] then this must be found in that which cuts below the level of their formal articulations and, therefore, in some primary experience, which is literally *in*articulate, or as James called it, "ineffable."[24] And this "ineffable experience" is, he says, the mystical.[25]

It is of little relevance that this précis of the origin of a modern conception of the mystical is manifestly oversimplified. It is not relevant here whether the misreadings of Julian's work that assume her shewings to possess (either on their authors' part or on Julian's) some character of epistemic independence relative to the common teaching of the Church do or do not in an explicit way rely on any such formalized religious anthropology, though undoubtedly some do.[26] What does seem worth noting, however, is a common tendency to suppose, in the manner of an implied assumption, that Julian's aporia should be construed as some sort of conflict between the authority of a primary datum of experience free of conceptualization and that of a doctrinal (and as it is implied, therefore secondary) conceptualization that is experientially empty. So understood, then, the aporia with which Julian sees herself confronted would turn out to be that between the authority of her mystical experiences and that of something external to it in its character as mystical, namely, the teaching of the Church.

This way of reading Julian's aporia will not do, even if the two sources of authority are accepted as being of equal weight, as Julian emphatically avers. Principally, this is because not only does she herself show no sign of understanding her conflict even remotely in such terms, but also, more importantly, because the way in which she does understand how the conflict of sources arises for her formally excludes any such construal of it. This is clearest in the way in which Julian employs the language of "seeing" so as to cut across two quite distinct, though intimately related, divides: that between the Short and the Long texts, and that between the shewings themselves and her attempts to grasp their meaning. The first is a question of how to understand the development of her thought over the twenty years or so that separate the composition of the two versions. The second is a more general question of Julian's understanding of the hermeneutics of her shewings. But in either case, the issue comes down to the significance of her frequently repeated employment of the language of seeing, for throughout her text, such and such is so, she will say, "as to my sighte," and otherwise, to the same effect, "I saw in my shewings . . ."[27]

In view of her frequent use of a metaphor derived from a form of direct and unmediated perception—seeing—to characterize her various insights, it is of course tempting to read her in such contexts as appealing to a primary datum of experience by contrast with the mediated, dogmatic formulas of Church teaching. But this reading will not work, first because it is not only in reference to the originating experiences of her shewings that she uses this metaphor of seeing, for she uses it just as frequently in reference to her own reflections upon those initial experiences. That is, Julian will say equally that she "saw" in her shewings truths that belong to them in their raw immediacy, and that she "saw" in them truths that came to her only after long, and sometimes painfully difficult, reflection on them. And she makes no difference between the two as to the meaning of "see," whether in its character as experience or from the standpoint of its truth-bearing properties wrung from that experience by much reflective labor.[28] On the one hand, then, she can speak of "this *sight* of the head bleeding," where the force of the "see" is directly visual, imaginative or, as she herself says, "bodily";[29] on the other, in this visual "seeing," "our good lord shewed a ghostly *sight* of his homely loving."[30] Again, in the same early chapter, she tells of how she was (literally) "shewed a little thing the quantity of an haselnot," in which she saw—and this latter seeing is clearly a mediated understanding of what she was immediately shown—"three properties: the first is that God made it, the second is that God loveth it, the thirde is that God kepeth it."[31] Here the word "saw" will do, whether its direct object is visual or propositional. And the layers of meaning of "see" are further piled up in the same passage, where she asks, concerning this vision of a hazelnut, "But what is that to me?"[32] and thus calls for further insight derived by yet deeper exploration of the vision's meaning, and, just for that reason, extending to the same degree the semantic embrace of the word "see."

But, there is more to it even than that. The passages in the first revelation from which the above quotations are taken belong in common to both the Short and the Long texts. Especially if we accept that the Short Text was written soon after the experiences that it recounts—though this is uncertain—then we might think that there is a reason for supposing that the Short Text lies in closer immediacy to those experiences, and so more appropriately reports them as a kind of seeing. But it is just such suppositions that cannot be supported by the evidence of the relation between the Short and the Long texts. For in a passage of extended meditation on that same first revelation, a passage that belongs only to the much later Long Text,[33] Julian tells us once again that she "saw" those further meanings "sothly."[34] If the same word "see" can do the epistemological work necessary for anything from the visual immediacy of the sight of a hazelnut to what comes to her by way of the meanings which that sight discloses after a minimum of twenty years of reflection on it, then the elasticity of the word has been made to extend, in practice, across a vast semantic range, heedless of any distinctions we might think fit to make between experience and its meaning, or between the immediacy of the visual and its theological mediation.

Nor is this a matter only of Julian's practice. So consistent is that practice that it is very hard not to discern in it a conscious, strategic, even a theologically educated purpose. And a clue as to the nature of that strategy is offered in the case Oliver Davies has made for understanding the relations between Julian's revelations and their interpretation as bearing symmetries with the relations between text and hermeneutic within standard medieval practices of biblical exegesis.[35] As I explained in chapter 1, where the medieval monk brought to scriptural commentary an apparatus of "four senses" and technical devices for their identification within the biblical text, Julian, Davies argues, brings a similar hermeneutical apparatus to bear not on a text but on the material of her shewings. The analogy should not be taken too far, but it may certainly be taken so far as to say that Julian's extended use of the word "see" as embracing both the text of her revelations and her long-term reception of it does indeed parallel the practice of the medieval exegete, who would have found it quite implausible to draw any sharp distinction between the biblical text as a primary datum of revelation and the Church's practices of that text's reception, as if either had any authority independently of the other. For in practical reality, the biblical text came to the medieval exegete physically as a codex of which the pages contained the bare words of scripture already "read between the lines" in the form of the interlinear gloss and surrounded by more ample glosses in the margins, a scribal practice that constituted, when standardized in the mid-twelfth century, what by the thirteenth century had come to be known as the *glossa ordinaria*. This compilation was put together from centuries of the Church's reflections and meditations, whether embodied in the traditions of patristic and early medieval scriptural commentary, in dogmatic decree, in liturgical practice, or in traditions of preaching. It was that single, many-layered reality that came to the medieval theologian as scripture, scripture as received by the Church, which displayed, even in its physical layout, both the text and its reception. It was known to the theologian with a "bodily" literalness and theological profundity as the *sacra pagina*, the "sacred page," the Bible as material object.

It is on some such analogy with the medieval practice of scriptural hermeneutics that Julian's compendious use of the word "see" is best understood, and that usage bears the strongest possible *dis*analogy with any attempt on our part to force some sharp positivist cleavage between the word "see" as implying some immediacy of direct experience and the subsequent interpretation of that experience.[36] Moreover, the analogy between Julian's practice and that of the medieval scriptural commentator turns the tables on the positivist account of the mystical, insofar as the word has any relevance to Julian's work. She, at any rate, appears to have hardly any use for the word at all.[37] But if we do insist on using the word "mystical" to denote any dimension of her theology, then at least we ought to employ it in some sense that she, as a medieval theologian, could in principle have recognized. And on the score of that, insofar as the word "mystical" entered the Western traditions of theology in the Middle Ages from Rufinus's translations of Origen, it denoted principally a sense of the scriptures that is hidden beneath the immediacy of the literal sense of the biblical text and extracted from the literal meaning only by a complex interpretative strategy. In short, the mystical for Origen is precisely the meaning you do *not* grasp within textual immediacy, and refers to the meaning released only hermeneutically from within a fractured, often inconsistent or factually implausible and so essentially problematic, surface meaning[38]—and the analogy with Julian is, in that respect, hard to miss. Moreover, insofar as the medieval meanings of the mystical derive from the theology of the Pseudo-Denys—and they do to a very great extent—they referred to the *mysterion* that likewise lay hidden. But for the Pseudo-Denys that hiddenness lay within the Church's sacramental liturgy, access to which is gained through, but escapes beyond, the immediate significance of the experienced material sign.[39] Finally, if there is any other medieval meaning of the word "mystical" that bears appropriately upon Julian's work, it will be that which it had for Thomas Aquinas, as also in her own different way for Julian's contemporary, Catherine of Siena: the mystical is the gift, the charism, of the teacher of the Church, who is given the hidden teachings of the Holy Spirit for the proclamation to, and thereby the building up of, his or her *evencristens*. And therefore, insofar as we could apply the term "mystical" with any degree of medieval appropriateness to Julian's theology, far from its being found in some immediate experiences recounted in her revelations, it would denote precisely that which she says she was prevented from experiencing in them, namely, that "great secret" referred to in chapter 1, hidden in the bosom of the Trinity. That secret, which cannot be known until the end of time, is the story within which alone sin's being behovely could be understood, if only we knew it—which, to be sure, we cannot know, not prematurely, not before the beatific vision. Nor, she adds, should we strive to know it.[40]

In short, if we are to say that there is any mystical meaning in Julian's text, then it consists precisely *not* in some immediate datum of experience as distinct from its interpretation but, on the contrary, in the hidden meaning that can be known to be there, but in its ultimate significance inaccessibly so, and known to be there insofar as we can know it only on the strength of an appropriate hermeneutic. That is to say, as disclosed by the progressive elaboration of the layers of meaning with which over twenty years or more she "glossed" her revelations.

And that, in turn, brings us back to the question of the terms in which to understand that aporia, which appears to set in opposition the authority of her revelations to that of the Church's teaching. Her revelations tell her that there is no anger in God. Both Church teaching and her quotidian experience of guilt support the idea that in our sinning we are blameworthy and will be punished for it. But on the account just given of the relation in Julian's theology between the revelations themselves and their interpretation, it turns out to be entirely mistaken to represent the conflict as occurring between two independent sources of authority, even if of equal but opposed weight epistemologically. Still less is the conflict well construed as that between the primary authority of her revelations as mystical against which is pitted the unequal, merely dogmatic authority of the Church. For the aporia is internal to a single, complex, indivisible whole—*her shewings as mediated to her through the teaching of the Church.* For Julian, her revelations have no meaning except as thus mediated. Her problem, the aporia, consists in the fact that, precisely as so mediated, her revelations seem to involve an intolerable internal contradiction. And that, the aporia itself, is what—if anything does in Julian—points to the mystical, to the unknowable secret withheld from us in time within the eternal wisdom of the Trinity. The aporia points beyond itself to the mystical, and the mystical is *in* the aporia. The mystery is discovered—one might say uncovered—by Julian the theologian, by Julian the mystical theologian.

The Reality of Sin and Manichean Imagination

Thus it is that we are brought back to the main substantive theological issue, to the question that so preoccupies Julian in the first half of her *Revelation:* "What *is* sin?" And so to the question left hanging at the end of the last chapter: in what sense may sin be said to be "real," given that it has "no maner of substance"? Two theological commitments appear to conflict in a manner that parallels the conflict between Julian's theological sources. For the ontological claim that sin lacks being seems challenged by the ordinary experience of evil in the same way that her describing sin as behovely is challenged by our intuitive moral sensibilities. Just as one might balk morally at the proposition that on any possible account of it the Holocaust could be behovely, so one might demur epistemologically at any such ontology of sin as would entail that that systematic orchestration of genocidal malice lacked reality. As the one proposition would seem to assault the conscience, so the other seems to be an affront to what one might fairly consider a commonsense ontology—that is, it seems an affront to our fundamental instincts about what our experience tells us.

For most people it will matter not that evil generally, and more particularly sin, may, or even must, be construed as ontological "privation," if the metaphysical arguments of the previous chapter fail to do justice to the plain experience of evil done. At the very least some effort must be made to close the gap between what logic requires and the revolt of experience against it. To be sure, as much as to any "plain" reader evil appears to Julian too to be far from "no maner of substance"; least of all does it seem to be "nought," as the Short Text has it. On the contrary, neither we nor she need be thought overcynical if, more often than not, it seems to us that it is sin, not love, that carries the day when it comes to what there is. For it is not only the amount of sin that seems to some to outweigh the quantities of love in our world;[41] it would also seem that

83

it is evil that better qualifies for the name of the real. For the images and tropes in which we spontaneously attempt to construe our experience of sin and evil all seem to possess a powerfully realistic force. Does not deliberate evil seem to have a real energy all of its own, a power that it lends to its perpetrators and to their actions? By comparison, love can seem less "realized" in the ordinary condition of things, more an unreachable ideal to be sought. Does not evil motivate and sustain purpose through hardships; indeed, does not evil seem the more capable of sustaining its purposes the more malicious its intent, as Iago is so much more sustained in his malicious and crooked purposes than is the better but weak and vacillating Othello in his sincere and straight ones? Would one not be inclined to say that, if anything, Julian's ontology is exactly wrong, and that the more evil an action is, the more "real" it is—that is, the more it has the character of a "dede"?

And it is the same with evil undergone. Any account of evil suffered that has us concluding that while the suffering is real its being evil is "unreal" would seem to be a distinction too preciously metaphysical, too ignorant of what is the more obviously plain truth, which is that when an evil action causes suffering to others it is the *evil* in it, not the action as such, that causes the suffering.[42] For it is not exactly the spouse's having had sex with another partner *simpliciter* that hurts, but its being an infidelity, a betrayal of trust, which does the damage, so that evil seems plainly enough to be not only a "something done" but also in its own right a cause, one that is capable of sparking off uncontrollably further combustions of malevolence. Evil, indeed, travels like a fire down long lines of consequence. In short, far from seeming unreal, evil visits us in our experience as if a force and, as we might be tempted to say, as if an agency, or at least a quasi-agency, like the plague in Camus' eponymous novel. For sure we know well enough how evil violates. And Julian's saying of sin that it lacks substance, "has no part of being"—which would appear to be the same as to say that it lacks reality—seems simply shocking in its failure to measure up to such facts as experienced for which we find quite natural verbal expression in a forcefully activist rhetoric of evil, in a sort of Manicheism of metaphor.

It might seem natural to derive a form of ontological Manicheism from such metaphoric construals of sin and evil, and it is clear that Julian's emphatic denial that sin shares any "portion in being" is at least negatively intended to resist any such derivation of a Manichean ontology from its spontaneously Manichean imagery. Such, at any rate, is my view. Striking, however, is the contrary interpretation of David Aers, who detects in Julian's account of sin an implicit and, as he admits, an unintended, ontological Manicheism,[43] a reading that we will have cause to discuss at some length in chapter 6. Though there I will contest Aers's reading, it must be conceded that, notwithstanding Julian's unambiguous rejections of a Manichean ontology, her language and imagery of sin are so emphatic as to the reality of sin as to convey the impression that she thinks of it as Manichees do, as if it were a real agent. And it does need to be said that just because pushing such language too far may well incur risks of a decline down ontologically slippery Manichean slopes—and I will argue that Aers is mistaken in supposing that Julian thus declines—there is no reason to deny a level playing field to a certain Manichean imagination. It is in fact almost impossible to resist construals of evil as an agency or a force possessing an energy all of its own. Nor ought we to do so, not at any rate if we are to understand the full intensity of the theological dilemma with which Julian perceives herself to be confronted. For this dilemma's two horns have equal power to impale, as we have seen, and the capacity of that horn to impale that consists in the Church's teaching about sin is witnessed by Julian's experience of sin's "sharp pain." Accordingly, she had no wish to deny that our natural rhetoric of evil holds any grip on how things are. At any rate it has grip enough on Julian.

Persistent as the tendency is to read Julian as a sort of theological

Goody Two-shoes, to interpret her assertion that sin "is no dede" as if it entailed a denial of the reality of sin, or as if it were some sort of naïve and theologically inspired refusal to acknowledge the quotidian experience of evil, is to do scant justice to what she plainly and repeatedly says about the matter. Still less does it deal fairly with her own sense of the stark theological predicament with which she is herself confronted if she is consistently to believe that in truth "alle maner of thinge shalle be wel." For on the score of the phenomenology of sin and evil, Julian is as full-blooded and emphatic as one could hope for. "For sin," she tells us, "is so vile and so mekille for to hate [so much to be hated] that it may be liconned to no paine which paine is not sinne. And to me was shewed none harder helle than sinne."[44] And again, she insists that "ther be many dedes evil done in oure sight and so gret harmes take that it semeth to us that it were unpossible that ever it shuld come to a good end."[45] If indeed sin is "nothing done," its "sharp pain" certainly is, for it is by that pain alone that it is known.[46] And though sin is nothing to God, she avers that it is certainly something for us, for it is "the sharpest scorge that ony [any] chosen soule may be smitten with."[47]

Moreover, Julian's sense of the power of evil, of its character as a malicious force, is not confined to such abstract generalities. It is for her an acute personal experience of conflict between the forces of good and evil. And if, as we will see, she firmly denies that sin itself is an agent, then sin possesses a vicarious agent who, even if she encounters him only in her sleep, is real enough to frighten her out of her wits. This agent is the devil, a monster as red as a Norfolk baked tile, freckled with black spots, and he seizes Julian by the throat in an attempt to strangle her.[48] It may be, as she says, that "pees and love is ever in us, being and working," but despite this fact, she adds, because of sin "we be not ever in pees and in love."[49] At one level she construes the relationship between love and sin as directly conflictual and absolute, that is, sin and love are in themselves mutually exclusive. Sin excludes the possibility of love; love excludes the possibility of sin. And as a result, in this life, Julian tells us, "we have in us a mervelous medelur [mixture] both of wele and of wo,"[50] experiences that sometimes, she adds (she is speaking of herself), follow one after another with alarming and dizzying rapidity: "And than the paine shewed again to my feling," she says, "and than the joy and the liking, and now that one, and now that other, diverse times, I suppose about twenty times."[51] Such is the tissue of our mortal experience in which "we stoned [remain] . . . all the dayes of oure life."[52] There is no escaping the drama of this conflict of forces—those of good and evil, love and sin—played out within our experience.

Our human experience of evil is, then, spontaneously Manichean. Evil confronts us as a powerfully malevolent force. It confronts Julian more in its character of the fallenness of the human condition as such than in the malice of individual actions, that is, more as being the sin that we are in than the sins that we do. This, we might say, is the "sin of the world," which is not exactly what we nowadays call "structural sin" *as against* individual sin, but rather that mysterious condition of things that is the source and origin of both. If it is also true that for Julian there is within us, in its own equally mysterious way, an original condition of peace—for "pees and love is ever in us"—then our total experience is dominated by two originals, such that "we stoned [remain] . . . all the dayes of oure life" in the crossfire of the conflict in which peace and love are engaged with sin. And if it is true that at some more fundamental level sin and love are not mutually exclusive, that not just the possibility but the actuality of sin lies enfolded within an all-encompassing love within which it is behovely, nonetheless that is not how it can seem to us, nor is that how it is with us. That sin is from all eternity defeated is, for Julian, a primal truth. But that truth does not entail for her the denial of the reality of our experience of sin. For our human condition in time-bound experience is of an order constituted by the conjunction, internal to it, of two opposed forces—sin and love—at permanent war with one another. Within our human experience, our reality, which is the condition of our mortality, is constituted neither by the power of love to the exclusion of sin nor by the power of sin to the exclusion of love, but by the unresolved conflict between them. At this level of our human experience, our human condition is essentially a *conflicted reality*. That is how we have to see things. Thus, no possible denial of the "reality" of sin is opened to Julian by her conviction of love's victory. That much, at least, would stand by way of intuitive support for Aers's reading of Julian as an implicit Manichee.[53] But only that much, as we will see.

Sin as Misperception: Dante's Inferno

That being the case, we are brought back to the question why it is that, given her vivid sense of the power of sin as a phenomenon of human experience and her emphatically "realistic" rhetoric of evil, Julian should in any way feel compelled to say that sin is nonetheless "no dede," has "no maner of substance"? In what possible senses does she mean that sin has "no part of being?" Does she mean that sin lacks reality in some other sense of "real"—other, that is, than that it lacks power, lacks effect? For power over the human will, effect upon our human condition, constraint upon human freedom—these she knows sin certainly to possess. There is one clear, and in my view defensible, sense in which it would be right to say that sin lacks reality, and it is perhaps the core of Julian's meaning. That is the sense in which to live in sin is in some way to live within illusion, a sense in which there is what one might call a sinful world of misperception. More to the point, sin makes us misperceive the nature of sin. Nor is Julian alone in her own century in construing sin's unreality in that way—Dante does too.

In canto 12 of *Inferno*, Virgil explains to Dante the cause of a landslide that had left an unstable bank of rocks strewn across their path.

Sometime between an earlier unaccompanied journey into hell and this one as Dante's guide, Virgil says,

> *there came One who gathered up from Dis*
> *the stolen treasure of its highest place.*
> *Moments before, a tremor in every part*
> *disturbed these fetid depths. The universe*
> *must then, I think, have felt that love through which*
> *it often turns (so some suppose) to chaos.*
> *At that same point, these age-old crags were rent*
> *and left both here and elsewhere as they are.*[54]

Virgil, of course, being a pagan and however rationally virtuous therefore ignorant of the full theological significance of Christ's harrowing of hell, knows of the event only in the general terms of the chaos that the irruption of perfect love causes to hell's violent regime. In hell, the presence of a perfect love is a destructive earthquake paradoxically turning its order into anarchy, which is, of course, to say that love reveals hell's bogus "regime" to be the anarchy that in fact it is. At any rate, this effect was inevitable, Virgil adds, "as some suppose"—the "some" in question being the philosophers of the atomistic school of Empedocles. For they "maintained," as Kirkpatrick explains, "that the existence of created forms depended upon the constant collision of streams of atomic particles. On this view violence is essential for the creation of all we know." Consequently, he adds, "any touch of love would paradoxically reduce the world to chaos."[55] Dante's hell, considered as an order, as a regime, is itself in that sense "Empedoclean" in that it is the very articulation of violence; it is, to use a phrase current in the theology of our day, structural sin par excellence; it is that parody of order of which alone sin is capable. And so, inasmuch as it is an order at all, it is but the intersection of multiple hatreds held in an (inevitably precarious) equilibrium by the overweening surplus power of diabolical counter-repression.

Dante's theological cosmology, of course, supposes exactly the reverse of the Empedoclean, for it is central to Dante's account of the order of the cosmos that on the contrary the universe—heaven, purgatory, hell, the human world and the angelic, all nature, "the sun and the other stars"—all are "moved by [an eternal] love."[56] Consequently, Dante's hell exists not otherwise than as everything whatever exists, that is, as the outcome of an overwhelmingly loving Creation. And this is so even though hell's internal regime-like order excludes all possibility of the love that created it. The divine ordering of the cosmos therefore includes hell as the site of its own exclusion. It is because of this disordered order of hell's internal regime that the effect of the irruption of the love that created it must be to loosen the grip of that violence that holds it in a parodic simulacrum of order, and so must visit destruction and chaos upon it. And therein lies Kirkpatrick's paradox. In relation to the order that sin constructs, the intervention of love can mean only its violent subversion.

For hell is above all a place of misperception, a place where all knowledge and all speech are grindingly out of joint because hell's order is structured upon a fundamental misreading of reality. Within the infernal conceptions of the damned, the divine order of the universe is turned upside down. The lost souls in hell know no order but that of their own violence, the source of which lies in the self-violations that are their sins. For this reason, they cannot see the more fundamental reality that Dante can see, namely, that even hell itself is part of the order of love. If hell were not at least a possibility available to free human choice, then something about the nature of the love that moves the sun and the other stars[57] would remain undisclosed. Being in itself a congeries of every variety of maliciousness, hell is intolerant of the possibility of love within its confines; nonetheless, hell's very existence bears witness to a love so all-encompassing as of necessity creating the space in which its inhabitants may endlessly rehearse their pre-mortem and final rejection of it.[58] The possibility of hell is an expression of the divine love, but everything in hell is premised on the refusal of the love that made it possible. For hell is hell because it is the condition of not being able to see the fact that love made it.[59]

No misreadings of the *Commedia* as a whole have a greater tendency to distort Dante's cosmic vision of the love that moves all things than those that assume that, whereas purgatory and paradise are expressions of the divine love, hell issues from something else, perhaps from divine justice or even from divine vindictiveness, as distinct from divine love. Such a reading of the universe of the *Commedia* is impossible, for the very reason that it is precisely that misunderstanding of things that characterizes the misperceptions of the damned. Besides, Dante makes his meaning plain at the very gates of hell, in the words of that famous inscription wherein we are told that is was not a vindictive and resentful tyrant but an infinite and eternally wise love, inseparable from justice, that made it:

> *Through you go to the grief-wracked city.*
> *Through me to everlasting pain you go.*
> *Through me you go and pass among lost souls.*
> *Justice inspired my exalted Creator.*
> *I am a creature of the Holiest Power,*
> of Wisdom in the Highest and of Primal Love.[60]

It is this paradox, then, that the lost souls can never see, or if they can see it cannot admit, or if they can admit it must reject. The ultimate gift of an all-loving God is the gift of the freedom to reject the love through which alone their freedom is in the first place made possible. That love is "primal," therefore, because it precedes and contains within itself the possibility of the sin of its refusal. In that sense, Dante's hell, just as much as his purgatory and paradise, represents not the defeat of love but its victory, a victory that the free rejection of it ironically concedes. Sin's defeat is ultimately its self-defeat. Sin is a defiance that concedes victory to that which it defies in the very act of its rejection—just as does the defiance of Satan in that other "divine" epic, *Paradise Lost*. Milton's Satan, for all his heroics, is in the end reduced to proclaiming even his evil as his good. Thereby, he concedes, for all his bluster, that he is but a parasite on what he defies.⁶¹

Dante's hell is not just a place of punishment inhabited by sinners. It is a place where sinners, by choice, inhabit their sins and live their lives structured by sin's distorted perceptions of love. That love they have to reject, as being an invasion of some imagined personal space independent of God, as a violation of their personal freedom and autonomy. But this self-deceived self-affirmation shows up in the refusal of the damned to accept that there can be any narrative other than their own, for they deny that there is, after all, any *divina commedia*. The damned all have their own stories to tell, and *Inferno* tells them. Each of them, from Francesca da Rimini⁶² to Ugolino,⁶³ know that those stories which they each tell of their fates recount not just why they were sent there to hell in the first place—that is, their specific sin—but also why they are held there without term in a condition of sinfulness, for the grip of hell on them is but the grip with which they hold onto their stories, without which they cannot imagine for themselves an identity or reality. They need their stories, stories of their own telling, and they need the misrepresentations that those stories tell. Hell is but the condition consequent upon their ultimate refusal to abandon that need. Hell, then, is the condition not of those who have sinned, for many who have sinned more grievously than Francesca and Paolo are not in hell but in a place of Redemption in purgatory. Hell is the condition of those who do not repent of their stories, who refuse the offer of their revision by the divine love, and insist on living by means of the story that sin tells, the story of the attempt to achieve a self-made significance independently of the story of the divine love. And you might even say that the free-will defense is the philosophical rationalization of that story, which, because of their refusal to abandon it, holds the damned in their place in hell. Hell is the place for those who can represent their freedom narratively, and choose it, only insofar as that freedom stands in the relation of mutual exclusion with the universal and omnipotent sway of the divine love.

Sin as Misperception: Julian

For Julian, as for Dante, what is "real" is the divine love. Sin, in being the refusal of that love, is the refusal of reality. To say in this sense that sin is unreal, however, is not to deny that it happens. Nor is it to deny sin's pain. For Julian, all the pain of the world is nothing but sin, nothing but sin's violence and violation. For this reason, if we are to understand—whatever we can understand—of that order which is ours premortem, the order which is but another word for what I called "story" in the preceding chapter, then we must grasp just how inappropriate, after all, is that Manichean metaphor I employed earlier in this chapter of "warfare" between love and sin, for it is sin alone that knows violence and wages war. Love knows only peace. Just as Dante's hell is a loveless place created by the same love that sin self-defeatingly rejects, so for Julian sin and love contest with one another within human freedom on terms that are at once asymmetrical and radically unequal. Asymmetrical, because if we are to capture the force of Julian's theological vision, we should say not that love and sin wage war upon one another, but rather that love wages peace upon the warfare of sin, subverts its simulacra of order by enclosing it within a *commedia*, a *commedia* that can appear to a sinful world only in the misperceived guise of violence. As Julian says, peace is "always in us." And the only thing that can separate us from that peace is the "wrath" that is only "on man's side," not at all on God's, and is there in us only "through sin and wretchedness." Sin knows nothing but anger with peace, while peace can show no anger with sin. And the conflict between sin and love is not only in that way asymmetrical but is also radically unequal, because we have to add that for Julian, in love's waging of peace against sin that is our human story, it is love that always has the upper hand. For sin is from all eternity foreseen by love, and for that reason, it is nothing in itself, even if what sin intends—that is, its nature as sin—is precisely the attempt to mean something in itself and independently of the love of God that foresaw it. Sin, on Julian's conception of it, is essentially parasitical for its meaning on that which, as sin, it denies. It may be that in our experience sin always wins. But beyond our experience lies the victory of love, for sin's victories are always pyrrhic.

However, if we are to say that sin is a *refusal of reality*, this does not mean that it is in any way an *unreal refusal*, for to say that to live in sin is to live within illusion is by no means the same as to say that sin is illusory. Refusing reality can have every sort of real consequence, can cause every sort of pain and suffering, can weave warps and webs of fantasy and illusion, can create and sustain whole regimes of deceit, can motivate personalities distorted by such fears and self-deceptions so as to generate all the world's violence, all the world's need for it, and all the world's untold numbers of cruelties—all of which can join up into interlocked systems, into self-sustaining structures, which conspire to be a world made out of the material of its unreality. Sin's world is the world of Plato's Cave, the world of prisoners who, locked into their illusions, will kill rather than have their illusions shattered. And yet, for all that, the unreality of that world can have the "real" force and energy, the "real" motivating power, even the bureaucratic efficiency that any Holocaust can—did—have. Dante's hell is but the apotheosis of that refusal of reality, the outcome of the choice finally to refuse the reality of the divine love, preferring one's own unreality to the divine reality as an ultimate condition. Hell is but a regime of the refusal of reality. Of course, then, sin is real, and there is nothing in Julian's theology that would suggest otherwise. But her saying that sin is "real" is perfectly consistent with her also saying that sin has "no substance, no manner of being," that is to say, it is perfectly consistent with an unambiguous rejection of Manicheism. Sin is real in the sense that an unreality can become the real substance of a person's or of a society's existence, a kind of *really lived refusal of the real*.

Nor is there anything very paradoxical in that conjunction of the "lived" and the "unreal," for we know the conjunction all too well at a personal level. We are, after all, quite familiar with the condition in which a person's actual life is embedded in, so as at least in part to be constituted by, a misperception of its own real nature. Sometimes this condition is at least semideliberate and so a kind of self-deception. For a person's actual life—its reality in the sense of what happens in it—can be organized around a contrived failure to see it as it really is, as when, out of fear of admitting it to myself, I refuse to believe that I am in love, or will not admit that I am motivated by self-interest, or some such. Really I am in love. But I live in and through the denial of this reality, so that in another sense my reality is constituted by the contradiction between what is really the case and my denial of it. My life is over-determined, as it were, by the conjunction of the disjuncts. And so it is that in such wise, I (insofar as I am self-deceived) act—indeed, I make a self who acts—out of the overdetermination of that contradiction. For in such cases I do really live in and through not just a conflicted motivation but an unreal, conflicted selfhood, and so in the medium of an impossible story. However difficult it is to get right the terms for the description of self-deception—after all, there is a paradox built into the very notion, as there is, say, in my own self-defeating attempts to hide my cigarettes in a place where I cannot find them—nonetheless, the phenomenon undoubtedly exists and gives at least a primitive experiential link to the notion of a lived, and so actual, form of unreality. For I, the self-deceived person, am both the real me I disguise from myself *and* the disguise with which I mask that reality. In fact, we might say that the really real me is the person whose selfhood is constituted by the contradiction between them. And so my conflicted actions arise out of that conflicted reality of my selfhood. Such is sin's persona.

Nor is self-deception at a personal level the only sort of case that might be described in terms of conflicted, lived unreality. Sin makes not only a self of its own. It makes a world for that self. For there are well-known forms of social relationship, not only at an interpersonal level but whole regimes, lived out in terms of fantasies and illusions and falsehoods, whether imposed by manipulative propaganda or of the kind that Marx ascribed to social ideologies, being "a society's natural and spontaneous mode of thought." And those falsehoods constitute the actual reality of those regimes, for which reason we have to say that their reality as social formations consists in lived forms of unreality. Sexual partners can sometimes achieve an uneasy equilibrium of known but unacknowledged mutual dishonesties; consumer behavior can be mediated through the manipulation of all sorts of fantastical desires and aspirations; whole social structures can achieve relative stability in the medium of collective and false national, racial, and religious identities. As we know and recognize such phenomena to be common enough, we should have no trouble conceding in principle the possibility of an individual life or a social formation lived in and through the contradiction between the reality that is lived and the unreality that is the very fabric of the life so lived. Such, at any rate, in its ultimate form, is the regime of Dante's *Inferno*. It is falsehood lived as relationship, self-deception lived as politics.

And I think that this is one central element in what Julian too meant by sin's lacking substance—that is, she means, primarily, the sinful condition of consciousness, sin as misperception of reality. And just as there is love's story, so there is a story of sin. Not, that is, a story that tells of sins, truthful or otherwise, a story that rehearses the historical record of human depravity, but rather the depraved story that sin itself tells, especially of itself. For the collateral effects of the sinful human condition are in part cognitive and cause the sinful to misperceive the nature of sin itself. And the story that sin tells of itself is necessarily also a false story of God. This would seem to be the shape, in general terms, of Julian's response to the problem of sin: the demand that the story of sin be told in all its demoralizing fullness—the acknowledgment of the reality of sin—does not require the telling of sin's version of that story, for that tale is told by idiots, its sound and fury signifying nothing. The story that sin tells, which both issues from and tells of wrath and violence (that are, in truth, "only on man's side") projects that wrath onto God, who can then be seen only as condemning us, so that within that story we can see nothing of that divine love for whom sin is nothing. Nothing, that is, except that persistent telling of the false story of God. The god of wrath and vengeance is the petty little tyrant godlet we choose out of the wrath of sin within us, a fabrication concocted as the objectivized counterpart to our own resentment. Such a god is truly diabolical and in two senses: first, this is god as only the devil can see him, and second, such a god is but the devil's—sin's—angered self-projection.

But concoction that such a god may be, the god we choose is the god we get, and hell is but the consequence of our sticking to a delusional story of divine anger and of God's vindictive desire to punish us. Some people, the Church teaches us, do, and others will, stick to their own sinful stories of sin and their corresponding theologies. The conflict between her perception of the divine love and the existence of sin and hell is resolved for Julian not by denying that there is sin, for it is not in that sense that sin is nothing, nor is it resolved by denying that there is hell. Julian can tell that story of sin with complete truthfulness, and she need not be deviated from it by anything she gleans from her shewings. I repeat: Julian is no optimist naïvely denying the reality of sin in the best of all possible worlds. Because of sin this is *not* the best of all possible worlds. Therefore, her story telling the record of sin does not require any absurd calculation of the ratios of love and sin in the world in favor of love—as if such calculations were either possible or meaningful either way. For Julian both sin and hell are real in the sense that both happen and the Church is right to resist the denial of their reality. But within every conscious decision to sin lies the decision to act within a story of selfhood and God that is unreal, false. It is a story in which, being of our own fabrication, the infinite compassion of God can have no place, for the story of that compassion is one that we could not possibly tell for ourselves. It could be told only by that infinitely compassionate God himself. And hell, for Julian, is nothing but our choice—endlessly, pointlessly, self-defeatingly—to rehearse the unreality of those stories that sin tells. Hell is the choice to live in the medium of our own nothingness and of the idolatrous theology of a God who annihilates. Sin is how we exclude *ourselves* from reality by preferring to inhabit the self-destructive unreality of the story that sin tells, by refusing to allow ourselves to be told by the story of compassion that the divine love tells. It is in that sense at least, then, that sin is "no dede," is nothing real. It is the attempt to place a nothing at the heart of the real. Necessarily the attempt fails. But the attempt itself is real enough. Indeed, attempting it and failing in the attempt are the only two things that we genuinely can do for ourselves unaided by grace.

What, then, are we to say about the conflict between Julian's theological sources, between what the Church and her experience tell her about sin and hell on the one hand, and what her shewings tell her about the love and compassion of the Lord who "sees not sin" on the other? To ask the question in another way,[64] what is the difference between what the Church teaches about sin, punishment, and hell, and "the story that sin tells" of itself? Though the full answer to this question awaits the next chapter, this much can be said at this stage: as to the relationship between what the Church teaches and what is revealed to Julian in her shewings, neither is true in separation from and disjunction with the other. In short, *only* both are true. For in fact what the Church teaches is both what Julian is shown of the divine love in her revelations—for it is through Julian's work that the Church teaches it—and the reality of sin. By contrast, what I have called "the story that sin tells" amounts to the one-sided narrative of sin and divine punishment *minus* what is shown to Julian in her shewings of love. Conversely, a naïve, sentimentally optimistic Julian is what you get from Julian's shewings *minus* what the Church teaches about sin and hell. Only the simultaneous telling of both is true, for neither is true unless the other is. Insofar as Julian's theology is constructed upon this dialectical two-sidedness, it is, as we saw in chapter 1, rooted in paradox, the paradox being that while each side is false without the truth of the other, yet we stand on no ground of vision (that is, of seeing), but only that of faith, from which we may understand the conjunction.

PART TWO

Sin and Salvation

CHAPTER FOUR

The Lord and the Servant

Is Julian a Universalist?

THERE IS A STORY that tells the record of human sin, and there is the story of that record as sin tells it. The first is real enough, for there are sins enough of which to tell, and they have visited much by way of consequence upon human history. But the second is a bogus theology of history equipped with its own accounts of selfhood and of God, and, as we will see, even with a kind of soteriology all its own. If in the first half of this essay I have sought to explain how Julian responds to an experience of sin that appears to undermine her confidence in her shewings of love, and to defend that response for consistency, then the topic of this second part has already been anticipated in what precedes it. For it has become increasingly clear that Julian does not perceive the existence of sin to be the greatest stumbling block in the way of her making coherent sense of her shewings. What proves a more troubling obstacle, rather, is a sinful theology of sin, the story that sin tells of itself. This story is constructed from a false theology of history and a false soteriology, and as such has no reality except in that secondary sense (identified at the end of chapter 3) in which it is possible to live within a false story and really live in a state of unreality. Moreover, the story that sin tells is not entailed by even the most truthful and undeceived record, while conversely, Julian's certainty that nothing can "be amisse" is not sustained on some naïvely optimistic amelioration of its horrors. As I have put it, the defense of Julian's theology of history is not premised on, nor does it entail, any form of "Holocaust denial." On the contrary, it is sin that cannot tell its own story, for the record of human sinfulness is least well told by sin's account. It is, in fact, what the Lord tells Julian that is the only true story of sin.

Above all, the story that sin tells is false not because it has no soteriology but because it perverts a good one. In the nature of the case a language that speaks of sin is innately theological. Atheists may be guilty of all sorts of crimes. But atheists cannot describe their crimes as sins. Only believers in some God can so describe their actions, because all sin is in some way a defiance of God, and the atheist admits of nothing to be defied. Sin is an attempt to establish an identity independently of God's power and love, an attempt to clear some space free of God so as to make room for oneself. To judge oneself to have sinned, therefore, requires the belief that there is a God to have been cleared out of the way. It is to judge oneself before God, to admit so to have construed one's identity as to have excluded from it a divine presence that threatens its imagined sovereignty. In general, then, to tell the story of one's sin is to affirm the existence of God. But to tell the story of God as sin tells it is to buy into a theological narrative that is inherently sinful—it is sin's cognitive collateral damage. It is to tell a story of self and of God as standing in relations of mutual exclusion, as if what were at stake is either my identity or else God's, either my freedom or God's providence. Sin's narrative is, then, both theological and perverse. It tells of a God whose eternal purposes for Creation are thwarted by sin, of a God angry for being thwarted and so punishing, threatening my freedom with extinction.

Within such a narrative it is inevitable that before such an overwhelming and infinite power, we creatures are but children, and cowering children to boot. The God of sin's story infantilizes us, reproducing and reinforcing the need to placate an implacable tyrant—and as end-lessly as fruitlessly. For the tyrant god's implacability is the *product* of the infantilism it reinforces: the two loop back on one another. It is for this reason that Julian's repeated warnings against maudlin wallowing in the mire of our own sinfulness have such urgent intensity. Wallow-ing in this way is not a misplaced or exaggerated form of humility, not even an understandably pious one. It is idolatrous, and she tells us that it is fiercely to be resisted, for "it is againe [against] truth."[1] It is not God who urges us thus to wallow. It is a diabolical temptation, "a foule blindhede," for the mud of sin sticks on those who wallow in it, trapping them in a vicious circle in which resentment continually reinforces the idolatrous doctrine of God that causes it.[2]

Julian sees no such God in her shewings. Neither, here, does her theology arise from any denial of the power of evil, whether of her own or of her fellow Christians. The Lord tells her that she will remain in sin's power in that she will continue to sin and, on her own account, sin she does—in fact, she says, "I shalle do right nought but sinne."[3] Nor does Julian deny that hell exists. The Church teaches that there is hell, and Julian believes the Church: "I beleved sothfastly that hel and purgatory is for the same ende that holy church techeth for."[4] But hell's existence is more or less self-created: to sin is to choose hell, to choose that there be hell, to live in an infantile world of unreality. In fact, as Sartre knew every bit as well as Dante, the only world that human beings can make for themselves independently of God is hell: "L'enfer, c'est les autres"[5] follows from the existentialist conception of freedom as possible only in a space cleared by the denial of God.[6]

Sin is in that sense the choice to make one's reality out of the un-real. And a loving God, who creates and sustains our freedom, allows the freedom to make just that choice. This God who loves us allows room for the possibility of an effective rejection. We can replace God as "Father," as "Mother," with a vindictive tyrant: and who, after all, mistaken enough so to conceive of God, would not, like Sartre, seek to occupy some higher moral ground from which to defy him? Within such a soteriology the choice of hell is not only the most natural one, it is the one that would appear to be required by any sense of human worth and dignity. All that Nietzsche ever denied in his rejection of Christianity is contained within that humanly destructive soteriology.[7]

Moreover, Julian appears to be certain not just of the possibility that God can be rejected, but that in fact at least some people actually make that choice, and that they get what they want—to be in hell. Disputed as the matter is,[8] there is much less textual support to be found in Julian's *Revelation* for the "universalist" doctrine that all will be saved and none that is as explicit as her emphatic assertion that many are not: "One point of oure faith is that many creatures shall be dampned—as angelis that felle out of heven for pride, which be now fendes, and man in erth that dyeth out of the faith of Holy Church—that is to sey, tho that be hethen—and also man that hath received cristendom and liveth uncristen life and so dieth oute of cherite. All theyse shalle be dampned to helle without ende, as holy church techeth me to beleve."[9]

Reflecting on the unequivocal character of that "many," and upon how common was the teaching among theologians and preachers alike that few are saved,[10] it seems hard to credit Julian with anything more than "universalist" inclinations, as Watson and Jenkins do,[11] that cause her once more to be puzzled by the apparent conflict between what the Church clearly teaches and what would seem to be implied in her shewings. The Church teaches that many are damned. Her shewings reveal to her a God whose love is so universal and inclusive as to be beyond the need even to forgive sins, never mind any desire to punish for them. But that is the point: the tension between her two sources is troublingly present in a way that it would not be were Julian to have seriously challenged the Church's teaching in a universalist manner. Moreover, what does seem to be clear is that her frequently repeated references to "alle that shalle be saved,"[12] though theoretically open to the possibility that every soul is to be saved, is more naturally read against the background of her unambiguous declarations that many are not. It is therefore true that, as Watson and Jenkins say,[13] Julian is caused to be anxious by the difficulty of reconciling the universal love of God with the fact that some place themselves by their own choices outside that love. But when she tells God of this anxiety Julian admits that "as to this, I had no other answere in shewing of oure lorde but this: 'that that is unpossible to the[e] is not unpossible to me. I shalle save my worde in alle thing, and I shalle make althing wele.'"[14] It does not seem right to conclude that the Lord's answer "I shalle make althing wele" entails that, contrary to the teaching of the Church, God will pull off the "impossibility" of saving everyone. It seems a more natural reading of what Julian says that the impossibility of which the Lord speaks refers to her problem of *seeing* how the damnation of many can be made consistent with God's making "althing wele," that what seems impossible to her is not an impossibility to God. All Julian is told is that God resolves her difficulty, not how. In effect she is told that a solution is none of her present business: the solution to her difficulty is "unpossible to the[e]."

What is her present business—because it is the proper business of the theologian—is that she should here, as everywhere, keep all the theological data in play—both that "alle maner of thinge shalle be wel" and that some souls are damned, not running with either to the exclusion of the other. And lying behind this inclusive strategy is at least the general principle that, whatever facts will be revealed in the final outcome, whether it will or will not turn out that there are "many," or even any, in hell, Julian does not conceive of the ultimate victory of love over sin as entailing that there could not be any souls in hell eternally damned, any more than, as we saw in chapter 2, her shewings allow her to think that "alle maner of thinge [could be] wel" only in a world without sin. Once again, Julian is steering her theological way between what she believes are two kinds of error: the first being that hell is an impossibility before the omnipotent love of God, the second that the price of human freedom is necessarily sin. Not the first, because in principle universalism—the doctrine that a loving and merciful God could not allow hell to exist—would seem to entail that any human refusal of God must ultimately be frustrated: like it or not, we will be saved. Maintaining that proposition seems to rule out a genuine option for human freedom and, therefore, would amount to the denial of sin's reality, for it would preclude the possibility of any effective rejection of God. And not the second, because, as we saw in chapter 2, Julian appears to see no problem in principle—that is, of conceptual consistency—with there being a world in which in fact everyone freely chooses only the good. In general the world's condition is governed neither by necessity nor by impossibility, but by willed fact—a state of affairs willed by an eternal and invincible love. All she needs to say—indeed, all she thinks we can say—is that as a matter of fact there is hell, because as a matter of fact people do exercise their freedom so as to reject God. And it is the particularity of those facts of the matter that set up a problem for any claim of faith to an assured victory of love. At all events, assurance of the victory of love can rest on no principle of the impossibility of hell or, conversely, of its necessity.

Julian, therefore, is told a quite different story of God from that which sin tells, and consequently her theology of history departs sharply from its account. Ultimately the true story of the human race—which is how everything that happens, including sin, is made by love—will be told in all its particularity. Event by event, choice by choice, each person's actions, however small or insignificant, will be rehearsed in their relevance to just that story of love that from all eternity was told within the very being of the Trinity itself. It is within that story alone that content can finally be given to Julian's "behovely," for it is only when we can finally enjoy the vision of the Trinity that we will be able to grasp just how everything that happens, one way or another, bears the meaning of love. We, however, presently live not within that ultimate reality, but at the crossing of its path with our temporality. Our present condition is essentially *pen*ultimate. For we are not in a position to tell the ultimate story—its plot is hidden from us. We are given only a story fragment, and our condition is defined by the partial character of the story as we possess it, both by what it can disclose to us and by what is implied by the very incompleteness of what it discloses. We can know by faith that our living within a story of love is "true." We can know by faith that it is "nothing but the truth." But we also know that our grip on that story captures less than the "whole truth." These, we may say, are the epistemological limits within which Julian thinks through her problems about sin, epistemological limits that are eschatological. They are neither more nor less than the limits of theology, for they are the limits of faith. And so, as we will see in the next chapter, they are the limits of life.

Dante and the Incompleteness of "Narrative"

As we concluded chapter 3 with Dante, so also may we begin this next. For if flesh and blood were needed to embody and give content in a fragmentary narrative to the skeletal framework of propositions—that sin is real but yet behovely—then no more comprehensive or bolder attempt to tell that story was ever made than by Dante in his *Commedia*. If anyone ever reinvented "narrative theology" after Augustine,[15] it is Dante; and no one but Milton has since dared risk comparison with the *Commedia*. But we would be sorely misled if we were to draw the conclusion from the appearance of completeness in Dante's *Commedia* that he imagines his narrative to be obedient to laxer eschatological constraints than does Julian hers. It is true that Julian's own narrative fragment—it is found in chapter 51 of the Long Text and consists in the parable of the "Lord and the Servant"—is by comparison perfunctory and drastically pared down, as it were demonstrating in its textual brevity the theological short-windedness that it argues for. Nonetheless, the theology of the *Commedia* and the theology of *Revelation* represent a common eschatology, a common conviction that the story of salvation can be told only *in part*, exceeding our pre-mortem comprehension.

Dante had entitled his work not *Divina*, but simply *Commedia*—the interpolation of the *Divina* was a later, sixteenth-century pious addition that has since stuck. One imagines that Dante himself would, however, have understood the title "*Divine* Comedy" to be rather more pleonastic than pious. On Dante's account, there is no comedy that is not the one and only divine comedy. For if there were no such divine story to be told as he tells it, then all that could remain is tragedy. Or perhaps it is truer to say that for Dante, were there no divine comedy, then there would be no story at all; there would be nothing but the tragedy that there is not even enough story to be told for tragedy to apply. That, after all, is the meaning of Dante's hell: its inhabitants, as we saw in chapter 3, live exclusively within their own stories, admitting no larger narrative into which their own stories are inserted and from which they acquire meaning, for they have no desire to live within any narratives other than those they themselves have composed, not even those of fellow human beings. In hell there are no "fellows," for in hell other people are hell, and the narratives of the damned amount to a cacophony of discordant, self-absorbed voices. The damned are thus condemned, but by their own choices, to live out their own meaning on their own terms, out of communion with God or any other human. And they get exactly what they have chosen—solipsistic meaninglessness, an abyss of loneliness. The self-enclosed and self-enclosing stories that the damned tell are not stories at all, and their attempts at self-justification ironically amount only to the justification—precisely on the terms they have sought to impose—of their own condemnation in hell. For here too in Dante's hell, as in Julian, the story that sin tells is of an angry God of whom just such a condemnatory judgment is to be expected. For all their self-justifying rhetoric, the souls in Dante's hell are really not at all surprised to find themselves there. For the standpoint of sin knows no other God. Within the dialectic of the story that sin tells, the self-affirmations of the damned require a tyrannical god who damns them, for they cannot construe their self-affirmations in any other terms than those of the exclusion of such a god. It is not exactly the god they deserve that they get, for, as Hamlet says, "Use every man after his desert, and who should 'scape whipping?"[16] What they get, rather, is the god that they insist upon.

On the other hand, it is not as if Dante represents himself as being, by comparison with the souls in hell, a theological know-it-all. What he can narrate is not the "master-narrative," and he knows it. As Kirkpatrick reads Dante's *Purgatorio*, this is not a place of punishment for sin, not even a temporary one. It is not even a place of sin's painful, fiery purgation—not exactly. Rather, it is a place of progressive, joyful self-discovery, a place for the recovery of self through the recovery of one's own excellence lost through sin; and so it is the recovery of our delight in God's own delight in our making.[17] Here, in purgatory, there are many souls the record of whose sins match in intensity and depravity those of the souls in hell. It is not the sins committed that differentiate purgatory from hell, but the story that is told of them, the narrative to which they belong. The souls in purgatory have all repented, that is to say, they are learning how to be able, and how to desire, to situate the record of their sins within the comedy of divine love that redeems them. The souls in hell can narrate their sins only insofar as they exclude themselves from that comedy. You might say that Dante's hell and Dante's purgatory are one and the same place, inhabited by one and the same set of "facts" of sin—what differentiates them is the wholly different theological stories the repentant and the unrepentant tell of those facts. You could go even further, to paradise—for the souls there do "remember" their sins in a way, as does Folco, for they are part of his story of Redemption. But Folco can now remember his "fault" with a smile, for now he can see that it has no significance in itself—as such it "does not come to mind," for as fault it has no story of its own to tell, its significance as sin being entirely contained within the story of divine love: "Here we do not repent, nay we smile," he says, "here we contemplate the art that makes beautiful the great result."[18]

Hell's stories cannot be completed, for the damned refuse to complete them. Purgatory's stories are completed in paradise. But not for Dante, whether the character in the poem or the poet who writes it. The epistemology of the *Commedia* is the epistemology of the as yet incomplete. For if it is not the epistemology of the damned in hell, which is interminably self-obsessed, neither is it the epistemology of the redeemed in paradise, which is eternally fulfilled in the vision of the other. As Kirkpatrick has suggested,[19] the epistemology of the *Commedia*'s composition is that of the souls in the purgatory of which it tells. Of course it is possible to read Dante's final vision of God recounted in the famous last canto of *Paradiso* as an extended gloss on the passage in 2 Corinthians 12:2–5 in which Paul boasts of his being taken up into the third heaven, there to have witnessed things that no mortal eye has seen or heard, things of which, having been seen and heard, no "telling" within our mortal condition is possible.[20] But if that is right, then insofar as *Paradiso* canto 33 can be represented as a gloss on that scriptural claim of Paul's, it is important not to forget that Dante's *Commedia* is, after all, a work of fiction, whatever else it is. Dante the poet does not claim actually to have enjoyed Paul's vision as Dante the character in the *Commedia* does. Dante knew that any such authorial claim in fact and in propria persona would have been seen by the theological consensus of his times as verging on the presumptuous, for Paul's rapture in 2 Corinthians forms a theological topos of an almost wholly exceptional character. For the mainstream theological tradition, Paul's rapture bears comparison only with the description of Moses in Numbers 12:7–8 as meeting with God "face-to-face,"[21] and even if there are some few others who make similar claims to the unmediated vision of God pre-mortem,[22] Dante knew that, with the exception of those two biblically warranted cases and perhaps a few others, *all* human experience of God pre-mortem is governed by the stricture of Exodus: "no one may see my face and live" (Exodus 33:18–23). Dante consciously wrote the *Commedia* under that general condition on the pre-mortem knowledge of God, and it is in that sense that the epistemology of the *Commedia*'s composition is "purgatorial." But even as regards Dante the character in the poem, the narrative of *Commedia* is dominated not by the finality of that vision of the last canto as such but by the ethical implications of it for how human beings are to live in communities of history and time with one another in any degree of adequacy to what that vision demands of them.[23]

Even considered internally within its fictional context, then, Dante's vision of the Trinity in incarnate human form—the chiasmic counterpart to Julian's statement that when she says "Christ" she means the whole Trinity[24]—is one before which, he says, "high imagination fails."[25] And just upon that failure of all language, that is, even of his poetry, it is his will alone that is "moved" by that same love "which moves the sun and the other stars."[26] For that reason the last word of the *Commedia* is not, after all, as in *Inferno* and *Purgatorio*, the "stelle" of *Paradiso*, but the silence that falls upon Dante and his readers thereafter, a silence that is made to bear the whole weight of the preceding one hundred canti that interpret it—a silence that, paradoxically, is the perfect word toward which all the *Commedia* aims. It is in that perfect word that is silence that the final perfection of community is realized, and the whole meaning of the poetic act itself consummated. In that sense at least, for all its structural completeness as epic, the *Commedia* is theologically an essay on the impossibility of narratival completeness. And the *Commedia* spells out the limits clearly, of theology and of language itself, limits that his poetry can reach out to but cannot pass beyond. Enormously longer than Julian's "Lord and Servant" narrative as the *Commedia* is, Dante's epic is still theologically but a fragment, and essentially so: for theology is essentially fragmentary. In fact you could say, and not misleadingly, that the *Commedia* is many words about the theological significance of two contrasting silences—or, more precisely, failures of speech.

For in Dante two silences face one another opposed across the vast narrative between the end of *Inferno* and the end of *Paradiso*, and they face one another as do two impossibilities of narrative. At one end of the scale, and falling below the possibility of narrative, there are the "non-stories" of the condemned in hell: so intense does the meaninglessness of hell's depths become that Dante confesses that he himself lacks the *rime aspre e chiocce*, the "harsh and grating rhymes," with which to describe it.[27] At the other end, there is the story that cannot be completed because its significance exceeds all narratival possibility. Poised in between these two silences is human speech, the one and only possibility of narrative, and so the possibility of the *Commedia* itself, which tells of the boundaries of silence by which it is contained on either side. Spiraling down from the wordy self-justifications of Francesca da Rimini,[28] through Ulysses' bragging, hyperbolic, and value-free quest for knowledge,[29] down to Ugolino's despairing refusal of speech to his starving children,[30] finally to the sullen, ultimate wordlessness of Satan,[31] self-invented narrative progressively reveals its own ultimate emptiness. Spiraling up through the painfully but joyfully acquired self-knowledge of the souls in purgatory, through Dante's equally painful reeducation by Beatrice[32] and the testing of his faith, hope, and love by Peter, James, and John,[33] his narrative meets its apotheosis in a silence as distant from Satan's as heaven is from hell, a silence not before an absence, but before an excess, of meaning. The narrative of love is the only narrative there is; but necessarily even that narrative falls silent as narrative when it meets with its full significance in the Trinitarian nature of God, for the weight of that Trinitarian meaning is, as both Paul and Dante say, more than memory can contain, and so is more than *any* narrative could bear. Necessarily, then, the *Commedia* is incomplete, for in its very incompleteness lies the meaning of the epic narrative. Or perhaps it is better put that the *Commedia* is complete in its demonstration of the incompleteness of its own theology. Vision puts an end to theology. For theology is story; and the vision of God is the end of story.

Julian and the Incompleteness of Narrative: The Lord and the Servant

Julian's narrative of the "Lord and the Servant" in chapter 51 offers no temptations of any kind to be read as complete. In anticipation of it, in chapter 45 she tells us that in all her shewings this parable would provide as much answer as was ever given to her perplexities,[34] those perplexities being powerfully restated in their most intensified form at the end of chapter 50.[35] Consequently, we might seem thereby to have been encouraged to approach the "example," as she calls it, with an anticipation of conclusiveness. But if there is drama to this parable, it is the drama not of climax but of anticlimax. The narrative content of the parable is as quickly told in Julian's words as in any conceivable précis: "I sawe two persons in bodely liknesse, that is to sey, a lorde and a servant. . . . The lorde sitteth solempnely, in rest and in pees. The servant stondeth before his lorde reverently, redy to do his lordes wille. The lorde loketh upon his servant full lovely and sweetly, and mekely he sendeth him into a certaine place to do his wille. The servant not onely he goeth, but sodenly he sterteth and runneth in gret hast for love to do his lordes wille. And anon he fallth into a slade [dell], and taketh ful gret sore. And than he groneth and moneth and walloweth and writheth. But he may not rise nor helpe himselfe by no manner of weye."[36]

Such is the bare outline of the parable's narrative—or, as Julian puts it, the "bodely liknesse" in which its spiritual significance is contained. Julian, of course, will occupy quite the longest chapter of her work elaborating that spiritual significance out of the minutest visual detail of the parable, for she says that she "had teching inwardly" over twenty years ("save thre monthes") to "take heed to alle the propertes and the conditions that were shewed in the example, though the[e] thinke that it be misty and indifferent to thy sight."[37] Much of that detail need not detain us, given our purposes.[38] What is central to the parable's meaning is its soteriological significance. Again, no paraphrase could combine compendiousness with precision as effectively as do her own words:

In the servant is comprehended the seconde person of the trinite, and in the servant is comprehended Adam, that is to sey, all men. And therfore, whan I sey "the sonne," it meneth the godhed, which is even with the fader; and whan I sey "the servant," it meneth Cristes manhode, whych is rightful Adam. By the nerehed [closeness] of the servant is understand the sonne, and by the stonding on the left side is understond Adam. The lorde is God the father; the servant is the sonne Jesu Crist; the holy gost is the even love which is in them both. When Adam felle, Godes sonne fell. For the rightful oning [union] which was made in heven, Goddes sonne might not be seperath from Adam, for by Adam I understond alle man. Adam fell fro life to deth: into the slade of this wreched worlde, and after that into hell. Goddes son fell with Adam into the slade of the maidens wombe, which was the fairest doughter of Adam—and that for to excuse Adam from blame in heven and erth—and mightily he fetched him out of hell. By the wisdom and goodnesse that was in the servant is understond Goddes son. By the pore clothing as a laborer, stonding nere the left side, is understonde the manhode and Adam, with alle the mischefe and febilnesse that foloweth. For in alle this, oure good lord shewed his owne son and Adam but one man. The vertu and the goodnesse that we have is of Jesu Crist, and the febilnesse and blindnesse that we have is of Adam: which two were shewed in the servant.[39]

Two features of Julian's theological elaboration of this "example" are especially worth noting right away: its markedly Trinitarian character (to which we will return later in this chapter), and the distinct absence, as medieval soteriologies go, of any trace of "retributionism," the proposition that God's Son had to take on the punishment for sin on behalf of all mankind so as to placate an offended Father. Julian's Christ does not "take upon himself" the blame for Adam's sin; rather, "excusing" Adam from blame "in heven and erth" wipes out blame altogether from the picture, because it wipes out the picture of God within which God's blaming us makes sense. God cannot be represented as paying for a sin to which God has in any case never attached a price. But the most striking feature of this parable is what one might call its eschatological collapsing of history, of time, and consequently of historical identities. The servant's being close to the Lord makes him the Son; and the servant's being on the Lord's left hand makes him none other than Adam; and Adam is none other than "every man." The servant's falling into a dell is Adam's falling into sin, and that is our falling into sin, which is none other than the Son's falling into Mary's womb, the Incarnation. Moreover, one can add—for reasons that will be made clearer in chapter 6 —that if for Julian these three "fallings" are at a very fundamental level but one, albeit multifaceted, reality, they are in turn one with that other "falling" of Creation itself, as it were "down" from the act of divine love, and brought into existence "out of nothing." Creation, Fall, and Redemption coincide, as Adam, "everyman," and Christ are one and the same. Ultimately, they are one and the same reality, all are but one event, one persona.

David Aers takes exception to this eschatological collapsing of the historical sequences of Creation, Fall, and Redemption into a single reality, for in it he finds Julian to have "set aside [the] . . . history of the covenant, God's relations with Israel, a history of God's faithfulness, mercy and judgment in the face of human unfaithfulness and repentance."[40] And to be sure, as it stands, Julian's parable sucks out all the elements of drama that are to be found in the biblical narrative of salvation history. But the criticism mistakes the point of Julian's parable, which is intentionally eschatological, not historical, intentionally embodying the ultimacy of the divine plan in which all is from eternity foreseen and, as foreseen, from eternity willed. Ultimately the historical sequence is a single event, as it is willed by a single willing, and short of an ultimate eschatological disclosure, Julian does not pretend to understand how these things are thus, only that, being so, it is possible to trust in the story that her example tells. In any case, if for God the events are all one, for us they form a sequence, a story told over time. The history of our salvation is the eternal will of God as narrated in time. And that soteriological sequence is linked with a narrative by means of connectives that are neither necessary nor arbitrary: that Creation is not contingently connected with the Fall; that we—everyman—do not just as it happens sin, but that in some way our sinning is tied in with Adam's; that the Fall is not contingently connected with the sending of the Son; that the Incarnation is not, as it were, a merely post-factum response of the Father to the human predicament, as if, caught unawares by how badly wrong things have gone with his Creation, the Father had adopted a secondary strategy of rectification, a sort of soteriological plan B. All these Julian sees in her example. They are not, then, just *events* strung along a temporal line, as if in some simple sequence of historically contingent causation, for they are all in some way eternally willed as one. Of course, for Julian they are events, with a history—and the temptation to see them in the way Aers appears to require as thus strung one-dimensionally along a merely contingent historical line is motivated by our sense that, if they were more tightly connected than by happenstance, there would be no room for the human freedom with which we have sinned, or for the divine freedom that creates and redeems. But Julian's example tells her otherwise. Creation, Fall, and Redemption are all, somehow, contained within one another, are in some unimaginable way a single divine action eternally willed in a single act of willing, such that Julian can say: "God doth *alle* thing."[41] The whole drama was, for Julian, foreseen, and being foreseen, created as foreseen, and out of, not in spite of, a drama of love, and so of freedom, divine and human.

Therefore, if these events are not connected by mere happenstance, neither are they connected by bonds of necessity; contrary to how Aers reads Julian, these events of salvation do possess for her real historical contingency. Julian does not offer as part of her struggle to make sense of the example of "Lord and Servant" any account of it in formally metaphysical terms such that these historical sequences are deducible a priori, whether from the divine nature or the human. Creation does not necessarily follow from God's being God; it is not a necessary truth that free human beings will sin, for every sin was freely chosen and might not have been; there is no obligation on God which requires that, human beings having sinned, they should be redeemed. All these are free acts, whether of God or of human beings, which means that there is nothing available by way of either natural necessities or moral obligation laid upon God to explain how they form a sequence amounting to a story; there are only the free acts from which they derive. For, in any case, sequences obedient to necessities cannot be stories. Julian deploys no intellectual resources to the understanding of her example other than the "teching" conveyed to her through the significance of its tiniest details. The example is all she has to work with, and what it tells her is that the coincidence of Creation, Fall, and Redemption is a work of love, not one derivable from any kind of metaphysical necessity or moral obligation. If none of this is but a meaningless de facto sequence, neither did any of it have to happen, the force of "have to" being inconsistent with its all being a free work of love on the side of the divine, or of free choice on the side of the human. By the nature of such love metaphysical necessity is ruled out and history allowed in.

Therefore, given that within this falling together of Creation, sin, and Redemption there is neither mere contingency nor ironbound necessity, we are led back to the proposition to the elucidation of which chapter 2 was devoted. We will make sense of this coincidence only in terms of the behovely, and of the behovely only in terms of a sort of narratival fittingness, and of narratival fittingness only in terms of the "constraints" of love. We are able to represent the mystery of divine providence as intelligible to us in any way at all only insofar as we can represent it in the form of a narrative—for history is, as it were, the narratival refraction of the divine eternity, as a single source of light might be refracted in the multiplicity of fragments of glass. Time is eternity shattered into fragments that we can piece together again only one after another in sequences as best we may. What is one in itself, a single willing of love emerging from the divine simplicity, can be perceived by us only in the time-bound fragmentations of historical succession in some way linked into a narrative. Moreover, this narrative is not one we can be told or tell as if from a position outside it, for we are internal to the story we tell, we are being told by it as we attempt to tell it. Perforce, the eternal knowledge and love that made all things out of love—the Trinity—is for us a narrative: and the nearest we can get to understanding the connective tissue of that narrative—its character of being neither necessary as opposed to contingent, nor contingent as opposed to necessary, but somehow both—is through concepts germane to its narrative character: the behovely, the conveniens.

Narrative and the "Logic" of the Trinity

And so it is that we get to the heart of the theological meaning of Julian's behovely. The behovely is the historical logic of the Trinity itself, the logic of the "economic" Trinity, of the immanent Trinity economically revealed through time and contingency. Its necessity is the necessity of love, for that is all the Trinity is. And its contingency is the freedom of love, for everything in the Trinity is love's freedom. Salvation history is but the Trinity narrated and, to switch metaphors, the historical map of the eternal Trinity is the behovely, and that map is love. In her shewings Julian sees nothing else but that love—she does not see the map, not at any rate the whole of it, even if she is shown that the whole of Creation is as tiny before the infinite love of God as is a hazelnut in the palm of her hand. But to know by faith that it adds up is not to see how it does so. She can see in the shewings nothing of sin,[42] nothing of anger,[43] nor even forgiveness,[44] and it is in these facts of what Julian sees and what she does not see that one of the two poles dominating her theological style is exhibited: its relentless theological apriorism.

On the one hand, then, there is no trace in Julian of a metaphysical necessity to the story of Creation, Fall, and Redemption; on the other, the significance of every a posteriori fact is trumped by the antecedent power of the love that foresaw and willed it. Everything in her *Revelation* begins and ends with what Julian saw in them, however mediated her seeing is by the second pole, the subsequent reflective—or, as Watson and Jenkins call it, "interpretative"—elaboration, grounded in the Church's teaching and in her own experience. As Watson and Jenkins put it, with perhaps an excessively one-sided emphasis on the first of these two poles (see chapter 2), "Constantly pushing away all specific reference to the world and its facts to focus on the single burning fact of revelation, the signature phrase of both works [the Long and the Short texts], used to introduce the most abstruse material, is 'I saw.'"[45] And it is certainly true that so far as concerns her shewings, all that Julian ever sees in them is the Trinity, and all that Julian ever reads from what she sees is that in the Trinity all is love, a love that is absolutely unconditional. That unconditional love is the whole content of what she sees. Everything else starts from and is conditioned by that sight. That is to say, in point of theological method, Julian's apriorism is an apriorism of love.

It is fair to say, however, that Julian knows how exceedingly difficult it is for us to take this proposition seriously, that God is *nothing at all* except love. It is quite beyond our understanding because it is quite beyond our own experience of the practical and constraining need to compromise in the conduct of our own affairs. It is difficult to conceive of a being wholly otherwise from us, a wholly unconstrained lover. It seems unimaginable that there should be a being of infinite capacity who has available every possible means to bring about anything at all that it is possible to describe, but should possess no capacity at all other than the capacity for love, should avail of no means whatever except love, and cannot bring about anything at all that is not love. For nothing at all that we know works that way. Julian herself notes how few lack difficulty in truly believing what she sees in the Trinity: "Though the thre[e] persons of the blessed trinite are alle even [equal] in the selfe, the soule toke most understanding in love. Ye, and he wille in alle thing that we have oure beholding and enjoying in love. And of this knowing are we most blinde. For some of us beleve that God is almighty and may do alle, and that he is alle wisdom and can do alle. But that he is alle love and will do alle, there we stinte [balk]."[46]

We, at any rate, know of other means than love. And we take care to use them, because for all that we would like to believe that all you need is love, we think it unwise to abandon all resort to prudent calculation and practical expediency, just in case love should let us down. Leaving aside, therefore, the question that otherwise troubles Julian so, that of the consistency of such belief with the reality of sin in the world, there is a prior problem for her with the proposition in itself that God is nothing but love. For that proposition is in the nature of things simply incredible—incredible because it is, for us, inconceivable. Yet this is what Julian sees in her revelations, or rather, it is what many years after their occurrence is "shewde" in her "gostly understanding" to be the hermeneutical key to them: that love is the *whole* meaning of everything shown to her: "What, woldst thou wit [know] thy lordes mening in this thing? Wit it wele, love was his mening. Who shewed it the[e]? Love. What shewide he the[e]? Love. Wherfore shewed he it the[e]? For love. Holde the[e] therin, thou shalt wit more in the same. But thou shalt never wit therin other withouten ende."[47]

We, however, cannot make do with this vision alone, because its unqualified purity is simply too blinding. As historical beings, we cannot do theology in relation to just this one pole of attraction, nor live on the basis of vision alone. We need a translation of eternity into time, and that means we need a story of their intersection. And that necessarily means that we make the meaning of our lives within a story of which we know only a fragment. For just as in Dante the vision of ultimate love is the end of the possibility of story, so the necessity of story excludes the possibility of a completed vision. Julian's example of the Lord and the Servant represents as having a visionary, timeless unity that which, in our experience, is extruded piecemeal across the continuum of time, for it is a vision that collapses into one another the historical sequences and identities by which, of necessity, our mortal experience is governed. And, again contrary to the view of Aers, Julian is emphatic: we do not live timelessly within that vision of timeless unity; rather, we live within our fragmented, time-bound experience of it.[48] Julian, I have said, is no mystic: at any rate she is no mystic if by that word is meant a person whose common Christian experience is the vision of such ultimacy as Paul's rapture into the third heaven, as if experienced otherwise than within and through our historical, and so essentially penultimate, condition. But then, on that account, no one except Paul and Moses ever was or could be a mystic. The mystical, as I have argued elsewhere,[49] is the incomprehensible depth of mystery within our temporal experience, not a distinct experience that bucks the conditioning of our temporality. So at any rate it would seem for Julian, just as it seemed for Dante.

For as I suggested in chapter 3, her *Revelation* consists in large part in her attempt to elucidate the mystical sense of her shewings in much the same manner in which the medieval scriptural commentator attempted to extract the mystical meaning of the scriptural text. And just as the scriptural commentator could gain access to that mystical sense only on the foundation of its literal, historical meaning,[50] so too Julian can find access to the vision of the Love that created, sustains, and governs all history only at those junctures in time at which that love intersects with the historical itself. Therefore, just as the eternally instant "now" of love is present to us only in the time-bound character of narrative sequence, so too is our experience of that vision of love available to us only in the form of a time-bound fragment. But for Julian it is a fragment that intersects with our lives in such ways that we can, after all, get a grip on enough of its meaning to know what it entails for us, enough to know what it entails for how we should live.

Human history, then, because and insofar as the Trinitarian love has intersected with it, is "salvation history." Indeed, human history is the eternal and internally self-constituted life of God in the form of story. And if the controlling logic of that story—that is, the logic that governs the mode in which the events of history are linked into narrative—is that of the behovely, then the content of the story line of that narrative is compressed into the example of the Lord and the Servant. Indeed, both the events of salvation history and their narratival logic as behovely are compressed into that example. Moreover, Julian's own proliferations of Trinitarian names (see chapter 1) are themselves her own renarration of those Trinitarian relations, her piecing together into a partial picture as much as she can see of the eternal love of God out of the shards of glass into which time has shattered it. It is a partial picture, of course. But it is still a picture.

How, then, does that divine love intersect with our historical experience? In what "fragment" is it revealed? Principally in a human disaster. What we can grasp is that the irruption of love into human history is subversive and catastrophically disruptive of the order that sin has constructed, just as in the *Commedia* Christ's harrowing of hell wreaks chaos and destruction upon its violent simulacrum of order. In short, the experienceable form of the divine love, that is to say of the Trinity, is the Cross. It is true that for Julian Christ died for our sins, and in this her theology of the Cross is quite traditional, just as in accordance with theological convention Julian envisages our sins as having been the cause of Christ's death. But there is another level of theological significance that runs through especially the earlier shewings, with all their graphic, not to say gruesome, representations of Christ's sufferings: at one and the same time those sufferings reveal the sheer gratuitousness of the Trinity's love and the necessity with which a sinful world has to reject it. That is to say, it is not just that our sins cause the Cross. Conversely, the Cross reveals sin for what it ultimately is, the refusal of an absolute and unconditional love. The world has no alternative but to punish such a love, for its character as "world" requires its failure to acknowledge its foundation in the refusal of unconditional love. And by "the world" here is meant what it means in John's Gospel, the order of sin that can and of course does admit love, but only up to a point, and only insofar as it is contained within limiting conditions. Insofar as the world's order depends upon a compromised love, an uncompromised love threatens it. And it is because a sinful world has to reject absolutely unconditional love that it can envisage no god except one who, correspondingly, loves only on the conditions of a quid pro quo, a god who therefore exacts compliance with a trade-off and punishes deviations from its terms. It is for just the same reason that a sinful world constructs a soteriology that corresponds with its perverted doctrine of a vengeful God appeased only by the sacrifice of his Son.

It is in some such terms that Denise Baker characterizes what she calls an Augustinian soteriology,[51] though with what degree of fairness and fidelity to Augustine's *ipsissima verba* is disputable, and David Aers certainly disputes it.[52] In any case, Augustine's soteriology thus characterized, Baker contrasts it with what, no less contentiously, she describes as an Anselmian doctrine of Fall and salvation, such that, whereas Augustine's doctrine of original sin attributes malevolence to both Adam and his descendents, Julian's "Anselmian" soteriology emphasizes the consequences of human separation from God, not the revolt of the will causing that separation. In short, whereas for Augustine it is sin that causes our human separation from God, for Julian the possibility of, and propensity to, sin can only *follow* from that separation. Julian, she says, "considers the suffering that results from sin not as a penalty inflicted by a wrathful God, but as the natural consequence of the sinner's violation of his or her 'feyer kynde.'"[53]

Augustinian or not, Julian knows exactly what is wrong with such retributive soteriologies. Anselmian or not, Baker's reading of Julian's soteriology seems exactly right in at least one principal connection. Both what is wrong with the one and right with the other is shown in the meaning of Jesus's parable of the prodigal son (Luke 15:11–32), which Julian's own parable of the Lord and the Servant is clearly intended to gloss. It is the prodigal son's separation from his father's house that is the cause of his sinful wasting of his patrimony, not his sin that causes the separation. In fact, according to the parable, the prodigal son's sin is in no way the cause of separation from his father, though the prodigal son supposes that it is, and so has to learn much about his father's compassion before he discovers that truth.

For though the repentant prodigal counts only on his father's gratuitous love, this is because all he knows is that he has no grounds for counting on that love based on his own merit: he too, like the servant in Julian's parable, is powerless to raise himself from his "dell." And in believing that through his prodigality he has lost the right to his father's love, he supposes that he possessed that right on condition of his earning it. Hence, when it comes to bargains, the prodigal son knows he has spectacularly failed to meet its condition on his side. Therefore, on the way home he plans to negotiate a second-best deal. He plans to ask his father to treat him at best as a hired servant, for within the limitations of his punitive soteriology he knows of no better deal on offer.

What is notable about this parable—because it is its point—is that the father does not share his prodigal son's soteriology. In fact, the father offers no word of rebuke at all. He does not even offer forgiveness. The father simply celebrates his son's return, for his repentant return is itself enough, it *is* his being forgiven. He offers no forgiveness after the event because he does not need to; the forgiveness was always there before the event of the son's betrayal, because forgiveness was in the very nature of his fatherhood. All the father needs is that his son should openly admit to his transgression of the trust placed in him, and that admission alone is enough to elicit his father's compassion.

By contrast, it is the dutiful and moralizing elder son who is rebuked for resenting his father's having thrown to the winds any decent sense of a properly ordered quid pro quo. He therefore angrily rejects the gratuitousness of his father's love as "out of order"—which, of course, it is.[54] In that elder son's resentment of the father's unconditional love, disruptive as it is of the world's compromised complacency, lies the source of the wrath and violence that is "only within us," and is not to be found otherwise except as projected by that wrath onto God as its dialectical counterpart. On the way home, the prodigal son too had anticipated a father like that, but, in the event, learned otherwise. The elder son, by contrast, remains fixed in resentment and learns nothing. Julian's God, by contrast with the elder son's, is recklessly in love. "The good Lord," she says, asked: "'Arte thou well apaid [satisfied] that I suffered for thee?' I saide; 'Ye, good lorde, gramercy [great thanks]. Ye, good lorde, blessed mot [may] thow be.' Then saide Jhesu, our good lord: 'If thou arte apaide, I am apaide. It is a joy, a blisse, and endlesse liking to me that ever I sufferd passion for the[e]. And if I might suffer more, I woulde suffer more.' He saide not, 'if it were nedfulle [necessary] to suffer more,' but, 'if I might suffer more.'"[55]

Cur Deus Homo? Julian and Duns Scotus

At this point Julian's soteriology edges onto ground intensely contested in theologies of the High Middle Ages concerning the terms in which appropriately to answer the Anselmian question *Cur Deus homo?*—why did God become man? J. P. H. Clark has suggested that Julian's answer to that question is closely related to that of Duns Scotus, and, having thus far read Julian's soteriology in Denise Baker's terms, we can see why. For Scotus, the Fall was not, as for the majority of medieval theologians, "the primary cause of the Incarnation." Rather, Scotus maintained, "Christ, and the humanity of which he is the head, is willed for the sake of God."[56] To put it simply, it is out of and for the sake of the divine love and goodness itself that humanity was created; and it was for that same love and goodness' sake, not for any contingent end of subsequent remedy of sin, that Christ was willed to become through the Incarnation humanity's head. If indeed within the wider perspective of humanity's predestined glory the Fall is foreseen by God along with its remedy; if indeed "it is in view of the Fall that Christ comes specifically as Redeemer,"[57] nonetheless, had, counterfactually, there been no Fall, the Incarnation was in any case eternally willed by God and would have happened simply because God out of an eternal love willed to close the gap of separation that had fallen between human beings and their Creator. According to Scotus, therefore, the Incarnation's "necessity" does not derive from the requirements of a fact, namely, the fact that humanity did fall, but—if indeed this is a form of "necessity"—as the simple expression and outpouring of the divine love as such. Or, as Scotus himself puts it: "incarnatio Christi non fuit occasionaliter praevisa," "the incarnation of Christ was not foreseen [as something that would happen] *as if occasioned by* anything."[58] Therefore, it was not occasioned by the Fall.

It is not difficult to see why Scotus should say such a thing, nor why Clark should observe similarities between his position and Julian's. But if there are similarities, there are also differences. On the side of similarities, Julian's soteriology is, as we have seen,[59] very far from envisaging the Incarnation as a kind of reactive response to the Fall, and it would seem that it was with a view to the removal of any such implication that Scotus insists that the Incarnation was eternally willed in the divine providence independently of the fact of the Fall, hence not *occasionaliter*. Of course, Scotus does not deny that the Fall was foreseen. Similarly, Julian's Lord and Servant parable lays great stress on the Fall's having been eternally anticipated. For his part, Scotus insists that God "preordained or foresaw [the Incarnation] . . . as a remedy against the Fall,"[60] and thus far he and Julian are in agreement. But where Scotus appears to differ from Julian is in his maintaining that were the provision of that remedy against the Fall to be seen as the primary motivation of the Incarnation, then you would have to think of the Incarnation as having been motivated occasionaliter, so as to be a contingent, reactive, response to Adam's fall, a "plan B" soteriology, as I described it earlier.

If in ruling out any sort of plan B soteriology, Scotus and Julian are in agreement, Julian does seem to differ from Scotus as to the grounds on which that conclusion is reached, and if it must be said that the difference is subtle, it is nonetheless significant. For Scotus, as Clark puts it, "Christ was eternally foreseen and intended by God to be the head of a glorified creation, in terms which imply that Christ's predestination to glory, and our participation in this, is primary, and that Redemption from Adam's fall is to be seen in this wider perspective."[61] Julian's answer to Anselm's question, on the other hand, does not seem to require the distinction implied in Scotus's answer, between "primary" and "secondary" motivations for the Incarnation. For Julian—as I put it in chapter 3—it is in a single and undifferentiated act of divine knowledge and love that both the Fall and its remedy are willed, and both are willed for what Scotus seems to think of as a primary motivation of the divine self-glorification by means of self-disclosure. And the reason why Julian would appear to have less need of this Scotist distinction is that she has less trouble with seeing the Fall as behovely, because for her the divine end of self-disclosure in glorified humanity is most fully achieved precisely through the single complex event of the Fall and its remedy. Creation, Fall, and Redemption are all of a piece with one another, embodying in their conjunction the primary and only motive of the Incarnation.

Of course, then, Julian agrees with Scotus that the Incarnation is not caused by the Fall, as if occasioned by a change in the divine plan; but this is not for Julian as it is for Scotus, because the Incarnation would have happened had Adam not fallen, but because God causes the lot—Creation, Fall, and Incarnation—in a single providential act of self-disclosure, as a single revelation of love. Within that providential act the Fall is indeed a crucial element, but not as if standing outside it and as if necessitating it causally. That, of course, was the principal burden of the example of the Lord and the Servant: Adam's fall and the falling of the divine Word into Mary's womb were one and the same falling. Hence Julian, unlike Scotus, has no need to distinguish between what God would have willed absolutely had human beings not in fact fallen, and a secondary motivation arising out of the fact that human beings did in fact do so. From all eternity "sinne is behovely." That is all we can know as governing the Incarnation's necessity, because all you need to know by way of answering Anselm's question is that "it is a joy, a blisse, and endlesse liking to me that ever I sufferd passion for the[e]." The return of the prodigal son is the greatest possible joy of his father: no banquet in the elder son's honor could have matched in joy the celebration of the prodigal's return.

For Julian, therefore, everything—Creation, Fall, Redemption, the Cross—starts from that unconditional love, shown forth most spectacularly, and paradoxically, in the prodigal son's narrative. And within history that narrative collides with the other story to be told, which is the elder brother's narrative—two narratives in contention over the same facts. This is our historic mise-en-scène, then—that of an order of sin that is constructed upon the necessity of binding love in conditions being disrupted by the inrush of a love that is absolutely unconditional. We are, as it were, poised on the cusp of the tension between sin and its order on the one hand and unqualified love on the other, living within the consequence of the disruption and violence with which that sinful order must respond to love's intrusion. That is to say, the Cross is exactly where we are situated historically, the Cross is the world-historical meaning of our mise-en-scène because it is the world-historical meaning of the Trinity. And that mise-en-scène also determines how we should live: poised in an eschatological tension.

The Defeat of Sin

Moreover, that mise-en-scène determines the broad structure of *Revelation* itself. Divided roughly in two by the parable of the Lord and the Servant, it can be said as a general truth that, at least in degree of emphasis, the first half of the Long Text is Christocentric, whereas the second half is focused on the Trinity. From the outset, however, Julian tells us of the principle governing the work's unity, namely, that "wher Jhesu appireth the blessed trinity is understand, as to my sight," and that "this was shewed in the first sight and in all."[62] As a rubric, this caution needs to be taken into account throughout the whole of *Revelation* and both ways round: when in the first half Jesus is spoken of, the whole

Trinity is meant, and when in the second half so much is said about the Trinity, it should be just as clear that it is only in Jesus that the Trinity is known to her. Watson and Jenkins get this partly right when they comment: "This hermeneutic principle, that references to Jesus also allude to the Trinity, is in operation throughout the work, allowing a revelation much of which seems only to concern the human person [sic] of Christ to be interpreted as equally applying to his divinity."[63] As far as it goes, I am sure that Julian would have agreed with a corrected version of this formulation of her "hermeneutic principle," since it is but an attempt—if theologically imprecise—to give expression to a principle, familiar within post-Chalcedonian Christologies, of what was known as the *communicatio idiomatum*. That principle affirms that whatever is truly predicated of the human *nature* (not "person") of Christ may be legitimately predicated of his divine person (not "nature"): hence, if it is true that the man Christ died on the Cross, then it is true to say that God died on the Cross, for the man Christ was God.[64] No doubt, as I say, Julian knew and accepted this Christological principle. But it is not exactly this principle that Julian is invoking when she says that where Jesus is spoken of the Holy Trinity is meant. What she is invoking is a principle even more fundamental to her theological epistemology, one that governs the basic structure of her work as a whole—the paradox that it is only through the human nature of Christ that the Trinity is known to her at all. Jesus is the revelation of the Trinity. Jesus's humanity is how the Trinity is revealed to us, and in no other way; and it is as the revelation of the Trinity that Jesus is who he is, for he has no other reality than in that revelatory fact.

But as we have seen, there is more to it even than that general principle of theological epistemology. What pulls together into a seamless theological unity the earlier "bodely" shewings of the dying Christ on the Cross (all too easily discounted, even with some distaste, as an exhibition of a typecast late medieval pious grotesquerie) with the later, more speculative, Trinitarian reflections, is a theological insight: that if it is alone in Jesus that the Trinity is revealed to us, then it is in his dying on the Cross that that revelation is given. In short, what Christians know of the Trinitarian nature of the Godhead they know from the Cross of Christ. This is the "Bonaventuran" shift from a formal epistemological apophaticism to a theologia crucis referred to in my chapter 1. At the heart of the structural unity of *Revelation* as text is that which is at its theological center point: the paradox that the visibility within history of the Triune Godhead, which is love, is to be found in the historical defeat of love by sin. For it is sin's pulling off the defeat of Christ's mission—the defeat, that is, of every kind of success as the world can understand it—that ensures that there is no possibility of that death's being understood otherwise than in terms of a purely gratuitous love: for it can make no sense at all on the world's terms, in the terms of the story that sin tells. That death had to be unintelligible, untellable in the terms of that story. It was unintelligible even to Jesus himself, for his dying words were a desperate plea for understanding addressed to his Father: "*Why* have you abandoned me?" (Mark 15:34). He died, his work completed, though no answer was given by way of reassurance. Jesus's death had to be unintelligible; for had it been intelligible it could be only because there was sense to be made of it within sin's narrative, and so it would owe something to that narrative—it would be behovely on sin's terms, perhaps as a heroic tragedy—and could not then possess that utter gratuitousness that alone could reveal that "love was its mening." Confronted by the radically subversive character of that revelation, all the world can do is concoct some cock-and-bull story—the Gospel accounts suggest that it took some seriously corrupt committee work to devise an even half-plausible version (Matthew 26:59–66)—designed to contain that subversiveness within an acceptable narrative. It is sensible, it was said, "expedient," that an innocent man should die for the good of the people (John 18:14). In essence, the story as sin tells it amounts to the reduction of the behovely to a matter of practical, political utility, to the replacement of the conveniens with self-serving expedience.

And so the Cross effects a twofold disclosure: it discloses the Trinity and it discloses sin for what it is, namely, the elder brother's refusal of the Trinitarian love, that mutual love of the Father and Son that is the Holy Spirit. Unable to bear the rival story—sin, after all, cannot afford to know its own nature, for that is already repentance—a sinful world reacts with violence, and so in that very act confirms the truth of the story it violently resists. Sin's victory is entirely pyrrhic, for it is precisely in that victory that sin destroys itself. The Cross is how sin is defeated: and by the defeat of sin Julian means not that after the Crucifixion there will be no more sin, for that is manifestly false. As Julian says, she herself, and everyone else, will go on sinning, so that in one sense things go on exactly as they had done before. But she, they, and we will do so only insofar as all fail to see that sinning has become strictly pointless, for it no longer has a story—its story has been evacuated of meaning, exposed as being of no efficacy, utterly impotent. It is as impotent and inarticulate as Dante's Satan, frozen into immobility in the deepest pit of hell. And though in possession of three mouths, none of them serve him with any capacity for speech but only to devour in a self-cannibalizing frenzy the three traitors, Brutus, Cassius, and Judas, who are the prize achievements of his erstwhile, now lost, power over humans.[65] This, too, is Julian's Satan, at whom she simply laughs, because all he does is now turned against him. The more he wins the more he loses, for "his [the devil's] might is alle lokked in Gods hande."[66] Robbed of its story by the power of the Cross's defeat, now indeed is sin "nought" except meaningless, self-inflicted pain. And in that pain is the compassion of the Father, Son, and Holy Spirit all the more revealed.

CHAPTER FIVE

Prayer and Providence

JULIAN IS A THEOLOGIAN. But is Julian's *Revelation* also a work of "spirituality"? The question raises another—namely, whether you could envisage a medieval writer composing a work of theology that is not a work of spirituality, or, on the same terms, a work of spirituality that is not a work of theology. The question is real, not merely rhetorical. Bernard McGinn has identified the first use of the word *spiritualitas* as early as the fourth century,[1] presumably as designating a way of life lived through the spirit—more or less, in other words, lived Christianity. The question is not whether there are authors who write about how to live a fully Christian life who would not best be described as theologians, for it is clear that, for any given account of "spirituality" and for any given account of "theology," there have been. The question is, rather, whether there have been theologians who have regarded the writing of theology as something other than the writing of spirituality, and if so, at what historical juncture it became possible and (as it seems today) defensible to do so.

As regards that question, Simon Tugwell has argued that the beginnings of a parting of ways between the theological and the spiritual are detectable as early as the thirteenth century,[2] and I myself have argued that the sundering of the ancient Dionysian pleonasm "mystical theology" into the distinct, when not oxymoronically opposed, topoi of "the mystical" and the "theological" is well under way in the fourteenth.[3] And though I have no intention in this essay of taking up the complex and difficult issues of meta-theology, either in today's terms or those of the late Middle Ages, it is at least worth noting what little value there is in such taxonomies of genre in connection with Julian's *Revelation*. Indeed, any sense of disjunction between the theological and the spiritual would in Julian's case be nothing but misleading, even if it is true that it is in her century that one begins to observe such disjunctions in some other writers.

The risks that the interpretation of Julian's *Revelation* would be distorted by way of such classifications of genre are most clearly seen when one notes the absence from her text of the classic descriptions of a spiritual trajectory so typical of many late medieval and early modern "spiritualities." Absent from Julian is any description of the "threefold way" of purgative, illuminative, and unitive stages to be found in the fourteenth-century Carthusian Hugh of Balma;[4] absent are the three rungs of the ladder of ascent to union with God—the animal, the rational, and the spiritual—of William of St. Thierry;[5] absent are the three kisses of feet, hands, and mouth of Bernard of Clairvaux's *Sermons on the Song of Songs;*[6] absent is the detailed mapping of the soul's "journey into God" of Bonaventure in the thirteenth century.[7] Nothing of these kinds is to be found in Julian: there is in her writings no sense of a delineable spiritual trajectory. Nor is there to be found in Julian anything of the kind that in the sixteenth century marks out a Teresa of Avila or a John of the Cross, in both of whom are to be found not only elaborations of medieval descriptions of and criteria for discerning the stages of spiritual progress, but also a new and distinctively early modern factor. For in John and Teresa the transitions from one stage to another are punctuated, as especially in John of the Cross, by a series of ever more radical spiritual crises—or, as he calls them, "dark nights of the soul." If there is in Julian little sense of a spiritual trajectory, and certainly no attempt to map one, it goes along with this that neither is there any trace in Julian's writings of spiritual drama.

To put it in other terms, if Julian's theology is marked out by its problem-ridden, aporetic character, it is to the same degree notable how that problematic is of a principally intellectually critical character, a problem of formal consistency between apparently conflicting teachings, not that of the soul's progression through a trajectory of personal spiritual crises. If, on any indicators in terms of which a Bernard of Clairvaux or a John of the Cross establish themselves clearly as "spiritual" writers, one is looking for a "spirituality" in Julian's *Revelation*, one will be sorely disappointed.

It is possible that some will see this as grounds for criticism of Julian. For it might seem that there is at this personal level a certain static character to the spiritual life as she describes it. As one reads that magisterially calm prose, one might admire the impassivity just as one is regretting the absence of the existential. It can seem as if, for Julian, everything that will ever be done has already been done, being from all eternity predestined; as if therefore there is no new reality to be sought, no struggle to achieve, no transformation to undergo, no new event that has to happen, for any event that matters to our salvation has already happened, and every person "who is to be saved" already predestined to be so. While I have been prepared to defend Julian's theology against David Aers's accusation that she "sets aside . . . history," it might seem less easy to defend her against an equivalent charge of having "set aside" all reference to a personal ascetical way—that is, of having "set aside" the equivalent, at the level of personal spirituality, of the drama, the *Sturm und Drang*, of salvation history.

It is of course true that at just one point late in the course of her shewings, Julian personally hits the wall and, sparing of self-reference though she more commonly is, she recounts in some detail how she was afflicted by a personal spiritual crisis that challenged her faith and her confidence in her shewings: she became temporarily convinced that they had all been but "ravings." And so, much ashamed, she confesses to a "religious person" visiting her on her sickbed that she had only imagined that she saw the cross bleed when it had been held before her face. Upon hearing Julian say this, the religious person "loght [laughed] loude and enterly [sincerely],"[8] and immediately Julian is filled with remorse at her lack of faith and wants to be shriven of her sin. The episode is over quickly, for soon enough the "good lorde" has reassured her: "'Wit it now wele, it was no raving that thou saw today. But take it and believe it, and kepe thee therin, and confort thee therwith, and trust thee therto, and thou shalt not be overcome.'"[9] And that is about as much personal "spiritual drama" as one is able to find in Julian's *Revelation*.

If, then, one is to find any meaning for the word "spirituality" in terms of which to represent Julian as a spiritual writer, it will have to be otherwise than on the progressive, developmental model represented by a Bernard of Clairvaux, or the crisis-ridden model of a John of the Cross. And there are other models, other "spiritualities." In *The Darkness of God* I suggested that one can find in Augustine's *Confessions* two "narrative models" intertwined within the structure of the story of his conversion—a model of "self-making" and a model of "self-discovery."[10] The first model picks up the elements of a forward-moving trajectory of events, intellectual, spiritual, and moral, as Augustine drives on from one lifestyle to the next, from his dissolute youth as a student in Carthage to the more disciplined life as a neophyte Manichee on through the ethical Stoicism of Cicero and the discovery of true transcendence in the "Platonists" and finally, through his encounter with Ambrose in Milan, on to the famous climax in the garden that leads to his conversion to Christianity. Here all is drama, event, predicament, crisis, and resolution—a dramatic tale that needs to be told in its correct temporal sequences, for it is the record of critical episodes of Augustine's life, the meaning of which can be grasped only in the course of their narration: the meaning is in the story. For only in their narration can they be seen to add up cumulatively to the story of Augustine progressively constructing a coherent selfhood out of the fragmented materials of that dissolute youth who, in Carthage, was scarcely a self at all—more a bundle of random passions reactive to the strongest stimuli. Here is Augustine the restless seeker, the man of passions, always moving forward through a succession of failed attempts to identify the true object of his desire, in which alone it can take its rest. This is the Augustine of the spirituality of "self-making," and if Augustine tells us from the very beginning of his narration of that life, so dominated as it was by his seeking, that "our hearts will not rest until they rest in You,"[11] then it is not the resting that strikes the reader as supplying the impetus of his trajectory toward God, for his is a nervous energy driving a relentless questing. That, however, is but half the story, and one might say the less important half. Moreover, it is a spiritual profile that, taken on its own, is unrecognizable in Julian.

The other half of the story—and the half instantly recognizable as exercising a profound influence on Julian—reverses all this. For it is only by the hindsight of his conversion that Augustine can review the course of that restless seeking, with all its apparent aimlessness and randomness, and now see it not as it had seemed to him at the time, to be the record of his seeking God, but as having been all along driven by the God of his seeking, working within the very seeking itself and not as if some object "outside" himself. That, after all, is the reason his seeking could be truly described as having been a seeking of God. "You were within me," he says, indeed, "more within than I was."[12] But "I was outside myself."[13]

At one level, then, Augustine's *Confessions* consists in a broken narrative primarily of fracturing interruptions, discontinuities, and crises, both of intellect and of spirit, but mostly of desire, of "loves"—it is this level that I have called his a spirituality of "self-making." At this level Augustine's seeking is driven by the desire to know the truth. But at this second, more fundamental, level—that of "self-discovery"—Augustine finds the truth of his desire. And so, with the autobiographical narrative completed by the end of book 9, in book 10 Augustine can now see his pre-conversion life to have been a meaningful whole, as having been driven by a purpose not of his own, its unhappy restlessness being a symptom of his failure to see how the divine providential wisdom was all the time working its way through his story's superficial aimlessness. He sought, but did not find, until by the grace of his conversion he came to realize that God had been there all the time, not principally as that seeking's object, but more fundamentally within the seeking itself as its source and ground. Here, in the discovery of his true desire, of what he "really" wants, Augustine at last discovers the true God, the God who answers to that truest desire.

It is in this connection that the similarity between Julian and Augustine is most revealing. What one attends to when remarking upon the relatively "static" character of Julian's writing is the obvious absence of the dramatic personal narrative of a spiritual journey such as one finds in the first nine books of *Confessions*. What one would be omitting to notice, were one to conclude that Julian's *Revelation* thereby lacks the character of a "spirituality," is that even for Augustine that autobiographical narrative of his life's restless "seeking" gets its meaning only from what, at the end of the questing journey, he there discovers, namely, that what he saw as a series of time-bound events constituting his personal life of struggle for the truth was in fact the work of the truth that was already there within him, waiting to be discovered. In noting the relatively static character of Julian's spirituality, therefore, we are noting a difference from Augustine in point but of emphasis, no more. For if we are to characterize Julian's "spirituality" in any terms at all that relate to Augustine's, then it is as a spirituality of self-discovery that that comparison can most directly be made, and perhaps even more, in the way in which the balance is struck, differently in each perhaps, but still struck in both, between the components of active seeking on the one hand and contemplative rest on the other, between Julian's "beseking" and her "beholding." And nowhere in Julian's *Revelation* is this interplay more evident than in her minitreatise on prayer, to be found in chapters 41–43.

"Seking" and "Beholding"

In turning to the topic of her ascetical and practical priorities, Julian does not turn away from the high theology of salvation history. Indeed, it is in the light of the eschatological character of the historical as such that we must read Julian's distinction between "contemplation" and "prayer," or, as she calls them "beholding" and "beseking," because contemplation and prayer both differ from and relate to one another in ways that parallel the relationship between the timelessness of vision and the temporality of our historical condition. Moreover, both pairs—time and eternity, prayer and contemplation—line up with the complex interplay in Augustine between the spirituality of "self-making" and restless "seeking" on the one hand, and the spirituality of "self-discovery" and contemplative rest on the other. All three pairs align, therefore, in that all three stand to one another as the eschatological "now" stands to the eschatological "not yet," as the contingency and freedom of human desire stand to the eternal and unchanging providential love of the Father, so that the structuring determinant of Julian's "spirituality" is none other than that of her theology as a whole.

Turning, then, to the distinction between contemplation and prayer as we find it in the Long Text, we see that Julian begins to clarify it in a passage of puzzling density in chapter 10, which opens with a troubling and frightening "bodely sight" of the face of Christ on the Cross. There she sees "dispite [contempt], spitting, solewing [soiling], and buffeting, and many languring paines, mo than I can tell, and often changing of colour. And one time I saw how halfe the face, beginning at the ere [ear], overyede [spread] with drye bloud till it beclosed into the mid face. And after that the other halfe beclosed on the same wise, and therewhiles it vanished in this party, even as it cam."[14]

Given Julian's usual procedure when her shewings present her with such minute physical detail, it would be reasonable to expect that she would attempt to extract from that detail a rich and nuanced theological interpretation. And this expectation is especially provoked since most of what follows is found only in the Long Text. Hence, there intervene between the shewing itself and her account of it many years of opportunity to reflect on what it could mean. This time, however, the meaning of the "bodely sight" quite defeats her, not only initially but even twenty years later. She tells us that she saw all this bodily but "swemly [sorrowfully] and darkely," and she "desired mor bodely light to have seen more clerly."[15] After all, it is a distinctly odd and certainly unconventional "bodely sight" as standard medieval representations of the Passion go, even in her visually imaginative times. But her request is answered only indirectly and comes in the manner of a gentle rebuke for her having supposed the meaning of the shewing to be so easily obtained, as if by right. She says: "And I was answerde in my reason: 'If God will shew thee more, he shal be thy light. Thee nedeth none but him.'"[16] Whereupon Julian perceives that what she is to reflect upon is not in the first instance the bodily sight itself but its theological obscurity and her total dependence on God if she is to make out its meaning. If God chooses to provide his light, then well and good. But if not, then all we can do is seek that light and patiently trust that it will be given. And if it is not given, then that—our not being given the light—is itself what we are given. "Light," that is to say "seeing" the meaning, will alternate with darkness and "seking" it, according to patterns entirely dependent on the will of God and certainly not on ours: "For I saw him and sought him. For we be now so blinde and so unwise that we can never seke God till what time that he of his goodnes sheweth him to us. And whan we see ought [anything] of him graciously, then are we stered [stirred] by the same grace to seke with great desire to see him more blissefully. And thus I saw him and sought him, and I had him and wanted him. And this is and should be our comen [usual] working [way of being] in this life, as to my sight."[17]

It is this pattern of alternation between "seeing" and "seking" and between "having" and "wanting" that turns out to be the meaning of the shifting image of Jesus's face, in which first one side and then the other appear to be caked in dried blood, the one and then the other disfigured, the one and then the other beautiful. The visual alternations match up with a chiasmic spiritual counterpart: "I saw him and sought him, and I had him and wanted him;"[18] and her vision of the Vernicle at Rome, the cloth with which according to legend Veronica wiped the face of Jesus on the way to Calvary and retained his image imprinted upon it, contained the same message of oscillation between consolation and anguish, between "having" and "wanting." The most beautiful of all faces appears on that cloth as distorted and discolored, constantly changing its hue, "sometime more comfortable and lively, and sometime more rewful [pitiful] and deadly [deathlike], as it may be seen."[19] Both visions, that of the face of Jesus on the Cross and that of his face on the Vernicle, teach her the same thing, that there "be two workinges that may be seen in this vision. That one is seking, the other is beholding."[20] Our "beholding" is of Jesus's fairness of face. The "seking" is aroused by "the rewlyhead [piteousness] and leenhead [thinness] of this image."[21] From one point of view, she says, it does not matter in which we are engaged for, short of the beatific vision itself, which is a pure contemplative "beholding," the one is as good as the other—"And thus was I lerned to my understanding that seking is as good as beholding, for the time that he wille suffer the soule to be in traveyle [labor]."[22] And it is true, she says, that fine distinctions between seeking and beholding seem, in practice, to matter little, "for a soule that only festeneth [attaches] him onto God with every truste, either in seking or in beholding, it is the most worshippe that he may do, as to my sight."²³ In any case, seeking has beholding as its end and purpose—it is "Gods will that we seke into the beholding of him," and it is entirely in God's hands whether we do or do not behold: "he shews us himself of his special grace when he will."²⁴

Nonetheless, although in these ways Julian has softened the hard edges of the distinction between seeking and beholding, the emphasis of this second shewing is distinctive: even if it is entirely in God's hands whether we seek or behold—that is to say, if it is a matter entirely of special grace whether our seeking in fact reaches its goal of beholding—still, what we can certainly do for ourselves is seek.²⁵ For "the seking is comen [available to all]: that, ech soule may have with his grace, and oweth [ought] to have, by discretion and teching of holy church."²⁶ For "the continual seking of the soule pleseth God full mekille [much]. For it may do no more than seke, suffer, and trust."²⁷

"Beholding" and Contemplation

There is no need, therefore, to exaggerate Julian's distinction between seeking and beholding in order to see the point of it, whether by over-emphasizing it as a disjunction or by inferring too many, or too drastic, consequences as flowing from it. For the point of it is clear, as is where the emphasis lies: absolutely, beholding is higher than seeking. But since what we alone can do for ourselves is seek, whether we are doing the one or the other is not up to us, but only up to grace. In the penultimacy of our condition, it is seeking rather than beholding that fits best with the eschatological juncture in which she, and we, are situated, though at first blush her priorities might seem surprising. For by the time Julian was rewriting in the Long Text this much-expanded reflection on her second revelation, she was living an enclosed life as an anchoress, a condition of life in which one might have expected her to give priority to the contemplative withdrawal from those active pursuits that are of their nature busy with seeking.

It seems to me not only possible but plausible to read Julian's discussion of the relation between beholding and seeking as a commentary on the well-worn medieval theological topos of the relation between the "contemplative" and the "active" dispositions.[28] It is not without justification that Colledge and Walsh's modernization renders Julian's Middle English "beholding" as "contemplation," for "beholding" is as good a Middle English translation as any of the Latin *contemplatio*. Shadowing any medieval discussion of contemplation is the story of Martha and Mary in Luke's Gospel (Luke 10:38–42). And in the tradition of interpretation with which Julian was no doubt familiar—it extends from Augustine[29] through Gregory the Great[30] to the standardized medieval glosses of Julian's own times[31]—Martha, "busy about many things," stands for the active life, and Mary, sitting still in conversation with Jesus, stands for the *unum necessarium*—the one thing essential—of the contemplative. And of course, it is Mary who is praised by Jesus for having chosen the "better part, which will not be taken away from her." For, as that tradition glossed, the contemplative life "begins in this life, but ends only in the next."[32] By contrast, the active life represented by Martha, who is busy with the affairs of the world, begins in this world and ends there: ultimately, the active life *is* "taken away"; it does not survive eschatologically. In terms of that tradition of contemplation, then, it might have been more naturally supposed that Julian, the enclosed anchoress and so by choice separated from the active pursuits of the world for sake of the contemplative life, would, like Jesus, praise contemplation more highly than seeking. But as we have seen, at best, it seems all the same to her in which of the two one is engaged, since it is not up to us to decide whether we are or are not given the grace of beholding. And whether or not that gift of beholding is given to us, we can always seek it. Perhaps in this shift of emphasis from contemplative beholding

to active seeking Julian is writing less for herself as a contemplative anchoress and more for the common condition of her readership, intending
to address her "evencristen," most of whom were in no position to enjoy
Julian's contemplative circumstances of life.

In the light of which, we can see very well why Julian would seem
anxious to avoid polarizing seeking and beholding. Laypeople cannot
be specialist contemplatives, and it would scarcely be in the interests
of an address designed for common Christian folk to place the activity
of contemplation beyond their reach, even if the specialist, monastic,
contemplative way of life necessarily is. Nor should we polarize them,
even in our understanding of the medieval monastic contemplative traditions. There was reason within those traditions themselves for resisting
any such bifurcations.

Among the books of the Old Testament most frequently singled out
by monks for commentary on the contemplative life, the Song of Songs
ranks among the highest in popularity.[33] Indeed, contemplative theology
in the Middle Ages is perhaps most distinctively characterized by the
importance attached to this explicitly erotic text, precisely because of the
openness of its affirmation of love as *eros*, as yearning or longing or, in
Julian's word, seeking. Nor is it difficult to see why. The atmospherics
of erotic tension that so dominate the text of the Song of Songs—the
rapid narrative shifts back and forth between beholding in contemplative
oneness the presence of the beloved, and languishing, "sick with love,"
in separation, with a consequent yearning for his or her return—these
exactly match the monks' sense of their specific eschatological situation,
set between time and eternity, in the regio dissimilitudinis, the "land of
exile," "unfamiliarity," and homelessness of which Bernard of Clairvaux spoke.[34] Contemplative religious, male and female, saw themselves
therefore as set in time between the presence and absence of the beloved,
for within time neither presence nor absence holds the ring unchallenged
by the other, and there will always be Julian's oscillations between them.

Julian speaks in exactly that Bernadine spirit when she tells us how on the one hand "I saw him" and on the other "sought him," "had him," and "wanted him," a spirit of eschatological in-betweenness that, as I have suggested, Julian herself took with her into her own distinctive situation of anchoritic in-betweenness. To the extent that the monastic tradition never set seeking and beholding in opposition, Julian had no need to do so herself, for that tradition placed seeking at the center of the contemplative drive toward ultimate vision on very similar eschatological considerations as does Julian. Contemplatives like Julian saw themselves as poised on an eschatological cusp formed by the convergence of the "now" of time and the "not yet" of eternity. And the dynamics of eros, and so of seeking, form a perfect match with that eschatological tension, thus giving the vocabulary of erotic tension a natural place within the monastic conception of the contemplative life.[35]

Nonetheless, in distinguishing seeking and beholding, Julian does want to highlight a nuance of difference between two eschatological dispositions. For if there is no good reason for overplaying that distinction disjunctively, then there is no better reason for ignoring it, even if the grounds for her distinction are not general but narrow and specific to her own theological project. While drawing upon the monastic tradition, Julian places the emphasis in her own distinctive way. For her, the emphasis is relentlessly placed on the incompleteness of the contemplative vision. If she sees one thing, this leads only to her not seeing another, and so to more seeking. Where the contemplative religious characteristically thought of contemplation principally in terms of rest as its goal,[36] Julian is endlessly, if not at all goalessly, restless. In this life, contemplative vision is for her always short-term, discontinuous, and incomplete, which, as we have seen, is another way of saying that we live within the particularity of story—and of that story we know, we live within the knowledge of, only a fragment. The characteristic spiritual disposition corresponding with such a sense of the incompleteness of our knowledge is therefore less that of a passive contemplative rest and more that of the busy disposition of endless seeking.

"Seking" and Prayer

Just as the decision of Colledge and Walsh to modernize Julian's "beholding" as "contemplation" seems reasonable, so it seems reasonable to connect what she says about seeking in chapter 10 of the Long Text with the formal discussion of prayer that opens the fourteenth revelation in chapters 41–43. At any rate, it would seem plausible to make this connection if one understands what she means by prayer in her narrow terms as petitionary or intercessory, rather than in the more relaxed terminologies of our own times wherein medieval distinctions tend to be blurred. That Julian should be construed as distinguishing between prayer and contemplation in an important bearing on her theological concerns should not surprise those who know the medieval traditions on which she draws, though it might surprise today's readers somewhat more, given that, as Simon Tugwell has noted,[37] we have generally collapsed the two together into one. Within today's literatures on the subject, one commonly reads accounts of "contemplative prayer," an expression that would probably have puzzled Julian, since it combines two sorts of assumptions about prayer neither of which she would appear to share: first, that prayer is a practice that, properly speaking or at least in its highest form, is contemplative; and second, correspondingly, that as a form of prayer, the petitionary sort is lower than the contemplative. Julian's concern to rebalance the relationship between prayer and contemplation is best understood otherwise and against the background of a set of distinctions to which she holds firm, although others, Tugwell argues, had already a century or more before her time begun to remove the boundaries between them in the way we have come to do so today. As we saw in chapter 1, those more ancient distinctions were laid out in a sequence sometimes said to form the "ladder of monks" (after the title of the eponymous *opusculum* by the twelfth-century Carthusian monk Guigo II[38]), identified by four "rungs": *lectio, meditatio, oratio,* and *contemplatio.*

It is not too difficult to find adequate modern translations of the first two rungs, if only for the reason that reading and meditation as the monk engaged in them were devotional and theological practices that belong too specifically to the monastic way of life to be practicable within today's lay conditions—they are just too time-consuming. Hence, not sharing the practices, we have had no reason to modify the terminology for them.[39] The monks, by contrast, did very little else but read and meditate. Day in and day out, the monastic *horarium* was filled with the activity of reading scripture, either slowed up in choir by their chant or on their own by the practice of vocalized reading sotto voce. And that slow reading, a "biting off," Guigo calls it,[40] spontaneously led to a meditative "chewing over" of the text read and to the conjunction of the two practices which, in turn, issued in a vast theological output in the Middle Ages: the monastic biblical commentary, which is essentially the lectio divina formalized. And if Oliver Davies is right,[41] then we can see a modified form of that literary output in Julian's *Revelation* itself, in which the material of her shewings does duty for the scriptural text. Had one been the commissioning editor of Julian's manuscript, one could aptly have suggested the title *Meditations on a Revelation of Divine Love.* Monks of her time would have known what to expect, and in that sense would have recognized the genre in which she writes. For Julian's *Revelation* is not just a text about meditation. It *is* a meditation.

But Julian's way of distinguishing between oratio and contemplatio is today much more problematic. As Tugwell says, until Bonaventure (among others) began a progressive expansion of the scope of oratio to include what Guigo had meant by contemplatio, "oratio" was best translated by our modern term "intercessory prayer." For prayer (oratio) meant "interceding with God," asking—or, as Julian calls it, "beseking," the natural expression, in practice, of her seeking. And this is clearly the sense in which Julian writes of prayer in her *Revelation:* prayer, that is, as distinct from contemplation, as seeking is distinct from beholding. Julian's "evencristen" are "besekers," even if not, therefore, less than contemplatives. For which reason she would not have shared either of our two contemporary terminological assumptions: not the first (that contemplation is a form of prayer), because contemplative vision (her beholding) is not the same as beseking (her prayer)—they differ as end and means are distinct; and not the second (that contemplation is the highest form of prayer), because contemplation not being for her a form of prayer at all, it is not as a form of *prayer* that she would have ranked "beseching" below contemplation. For, as we have seen, Julian does not rank seeking below beholding in any practical context, even if in the abstract she does.[42] The monks did rank them thus hierarchically, for they envisaged oratio as rising up on the monastic ladder to contemplatio as to its fulfillment, just as lectio leads to meditatio and meditatio to oratio.[43] Nor would Julian's reasons for differing on this score of monastic priorities have been merely lexical. Given her theological description of our human mise-en-scène, beseking, not contemplation, is the most natural expression of it, even if on some absolute scale contemplation is a higher activity. For "beseeching," as I have said, has the more appropriate eschatological fit. And this is for a reason that goes far beyond the lexical, since it is fundamental to her theological purposes.

Prayer and Eschatology

Turning, then, to Julian's short tract on prayer, its relevance ought to be immediately clear. It opens the exposition of the fourteenth revelation whose center of gravity is the example of the Lord and the Servant. And if we are to take seriously Julian's rubric that it is in that parable that she finds all that she was ever to be told of how the divine meaning of the human narrative is disclosed to us, then the theological relevance of the interlude on prayer will be found in that connection too. What Julian tells us is that it is above all by means of petitionary prayer—"beseking"[44]—that we situate ourselves appropriately at that juncture where the eternal will of the Trinity and our messy historical contingency intersect. It is by means of a sort of pedagogy of prayer that we learn, in ascetical practice, how to incorporate into our lives the eschatological tensions between eternity and temporality, between the divine providential purposes and our human agency. Hence, insofar as we can get prayer right we can get the poise right—for prayer, properly understood, gets the eschatology right. As Julian sees it, beseking is the human practice, in miniature, of the providential purposes of divine love. One can go further: for Julian, petitionary prayer is a principal means by which the divine love achieves its providential purposes.

It would not be in any way misleading to say of Julian's *Revelation* that if it has any one central theme, it is that of the theological virtue of hope, of which her much-repeated refrain that "alle maner of thinge shalle be wel" is the typical expression. The common medieval understanding of hope was as one of the three theological virtues, along with faith and charity, and as such it was the gift of entirely an unmerited creaturely participation through grace in the being of God. More specifically, just as faith is our creaturely participation in the divine self-knowledge, and charity is our creaturely participation in the Trinitarian being of God, which is love, so hope is our creaturely participation in God's relation to time, which is the eternal divine providence. Hence, it is in hope that Christians stand in a relation of adequacy to their fundamental condition of temporality; it is in hope that the eternal divine providence intersects subjectively with our time-bound condition; and it is through hope that we are able to read the disjointed narrative of our temporality—"the story of sin," as I have called it—no longer in

SIN AND SALVATION

terms of the "story that sin tells" but as having only one source of meaning, which is love. Moreover—and here I continue to compress some complex and profound topoi of classical patristic and medieval theology—if it is in hope that we humans are given the gift of participation in the divine relation to time, then from the point of view of the human power in which that grace does its work, it is memory that is given that capacity. For, as human powers go, it is by memory that we relate to time. The theological virtue of hope, we may say, "deifies" memory and draws it through participation into the eternal providential purposes.

This theme of memory is once again profoundly Augustinian. When Augustine finally discovered God, it was, he said, through the restoration and healing of memory.[45] In fact, he thought that memory was the seat or ground of all intellect and desire, for intellect is but memory's eros; intellect is memory's seeking itself out, it is memory's desire to reconnect its broken lines of continuity with its own source; intellect is a kind of nostalgia for its own cause and origin. And that cause and origin is the divine light of truth that is in our minds but not of them, at once the cause and object of intellect's desire, at once "familiar" and "strange," "ever ancient, ever new."[46]

But if we are to say that for Augustine memory is a sort of nostalgia, then we will have to say that it is, paradoxically, a nostalgia not only for an unremembered past but also for an as yet unrealized future—or even more expansively, that memory is time's desire for eternity. For Augustine abandoned as inconsistent with his Christian faith Plato's teaching in the *Meno* and the *Phaedo*[47] that our souls had once known all truth in a prenatal condition of separation from the body, and had been caused to forget it all through the catastrophe of birth in a material body. For Augustine, our origin in the eternal wisdom of God lies not alone in the past, because our origin is inscribed in our present reality, which is a yearning for the future. We are beings both of eternal origin and of eternal destiny but inserted into contingency and time, and it is that very contingency and temporality of our worldly condition that "reminds" us of an incomprehensible otherness, a strangeness of possibility that is at once beyond us and at the same time familiar, like the strange familiarity of a home we eventually return to after a long journey abroad. That familiar otherness is also like a horizon surrounding all our knowledge but never to be captured within it.[48] As Bonaventure, centuries later but following Augustine closely, put it: the light in which we see can never be itself the object of our seeing.[49] This horizon, this light, indeed has a name—the name of "God"—but all the same it is a name the meaning of which is incomprehensible to us; it is known because it accounts for what we do know, but it is not itself one of the objects known, just as we see light only in its reflections struck off opaque objects. Light cannot be itself one of the things seen. Indeed, if we could see the light as an object, then we would be unable to see anything else in it. Thus it is that we "remember God"—because everything whatever reminds us of him.

It is true that Julian does not, as Augustine did, make memory a central and explicit topos of her *Revelation*. But in a way this was hardly necessary, because there are some obvious senses in which the work as a whole is an exercise of memory's power. First, at a relatively simple level, the Short Text itself, and the Long Text by considerable extension of it, are exercises in an increasingly profound retrieval of some initial experiences remembered—the retrieval progressively of a depth within those experiences, "ever ancient," because that depth was always somehow there within them, but also "ever new," because newly recovered. But second, there is the more fundamental sense in which memory plays a central role in Julian's theology, as it explicitly thematizes, as Augustine's *Confessions* did, the relation between the divine eternity and the necessarily narratival form in which we humans gain any grip on it. For Julian, just as emphatically as for Augustine, our experience of eternity is time-bound. To be sure, it is only through memory that past, present, and future have any possible relation with one another;

indeed, we have to say that only for a being equipped with memory can there be any past, present, or future.[50] But we do not "remember" the past, the present, or the future abstractly as time, but only as past, present, or future events in time. Moreover, every act of remembering is itself situated within the temporal sequences that it constructs. Consequently, acts of remembering themselves are events within the time that they recall. We are, thus, creatures of time, if even our power to relate to time through memory is itself a time-bound relating. And so it is that memory's desire for eternity too is a time-bound desiring, a "seking." If it is true that Henry Vaughan "saw eternity . . . like a great ring of pure and endless light," then it is also true that it was *"the other night"* that he did so.[51]

The theological virtue of hope does nothing to remove our time-bound creaturely condition, nor, therefore, the necessity with which we are creatures of narrative. Hope does indeed transform memory, and so the possibilities of narrative eschatologically, but not so as to set us in some vantage point of eternity as if we could occupy "God's point of view." Eternity is not a "vantage point," the expression "the vantage point of eternity" being an oxymoron. And God has no "point of view." It is creatures, not God, who see things this way *rather than* that, now *rather than* then, from a vantage point, from a point of view. Short in effect of describing God as just another creature, or of describing God's knowledge as just a maximized form of human knowing, we have to say that God sees in a single act the whole reality of which we can see at best some part, and then we see events only from within "points of view" sequentially strung out over time. For our part we must strain as best we can to connect them, sometimes with the scientific apparatus of causality, sometimes with the logical apparatus of inference, sometimes by means of a "story." Eschatology neither suspends time nor displaces sequence by means of eternity. Eschatology is eternity in the form of time, constituting some depth within it. And hope is our access to that depth.

And here, let me note on the subject of eschatology how markedly Augustinian Julian's is; and also how both his and hers differ in comparison with some eschatologies today. Within some contemporary theologies it seems to be thought—or perhaps it is rather unthinkingly assumed—that "eschatology" has something particularly to do with the future. They are, as it were, "one-ended" eschatologies, horizontal and sequentially linear in the temporal direction of their movement toward a future "end-time."[52] For theologians who think of eschatology (implicitly or otherwise) in terms of a single forward direction of time's arrow, the association so naturally made in patristic,[53] medieval,[54] and some early modern[55] theologies between the eschatological virtue of hope (on that modern conception uniquely future-directed) and memory (on that same conception unidirectionally past-related) is unintelligible. But for Augustine and Julian, it is the case neither that eschatology is forward-related to just one future time,[56] nor that memory is backward-related just to the past. As to memory, it is Augustine's sense that it embodies the power of human relating to time as such, and not to past time principally—for without memory, there could not be any time at all, and so no past time. And as to the eschatological, it is the relation of eternity to all time, a relation that is itself temporal, that is, mediated by past, present, and future. There is, therefore, a double dimension to time in Augustine—and, as we will see, in Julian too. On one axis, memory grounds time's possibility as such, and so it grounds time's one-directional trajectory through past and present to future; and on the other, it is in memory's construction of time that eternity eschatologically intersects with time's every moment. There, in memory, does the theological virtue of hope do its work: it grasps all time *as* eschatology.

And so, to complete the circle of connections thus very schematically set out, prayer as petition is the natural expression of hope; prayer, as Julian sees it, is hope's eschatological "beseking"; prayer, therefore, is, as George Herbert says, "the six daies world transposing in an hour,"[57]

God seen "in a pointe," as Julian says.[58] And it should be noted that in this she is, as usual, in accord with the standard theological taxonomy of her day. For medieval theologians commonly set their discussions of petitionary prayer firmly within the context of hope, as did Thomas Aquinas in his *Compendium theologiae*.[59]

The "Grounde of Our Beseking"

Prayer, then, for Julian means petition, "beseking" in hope. And if its relevance to the fourteenth revelation is found in the fact that the example of the Lord and the Servant spells out (in the collapsed timelessness of contemplative vision) the foundation of her overarching theology of history, then prayer as beseking is the form in which that vision of the eternal divine providence intersects subjectively with our temporal experience so as to become a narrative through which we are inserted into that eternity. And if in this way prayer is, as writ small, that which the parable writes large; if prayer is the eternal providence of God as experienced within our temporality; if prayer is the collapsed unity of contemplative vision extruded across narrative sequence; if prayer is memory's nostalgia within present time for past origin and future destiny; if, in short, our prayer is nothing other than that prayer that is the Trinity, the mutual indwelling of Father, Son, and Holy Spirit insofar as it is present within us, then we can expect that all the theological tensions embodied within that grand providential narrative will be replicated within every episode of prayer in which that vision is writ small. Hence, we should expect that if that grand providential narrative is, after all (at any rate in our finite capacity to receive it) not so grand, if it is necessarily an incomplete disclosure, then so too will petitionary prayer arise from within a corresponding sense of that same incompleteness of our knowledge and therefore from a sense of dependence and need. And so prayer will take the form principally of seeking in trust, that is, of hope and beseking. And if above all that fragmentary vision of the divine love on the strength of which God tells Julian that nothing is amiss stands by virtue of its incompleteness contestable and contested by the experience of so many things going wrong, then we will expect Julian to advert to the most obvious of facts about the human experience of petitionary prayer—namely, that if prayer arises out of hope, then that hope is contested by the apparent inefficacy of our beseking. To say the least, beseking itself does not seem always to set things right. For the trust in which it is founded is always challenged by the facts as they turn out.

And so advert she does. Immediately it is forced upon her that as much as we "beseke," too often, as far as we can see, it is to no avail. The odds as to the outcomes of our beseking seem, she says, so heavily stacked against trust that they lead as often as not to discouragement. At its simplest, the problem of petitionary prayer is that for all anyone can tell as they observe how things fall out, praying seems to make no difference to anything. And she is of course right, so far as experience goes. It is the obvious but real problem for any theology of petitionary prayer that the chances of what a person prays for happening would seem not to be calculably different from the chances of its happening if he or she had neglected to pray for it at all. On the one hand, then, "if we pray and se[e] not that he do it, it maketh us hevy and doughtfulle"; and on the other, "if we se[e] that he doth it and we pray not, we do not oure det [duty]."[60] Now, the natural question that arises for anyone, "What difference does prayer make?" is also a problem for Julian, who has been told, as Christians are, that their prayers are always heard, that their desires are known to their Father before they themselves know them, and that they are provided for from all eternity. She tells us: "Althing that oure lorde hat ordained to do, it is his wille that we pray therfore either in specialle or generalle."[61] But when someone asks God for things, how can anyone tell what his answer is when there appears rarely to be any discernible, and never a certain, relation between what one prays for and what happens?

Julian is acutely aware that in practice the relationship between asking in prayer and receiving rarely seems to work out the way we think it has been promised it should, not in most people's day-to-day lives most of the time. In fact, it is probably true to say that most Christians are at best prepared to say that their prayers are "answered" only when they get exactly what they prayed for: and even then, what happens could have happened anyway, had they not prayed. Statistically, "successful" petitionary praying is a hit-and-miss business. In moments of fine prayer, Julian tells us, a person may feel a particular intimacy of and with God.[62] But otherwise than in such comparatively set-piece and staged occasions of contemplative peace, prayer—"my lament / Is cries countless"—and whether or not "countless cries" make any difference to what happens seems, in practice, impossible to say—for they are "like dead letters sent / To dearest him that lives alas! away."[63] As with how things turn out generally, so in particular with petitionary prayer—there seems to be little consistency in our relationships with God. And that, Julian admits, can trouble us. For if Christians are inclined to think that the love of God is possible, then the thought will probably come to mind unforced that the divine will should be a trifle less indeterminably elusive than it is in their experience. After all, we know that we would not get on very successfully loving any other person, a spouse or a friend, say, if getting on the inside of their reactions were quite so random an affair as ours seems to be with the will of God. So Julian knows that the ordinary practical problem with prayer is no different from her general problem with her shewings themselves. And that problem about prayer concerns how to put these two things together: God's promise that he answers all prayers, because from all eternity he has willed to do so, with the apparently random cussedness of what actually happens.

Of course, as Julian notes, one response to this predicament is to say: our prayers are always heard, and they are always answered, but we do not know how. And she agrees, adding that we should not need to know how, for what else is faith but putting complete trust in God's promise to care for us? And what happens in the event is beside the point, since whatever happens is always a gift from a loving God in answer to prayer. And that seems right, if only because at a meta-level, that is to say, insofar as we can redescribe the particular things that actually happen as having a higher level of meaning within a larger story, that is all you can say: that "everything is all right, only we can't see it." But here too, as before, it can seem intolerably a priori—too disengaged from experience—just to say everything is all right because there is a loving God who cannot let us down. Of course it is true, Julian says, that whatever happens, nothing is amiss. Either you can say nothing is amiss, or else there is no God, and nearly everything is badly wrong. Either, as Dante implies, there is a divine comedy or else the story is nonsensical. The logic of the situation is as simple as that.

But as over and again we have seen, so one-sidedly an a priori visionary logic cannot be enough for Julian, for on its own, it cannot resolve the conflict it appears to be in with the sadder facts of experience. For even if everything's being all right seems fine to say at this "second-order" level, Julian knows that it is not so easy to concede it at the primary level, the level of day-to-day experience. For one thing, to say "Everything is all right, only we can't see it" would appear to explain nothing actual, and would seem to be rather like saying, "Everything just appears on the surface to be differently colored—red, blue, green, or whatever—but deep down everything is really green, its just that we can't see it." The point about colors is that they just are the objects of sight: the expression "an unseeable color" is an oxymoron. And a notion of faith correspondingly disconnected from anything in our experience would appear to reduce it to an idle cogwheel, spinning around smoothly enough on its own axis, but disengaged from the machinery of experience: it contributes nothing to how the thing works.

Nor, for that matter, only theoretically, but also practically. Things do go badly wrong: the parents pray incessantly that their young married daughter, the mother of two little boys, will not die of cancer—and she dies. Then Christians are taught to say that their "faith is being tested." And it is. But it could not be tested unless there were, after all, some sort of real connection between God's providence, what we pray for, and what actually happens. But if there is some such real connection, it must be deeply mysterious, as we know in the most painfully practical form when we try to find words of consolation for the parents. Vacuous second-order platitudes about "faith" butter few first-order emotional parsnips. So what is one supposed to say? Is Julian supposing that we must inform the parents of what's *good* about their daughter's death, just in case they had failed to notice?

Then Julian notes another sort of reaction that is sometimes provoked when what people pray for fails to happen, and it is that perhaps they did not pray well enough. One thinks: Perhaps I prayed with an insufficiently high-grade level of motivation, or perhaps not persistently enough, or with too much doubt for it to have been done out of real faith; or, perhaps it was just that I am not worthy enough to be heard. For "oftime oure trust is not fulle. For we be not seker [certain] that God hereth us, as we thinke for oure unwurthinesse, and for we fele right nought [nothing at all]."[64] And this sort of reaction can show itself in an anxious attempt to put pressure on God, perhaps as one sometimes hears people say they have done by offering him a trade-off: Grant me this, and I will definitely give up smoking, or hereafter be polite to my mother-in-law. But Jesus cuts off that line of escape. "Do not pray as the pagans do," he says, "babbling," thinking that "by using many words they will make themselves heard" (Matthew 6:7).

And it is with that contrast between what Thomas Aquinas calls

"pagan" or "Egyptian" prayer[65] and that of Christian hope that we get
to the heart of Julian's understanding of beseking. Prayer, for Julian, is
not something *we* do; it is something that *God* does. Thomas explains: it
is not the case, as the pagans think, that you can get the gods to change
their minds by offering them sufficient quantities of prayers and sacri-
fices by way of inducement. Rather it is that God is minded from the start
to bring about what he wills by means of our prayers[66]—which is merely
Thomas's expansion of what Jesus went on to say as Matthew reports
him: "Your Father knows what you need before you ask him" (Matthew
6:8). It is the Father's knowledge of what we need that is the cause of our
asking. And Julian's theology of prayer is fully in accord with that of
Thomas: "Alle thing that oure good lord maketh us to beseke, himself
hath ordained it to us from without beginning. Here may we than see
that oure beseching is not the cause of the goodnesse and grace that he
doth to us, but his proper goodnesse."[67] For Julian, God chooses our
prayers as the instrument of his will. Her praying does not effect a causal
influence on divine providence. Divine providence causes her praying. It
is God who brings it about that we pray in the first place, for we pray out
of grace, which is his alone to give. It is because the initiative of prayer is
not with us, but with God, that Julian can be so certain that God gives
us what we beseech in prayer. Hence, just as Augustine saw that it was
within his seeking—as its ground—that God was to be encountered
before ever he could be discovered as that seeking's object, so the Lord
tells Julian: "I am the grounde of thy beseking. Furst it is my wille
that thou have it, and sithen [next] I make the[e] to wille it, and sithen
I make the[e] to beseke it—and thou besekest it! How shoulde it than
be that thou shuldest not have thy beseking?"[68] As Thomas did before
her, so does Julian reverse the "pagan" order of prayer's causality. God
infallibly grants what we want *by means* of the prayer that God causes
to arise from that wanting: "And therfore he stereth us to pray that that
liketh him to do, for which prayer and good wille, that we have of his

gifte, he wille rewarde us and geve us endlesse mede [reward]."[69] Our prayer is the instrument of God's will, not its cause. "For whan a soule is tempted, troblede, and lefte to itselfe by unrest, then is it time to praye to make himselfe suppul [supple] and buxom [obedient] to God. *But he by no manner of prayer maketh God suppel to him. For he is ever alike in love.*"[70] Prayer is not how we get God to do things for us. Prayer is how God gets things done by means of us. "[Deus] vult . . . hoc esse propter hoc: sed non propter hoc vult hoc," as Thomas says: "[It is true that] God wills this [to happen] on account of that; but it is not on account of this that God wills that [to happen]."[71] And as in general that seems true of the divine providence itself, so it is true of our praying within the divine providence. As we might paraphrase: it is true that God wills this to happen as caused by our prayers, but it is not true that it is as caused by our prayers that God wills this to happen.

But even if that last is true, it still does not address the problem with which Julian began her discussion of prayer, namely, of the apparent discontinuity between what we ask for in prayer and what God brings about by means of our asking. How can it be true that, as I just said, God infallibly grants what *we* want by means of our prayers? Petitionary prayer, at any rate prayer that arises out of our specific desires, would seem to be pointless if all that could be said of it is that by its means God grants what *he* wants, whether or not it is what we prayed for as being what *we* want. In that case, it could make no sense to pray for what we want at all, but only that the divine will should be done regardless. And if that is all that Julian is saying, then will it seem that she has progressed no further beyond the conflict between that fine theological platitude about nothing being "amisse" and the plain facts, namely, that things go badly wrong in spite of our prayers?

Perhaps not. For it does not seem to be in the same way paradoxical to say that God always gives us what we want, only we are often unable to see it, as it does to say that everything is colored the same color in an invisible sort of way. And this is because while colors come only as they are perceived, our desires do not always come as we experience them. Our desires are often lost in a tangle of misperceptions. We are a mystery to ourselves. We do not always know what we want, and sometimes this is a straightforward case just of being undecided whether we want this rather than that, like being undecided whether to take a job offer or not. But sometimes it is more like this: we thought we knew what we wanted, only when we get it, it turns out that in truth we did not and that we "really" wanted something else; we were mistaken about what we wanted. Or sometimes it is as when I realize now that I was in love with so-and-so, though at the time I did not know it; I thought it was just friendship or some such. In such cases, our not knowing what we want is not that we are undecided as between two or more *known* wants; it is rather that there is something that we want, only we do not know it.

Now, ex hypothesi, we cannot pray in this sense out of our true desires if we are in ignorance of what they are. We can pray only out of the desires we actually experience, often desperately, and that, I think, is more in line with Julian's understanding of prayer, as arising out of our fraught and problematic human condition. We should pray out of our actual desires, however mistaken and self-destructive and confused, for all we know, they may be. As she says, "the goodnes of God is the highest prayer, and it cometh downe to us, to the lowest party of our need."[72] At any rate, honesty would seem to require it, in preference to a certain kind of theological and spiritual snobbery and high-mindedness on which account some seem to think it vulgar and cheap to pray out of our unworthy and narrowly selfish or just plain muddled desires, and that we should pray only out of desires that God might be supposed to approve of, even if in truth they represent the last thing we would want God to pull off. Such an attitude would seem to resemble more that of the Pharisee, who prays out of pretence of virtue, than of the publican, who prays honestly and as he really is.

Besides, there is no practical alternative to praying out of what you think you want. Thomas Aquinas comments that Jesus's prayer in the garden at Gethsemane was prayed in accordance with a purely "natural" animal desire ("secundum sensualitatem"). For, as any animal naturally does, he feared death, and he, as we would, shuddered at the price the divine will seemed to be exacting.[73] His prayer to his Father was not, after all, very pious. All he could manage by way of prayer was the shuddering itself—he pleaded that his Father take the chalice away from him (Luke 22:42). And Augustine comments that this shows that we ought to pray for whatever we want, even when we know it is contrary to the will of God.[74] For that felt discrepancy between our will and the divine will is what becomes the prayer itself.

But there is more to it than considerations of plain honesty and truthfulness. It has to do with the very nature of prayer itself. Thomas explains that "oratio est quodammodo interpretativa voluntatis humanae," "prayer is a certain kind of interpretation of human desire," implying that our desires need interpretation, and here, Thomas means by "oratio" what Julian means by "beseking": petitionary prayer.[75] To be sure human desire does need "interpretation," for, as texts go, human desires are an opaque palimpsest, texts deep with meaning but written over by trivia. It is only if prayer issues from the often confused, inconsistent, frequently superficial, and low-grade experienced neediness of human beings that they will discover deeper levels of desire, interpreted as they are prayed for, revealing an agenda often masked by the perception of immediate want and need. In that sense petitionary prayer is indeed, as George Herbert says, "the soul in paraphrase."[76] Answers to prayers, on this account, are like the perfectly judged gifts given to us by those who know us best. They do not simply answer to our known wants. Their being given reveals to us wants for which, as Paul says, "we do not know how to ask" (Romans 8:26). The perfectly judged gift discovers our desires for us. Routine and thoughtless gifts merely flatter our desires as they are experienced.

As Julian says, when our prayers seem not to be answered, it is not the facts that are out of line. To suppose that is rather like supposing that I got all the lottery numbers right this week, and what a shame it is that the machine got them so wrong. It is not the facts that prayer changes, it changes us. It is not, Julian says, that God only erratically gives us what we want, but that he always does, so that we can learn from what he gives us in answer to our prayers what our true desires are. It is in that way that our "beseching" both arises from and interprets our desires. The cog of faith does in that way engage with the machinery of desire. Not superficially to meet them, however unreal they may be, nor as if absurdly to say that a parent could possibly, at any level, desire their daughter's painful death, but so as to say that it is on the Cross of that pain, the pain accepted as the Cross, that our wants are transformed into our truest desire, our truest happiness.

Prayer and Providence

On Julian's account, the symmetry between providence on the universal scale and the prayer of "beseching" on the particular is therefore exact: they intersect at a midpoint upon a continuum. For just as on the scale of the grand providential narrative of Creation, Fall, and Redemption, all is done from eternity in the eternal wisdom and love of God, so from eternity is it willed that we should pray. And just as every event in time is caused by that divine love, some things by means of this, some things by means of that, so some of what the divine love brings about is done by means of our beseking, of which that same love is the "grounde." Just as the divine love, therefore, uncreatedly causes all created causalities, so it causes the very desire out of which we pray, and as it causes that desire, infallibly it meets the desire it causes. For the Lord, being "the grounde of our beseching," necessarily gives us what we beseech as having been eternally willed to be ours. Through prayer, then, eternity and time meet in the contingency of human desire, and the discovery of the eternal meaning of time is made within prayer's interpretation of desire's contingency. And it is here especially that Julian's account of petitionary prayer meets with Augustine's, each in its own way setting in relationship with one another the spirituality of "self-making" and the spirituality of "self-discovery." For both Julian and Augustine, what we most truly want is always in some way latent within the fractured, wayward narrative of what we experience ourselves to be wanting. For Julian, as for Augustine, whatever it is that we want, the true meaning of all our desire is the desire for God, because all our desire is from God. It is in this sense that Julian can say "God doth alle thing," for he "doth" not only outcomes. He "doth" also the means by which those outcomes are achieved, most especially by means of the prayer that issues from our free desire. And at least in principle we now know better than to conclude from God's doing "alle thing" that we do nothing, or nothing freely. For our free response to the divine providential wisdom is at the very heart of what that providence provides. If God does everything, so also do we.

CHAPTER SIX

Substance and Sensuality

"I SAW HIM AND SOUGHT HIM, and I had him and wanted him." Two features come most readily to mind as guiding motifs of Julian's spirituality. The first is trust in a given reality known and possessed, trust in the divine love that, being already fully given, is there for the taking: "I saw him and I had him." The other is desire for a consummation of that love not yet fully achieved: "I sought him and I wanted him." What is had and what is sought are one and the same—him. Moreover, these two pairs of terms, "saw" and "sought," "had" and "wanted," line up broadly with Julian's distinction between "beholding" and "beseking," a distinction that in turn corresponds with more general medieval ways of distinguishing between the "not yet" of intercessory prayer and the "now" of contemplative vision. Hence, just as it is misleading to overstress the distinction between prayer and contemplation, important though it be to distinguish them, so it is in the same way misleading to cast Julian's beholding and beseking in opposition to and exclusion of one another, for each entails and contains the other. What Julian beholds is that which is the ground of her beseeching; what she beseeks in prayer is to return to that ground: she had him *in* her seeking, and she wanted him *in* her having him. Correspondingly, the meeting between trust in what is already given and desire for what is not yet possessed defines the poise and balance of Julian's spirituality. In short, hers is a spirituality of hope in its most general character, and of prayer in its implications for ascetical practice.

As I explained in the previous chapter, the interplay of the prayer of beseeching with contemplative beholding, between desiring what is not yet come and trusting in what already is, is a sort of microversion of the dynamic interplay, writ large, between the eternal immutability of divine providence and the contingency of human history—and so between that providence and human freedom. For, as I put it before, it is in prayer that eternity and time meet with the contingency of human desire. Prayer is a practice of interpreting human desire, a practice that draws us back through the tangled thickets of wants and needs as we experience them to our truest love and to where we are most truly ourselves. And as eternity is mediated by time in the contingency of desire, so desire is transformed by the eternity it mediates. What I most truly want is also that which is already given.

The purpose of this chapter is to take one further step down into the foundations of the convergence between divine providence and human desire as Julian understands them. It is a step that will take us through her theological anthropology back to the starting point for everything in Julian's theology—the Cross of Christ. For just as it is in and through that very particular event in time that all history and all time are transformed into salvation history; just as it is through the Cross of Christ that a seemingly ad hoc narrative of contingent (and for all that one might otherwise have known, random) outcomes is shown at last to be the one and only divine comedy eternally willed by an immutable love, so it is that through that same Cross our human nature, disrupted and fragmented by sin, is restored and returned to its eternal source in God, so to its true selfhood—or, otherwise put, to its true desire.

That further step into Julian's theological anthropology therefore needs to be taken if we are to understand how Julian's theology of Creation, providence, sin, and Redemption cashes out in terms of lived practice and personal spirituality. For those intersections and identities at the macro level of salvation history between Creation, Fall, Incarnation, and Redemption that are the theme of the parable of the Lord and the Servant are also intersections and identities that are replicated in each soul that is to be saved. But, in turn, to take that further step into Julian's theological anthropology requires achieving some degree of clarity about perhaps the densest and most obscurely difficult of all her teachings, combining two related themes. The first is the theme of "the godly wille," a will that is to be found "in ech a soule that shall be safe [saved]."[1] The second is expounded in an extended development of the distinction and interrelations between our "substance" and our "sensuality." But in neither case is clarity about Julian's teaching easily won. For the way to clarity about the twin teachings concerning the "godly wille" and "substance/sensualite" may first seem blocked by issues of interpretation as to how they relate. But then, no sooner may some clarity on that score seem to have been achieved than we are faced with serious issues of substantive doctrine, that is, of the Christian orthodoxy of Julian's theology.

The "Godly Wille" and "Substance": Are They the Same?

Julian's doctrine of the godly will is introduced as early as chapter 37 of the Long Text, and is then expanded with full complexity in chapters 53–57. In chapter 37, she tells us: "In every soule that shalle be saved is a godly wille that never assented to sinne, nor never shalle. Right as there is a bestely wille in the lower party [part] that may wille no good, right so there is a godly will in the higher party, which wille is so good that it may never wille eville, but ever good. And therfore we be that he loveth, and endlesly we do that he liketh."[2] The formula is repeated in chapter 53, with the important difference that the sharp contrast between the "godly" and "bestely" wills of the earlier passage is omitted from the latter, and later in this chapter I will give attention to the significance of this omission. In chapter 53, then, she says: "I saw and understode full sekerly [certainly] that in ech a soule that shall be safe [saved] is a godly wille that never assented to sinne, ne never shalle. Which will is so good that it may never wille evil, but evermore continually it willeth good and werketh good in the sight of God."[3]

Immediately she draws this teaching in under the wide span of her doctrine of divine providence and governance when she says that the presence of such an indefeasibly good will in "ech kinde that heven shall be fulfilled with" follows from the doctrine of providence, for by "Goddes rightfulhede [perfection]" those who will be saved must "be knit and oned in him, that therein were kepte a substance which might never nor shulde be parted from him, and that thorow [through] his awne [own] good will in his endlesse foreseeing purpose.... For I saw that God began never to love mankinde. For righte the same that mankinde shall be in endlesse blesse [bliss] fulfilling the joy of God (as anemptis [regard to] his werkes), righte so the same mankind hath be, in the forsighte of God, knowen and loved fro without beginning in his rightful entent."[4]

Such, compendiously stated (we might also think a little obscurely), is Julian's doctrine of the godly will—that is, her account, as I paraphrased it, of "what you really want." This godly will is the level of true desire that is indeed there already in us. And yet it needs to be sought, because its presence within us is far from always evident and we must work to gain access to it.

On the one hand, then, it is "had." For whatever else we desire, Julian seems to think, we do desire God. For this reason, it appears that for Julian we do not have to somehow get ourselves to love God, as if that were our moral or ascetical-spiritual goal or, for that matter, as if it were even possible for us. There is nothing that we have to get ourselves to do except allow ourselves to be drawn by grace to see that we love God anyway, for loving God comes with our being created by

God's love for us. It is only sin that prevents us from seeing this and causes us to misrelate to our selves and our truest loves. Therefore, our love of God is in that sense "had," always there within us, even if only at the deepest and nonapparent level of desire.

On the other hand, it is also always to be sought, because in what Julian calls our "sensual" being, that is to say, in our time-bound historical experience, we live out of kilter with our truest desire. And so we need to work back from our desires as we experience them in our contingent, historical existence (prone as they are to all sorts of deformations, miscues, illusions, and fantasies), to that true desire that is always for God. And that given desire for God, both had and needing to be repossessed, is, Julian says, a godly will.

Now, it is a widely accepted interpretative assumption—though we will find it to be problematic—that what Julian says about our godly will is also true of what she calls "oure substance."[5] There are indeed good grounds for this assumption. Speaking of the godly will in chapter 53 of the Long Text, Julian tells us:

> For or [before] that he made us he loved us, and when we were made we loved him. And this is a love made of the kindly [essential, natural], substantial goodnesse of the holy gost, mighty in [by] reson of the mighte of the fader, and wise in minde of [in accordance with] the wisdom of the son. And thus is mannes soule made of God, and in the same pointe knite to God.
>
> And thus I understode that mannes soul is made of nought. That is to sey, it is made, but of nought that is made, as thus: whan God shulde make mannes body, he toke the slime of the erth, which is a mater medeled [mixed] and gadered of [gathered from] alle bodely thinges, and thereof he made mannes body. But to the making of mannes soule he wolde take right nought, but made it. And thus is the kinde [created nature] made rightfully oned [to be united]

to the maker, which is substantial kinde unmade [essential uncreated nature], that is God. And therfore it is that ther may ne shall be right noughte betwene God and mannis soule. And in this endlesse love, mannis soule is kepte hole, as all the mater of the revelation meneth and sheweth, in which endlesse love we be ledde and kepte of God, and never shalle be lost.[6]

Here, it would seem, Julian locates the deepest ground of the soul's unbreakable oneness with God in the act of Creation ex nihilo. As there is nothing between God and the soul in the soul's creation, so there is nothing that can ever get between the soul and God so as to break apart that primordial unity. Hence, there is no gap between God and our godly wills into which sin can insert itself. Significantly, in a gloss on the last sentence of this passage, Watson and Jenkins add: "The safety of the godly will derives from the moment and mode of humanity's creation,"[7] which appears thus to reinforce the reading that it is simply insofar as we are created, not specifically insofar as we are redeemed, that the godly will is unbreakably "oned" with God, and the created nature united with the uncreated. After all it is, Julian says, the "kinde," the "created nature," which is thus "oned to the maker," which is "substantial kinde unmade."

The interpretation that the presence of a godly will in us is founded in our created existence is further reinforced if we accept the assumption that for Julian godly will and substance refer to the same thing. If indeed there are in this assumption difficult issues both of interpretation and of theology, we can safely say that although manifestly the terms "godly wille" and "substance" do not mean the same thing (for "will" is a psychological term, "substance" prima facie a term of ontology), when Julian says, "and thus is mannes soule made of God, and in the same pointe knite to God," she refers in the same breath to our substance and to our godly will, because in either case, she is referring to that in the human being which is a trace of its creation ex nihilo. Because we are "made" *by* God, who "toke right nought" in making us, then necessarily we are "made" *for* God. We naturally desire an end that is laid down in our beginning, as T. S. Eliot wrote, consciously having Julian in mind.[8]

Hence, there is plausibility in the appeal that Watson and Jenkins make to the long tradition of Christian Neoplatonism in their explanation of Julian's meaning.[9] "Or that he made us he loved us," Julian says, and it seems clearly right to see here a reflection of the common Scholastic doctrine, no doubt Platonically inspired, of the soul's "virtual" existence in the eternal wisdom of God. In its exemplary character as the pattern or idea upon which we are created, the soul is eternally identical *with* God, for anything *in* God *is* God. We are eternally thought before we are made; we are eternally loved as we are thought; and God's thought and love for us are God. We are, insofar as we exist in our creating source, divine, so Julian seems to say, along with the conventionally orthodox opinion of her times—there is nothing theologically controversial here.

But the pressure of this Christianized Platonism would appear to exert a more powerful influence upon Julian's theology of Creation than merely to rehearse the widely accepted Scholastic truism about the soul's "virtual" *pre*existence in the mind and love of God. For Julian says more than that God made us in time on the pattern of the divine eternal idea of us—as if to say that in our eternal preexistence in the divine mind and love we were one with the God who thought and loved us, but now in our creaturely existence in time that primordial identity with God is fractured into distinction; or as if to suppose that in our created existence our identity with the uncreated Godhead is lost in the abyss of the most absolute of all distinctions, that between Creator and creature. For Julian, as for the common Christian-Platonist, what we most truly are in our historical created existence is what we are in our origin in God. Therefore, our eternal being in the thought and love of God is not something "kenotically" abandoned in our creation.[10] It is what we most really are in our present historical existence; it is our "substance." This would appear to be what Julian has in mind when in chapter 51 she collapses the identities of the Son, Adam, and everyman into the single identity of the Servant. And it seems that it is what she means in chapter 54 when she says: "A hye understanding it is inwardly to se and to know that God, which is oure maker, wonneth [lives] in oure soule; and a higher understanding it is and more, inwardly to se and to know oure soule, that is made, wonneth in God in substance—*of which sub-stance, by God, we be that we be*. And I sawe no difference betwen God and oure substance, *but as it were all God*."[11] Watson and Jenkins aptly gloss: "This perception (of identity between the soul and God) seems to follow from the claim that 'or that he made us he loved us,' for if there is divine love for a soul not yet made, it can be argued that what God loves in the soul is unmade, that is, part of God."[12]

The gloss is apt because it accords with what seems clearly to be Julian's line of thought: from all eternity, God loved us; in our eternal existence in God we are one substance with God, for everything true of God is identical with the God it is true of; God loved us into existence in time; within that temporal existence, there remains in us a trace of our origin, a place in us where the distinction between God and our souls is dissolved, and that place is our substance, "of which, by God, we be that we be." In that place, in our substance, all is God. And insofar as we desire from that place, as our desire arises from our godly substance, that substance is also well described as a godly *will*. Hence, it is not hard to see how, though differing in emphasis, the two terms could have the same reference. For if we think of the godly will as consisting in our truest, most real desires, and our substance as what we most really are, then their identity of reference would lie in the identity of our most real desires with our most real being: what we most truly are is what we most truly desire. That is to say, not only do we desire to be what we most truly are; we are what we most truly desire. And this is plausible, both as a doctrine and as an interpretation of Julian's meaning.

However, just if this is a plausible reading of Julian's meaning, there remain a number of problematic issues as to the orthodoxy of the substantive doctrine itself. It can seem theologically unsustainable, for on the assumption that the two descriptions "substance" and "godly wille" are taken to be identical in reference, conclusions might seem to be entailed that would be undoubtedly heterodox on almost any standard of Christian orthodoxy. Conversely, it might seem that the Christian orthodoxy of Julian's teaching can be defended only if that identity of reference is challenged, contrary to the weight of scholarly opinion that supports it.

Leaving aside for the moment the issue of interpretation, questions as to Julian's orthodoxy are far from merely rhetorical, and on three closely related doctrinal fronts doubts can arise. The first is caused by some of Julian's statements about our substance that by the standards of the later Middle Ages can seem to imply that between the soul and God there is, or can be, a "formal identity"—a teaching that had in her own times come to be judged as heretical, at least in some forms. A second doubt challenges Julian's doctrine of the Fall, raising the question whether the teaching about the godly will is not implicitly Pelagian; and a third questions whether, in at least some of the formulations of their relationships, the distinctions respectively between substance and sensuality and between godly and beastly wills are not in one or more unacceptable ways dualistically constructed.

Issues of Orthodoxy I: Is Julian an Auto-Theist?

Whether Julian's teaching about the identity of a person in his or her substance with God crosses the boundary of orthodoxy arises out of Julian's startlingly emphatic statement that by virtue of our very creation, we are so united to God that she could see "no difference betwen God and oure substance, but as it were all God." Robert Lerner devised the neologism *auto-theism* as the name for heterodox versions of those teachings in the late Middle Ages that appeared in one way or another to affirm the "formal identity" of the soul, or perhaps of the perfected soul, with God.[13] Reading Julian within the context of the theological controversies in her own fourteenth century, such a statement, to say the least, was bound to have raised a theological eyebrow, since it appears to affirm just that heretical teaching of the "formal identity" of our substance with God. It arouses the suspicion that on her account of "oure substance," the most fundamental distinction of all—that between the Creator and the creature—is obliterated. In the early fourteenth century, the threat of such heresies was thought to be very real—they were roundly condemned by the Council of Vienne in 1311–12 as the "Free Spirit" heresy—even if the threat existed more in the perceptions of hyperanxious minds of certain defenders of orthodoxy than in reality.[14] Moreover, this supposedly heretical teaching was thought to have some influential defenders, as is attested by the fates of Marguerite Porete (burned at the stake in Paris in 1310),[15] of Meister Eckhart (some prima facie heretical propositions of whose teachings were condemned by a papal commission in Avignon in 1329),[16] and of Julian's contemporary, Jan Van Ruusbroec (against whose supposed "Free Spirit" teachings Jean Gerson polemicized in the early fifteenth century.)[17] Of course, it is not beyond dispute today, nor was it in their own times, that the views of these and other theologians in the late Middle Ages were in fact heterodox. Most scholars today believe her theology to fall, if not entirely comfortably, within the bounds of orthodoxy, and Marguerite had her own defenders in her lifetime;[18] Eckhart protested against mis-readings of his views in his *Defense;*[19] and Ruusbroec had a powerful ally in his undoubtedly orthodox compatriot of the fifteenth century, the Carthusian Denys van Rykel.[20]

In any case, the teaching that within the human soul there exists a place where God dwells unthreatened by the possibility of sin (because the Creator's activity of making the soul out of nothing leaves, as it were, a trace of the divine nature in the human soul thus made), if not a commonplace of late medieval theology, was not novel in the fourteenth century, and certainly not to Julian. In fact, it had an ancient and pre-Christian lineage, stretching back at least to doctrines in Plato of a divinely erotic element in the soul,[21] and through the Platonic traditions in Plotinus[22] and Proclus,[23] and from Proclus via the Pseudo-Denys[24] into the Christian traditions. It is there too in Aristotle's assertion in the *Nicomachean Ethics*[25]—a text undoubtedly still under more Platonic influence than Aristotle liked to admit—that in its act of contemplation of God the human intellect shares some of the divinity of the God contemplated. The doctrine of a quasi-divine place in the human soul passed into the Latin Christian traditions, and quite apart from those fourteenth-century forms that at least some believed to be heterodox, it is found in an impeccably orthodox form in Augustine. Augustine argued that the human mind would not by itself and of its native powers be capable of judging finite and changeable created things as to "good," "better," or "best" were there not present within it the uncreated and unchangeable light of eternal truth providing the means with which to do so. For human reason in itself is just another of those changeable things, and a measuring rod itself subject to change cannot be a standard by which to judge the changeable.[26] That same Neoplatonic teaching is to be found in Bonaventure's exemplarist theological epistemology wherein the light of truth by which we can see the created world cannot itself be one of the created objects seen.[27] In some way, therefore, the presence within the human mind of the "eternal light of truth" is a necessary condition of our human, finite, and created ability to know even creatures.

None of these, however, maintained that the divine trace left in every human soul by its creation out of nothing was itself an *uncre-ated* element in the soul, as Eckhart appeared to say. For what caused him to fall foul of inquisitors, first in Cologne and then in Avignon, was his maintaining that, as Pope John XXII put it in the bull *In agro dominico:* "There is something in the soul that is uncreated and not capable of creation; if the whole soul were such, it would be uncreated and not capable of creation, and this is the intellect."[28] *In agro dominico,* of course, recounts secondhand what the inquisitors in Avignon felt to be at least misleading in Eckhart's views, but the bull's précis hardly does injustice to Eckhart, for in many of his sermons he makes similar statements: "Sometimes I have spoken of a light that is uncreated and not capable of creation and that is in the soul. I always mention this light in my sermons; and this same light comprehends God without a medium, uncovered, naked, as he is in himself."[29]

But if many things are unclear about Julian's position on the iden-tity of our substance with God, one thing is certain: she does not share Eckhart's opinion, if such it be, that in our substance we are *uncreated.* Watson and Jenkins, commenting on the crucial phrase in Julian "and I sawe no distinction betwen God and oure substance, but as it were all God," can confidently (and rightly) assure us: "If this perception [that is, her inability to *see* any distinction between God and our soul] were made into a theological claim, it would thus lay *A Revelation* open to the charge of auto-theism, the heresy for which Eckhart and Marguerite Porete were found guilty. For Eckhart, God and the soul are ultimately united 'without distinction,' so that the claim that part of the soul (what he calls its *scintilla,* or spark) is uncreated being, or God, is correct. Here, though, Julian's perception remains only that, and *A Revelation*'s argument as a whole, in which the soul is able to render God worship and a place of 'wonning,' has no place for understanding the soul as anything other than a created entity."[30]

In my view, Watson and Jenkins are right, but for reasons that they do not themselves fully explain. It is true, as they say, that a distinction is needed between what Julian can perceive and what she may legitimately claim for that perception in terms of theological doctrine, and Julian herself is clear that no doctrine of the "formal identity" of an uncreated part of the soul with God follows from her failure to see any distinction between the soul's created substance and the uncreated God. For that very distinction is implied in the theologically qualifying next sentence, in which Julian tells us that though she cannot "see" the distinction, "[her] understanding toke that oure substance is in God: that is to sey, that God is God and *oure substance is a creature in God.*"[31]

Indeed, it is not difficult to show the consistency of Julian's position. She seems untroubled by the combination of propositions that God and the soul (more specifically, God and our substance) are distinguished as Creator and creature, and second, that the distinction is one that she is unable to see. As I have argued elsewhere,[32] Julian is quite right: the distinction between creature and Creator is impossible to see. But this is not because the distinction does not exist. On the contrary, it is because it is too absolute, too total, for our minds to grasp. Our minds can take hold only of finite created distinctions, distinctions that obtain between things that differ in this or that respect. I can literally see the difference between red and green because they differ as colors do. I can see, in the sense that I can conceptualize, the distinction between what it is for something to be red and for something to be circular because they differ as colors and shapes do. Differences can be discerned only against shared backgrounds in the manner that colors and shapes differ as characterizations of surfaces. But we cannot discern in that way the difference between God and creature, not because that difference is reduced to zero, but because it is maximized to an infinite degree, that is to say, because there is not and cannot be any common background between God and creatures against which their distinction can be measured. The phrase "infinite degree" makes the point. "Infinite degree" is an oxymoron: infinity is *not* a "degree" at one end of a continuum occupied at the other end by the finite. To be on a continuum of any kind is to be finite. The infinite is off every possible scale (whether of comparison or contrast) with the finite. As the Pseudo-Denys once said: God, the "Cause of all," is "beyond both similarity and difference."[33] So Julian's position is perfectly consistent in the terms in which Watson and Jenkins explain it: she can insist that the distinction between God and our substance is imperceptible, because God and our substance do not and cannot differ as kinds of thing differ, since God is not a being of any kind, cannot belong to any species. Julian can say that in our substance we are all that God is, for we are as creatures all that God is as Creator, that is, in our substance we are not distinguishable from God—*except* infinitely. Julian is no auto-theist.[34] But then, it is arguable on the same terms that neither is Eckhart.[35]

Issues of Orthodoxy II: Is Julian a Pelagian?

More threatening to Julian's claims to doctrinal orthodoxy is her teaching that, if only in some part of ourselves, whether in our godly will or in our substance or in both, we are preserved from sin. For if that is the case, we might well ask why in *any* sense at all the Incarnation, and by means of it our Redemption, is necessary. Is not the inference inevitable that if we are in some part of ourselves, that is, within some of our created human powers, free from sin, then we can be saved by virtue of those same natural powers? Moreover, would not the universalist conclusion follow that if all are in any part of their created being free of sin, then everyone whatever, being thus created, is saved by virtue of their creation?

Read in such terms, there is no doubt that Julian's doctrines of the godly will and substance must entail heterodox conclusions—even if Julian herself can be defended against accusations of having herself drawn them. In fact, what makes issues of interpretation of Julian especially acute is that in the light of the overwhelming evidence of her text she can be so defended. For there is not enough textual evidence in her *Revelation* to support the proposition that Julian is a soteriological universalist (as we saw in chapter 4), even less to support any accusation of Pelagianism, and none at all that she is both. More than that, far from conceding to any such conclusions, she emphatically denies them. As to the doctrine of substance entailing a universalist soteriology, Julian is certain that many are damned; and as to the godly will doctrine being Pelagian, Julian is certain that we are so fallen as to be helplessly prone, emphatic that "notwithstanding this rightful knitting and this endlesse oning, yet the redemption and the againe-buying of mannekinde is needful and spedful in everything."[36] But how can we say both that through Adam's fall our necks are so stiffened as to be completely turned away from the Lord, and at the same time that through our creation there is some part of us that is always—despite the Fall—turned toward the Lord and never loses sight of his face? Is Julian's theology defensible doctrinally, then, only on terms that convict her of radical inconsistency? How are we to understand the godly will doctrine? How are we to understand Julian's teaching about "oure substance in God"? And how are we to understand their relations with one another? Can Julian's text be construed as internally consistent? And if it can, how can it be so construed as to be externally consistent with canons of Christian orthodoxy?

Julian's Augustinian Sources

The sources of Julian's doctrine of the godly will would seem to be primarily Augustinian. In fact, it would not be misleading to consider this doctrine as an extended gloss on Augustine's confession before God that "you have made us for yourself, and our hearts will not rest until they rest in you."[37] We are thus made for God, and, being made for

God, our being created thus and to that end is that in us which cannot be unmade. And our being for God *is* something in us; it is that in us which answers to our making, the force of that "in" being the primary meaning of Augustine's central motif of interiority. Augustine knows this, he tells us, because he experiences a restlessness that derives from his failure to find that point of inwardness in himself that is his created response to the call of his making: his seeking had all too often been for that which was "outside" him. It is even the case that it was there, outside himself, that he sought for God, for he knew how inclined he was to "rush upon the lovely things of the earth" and mistake them for "the beauty [in itself] ever ancient, ever new."[38] And in the same way as our experience has fallen away from the source of our being in God, so, speaking more universally, do our misguided theologies fail to answer to our truest desires: we seek God as if an "object" over against us. In short, our desire, our seeking, can face two ways simultaneously: one side faces toward God, as to the beginning and end of our desire, for that in us which is our "making" exists in us in the form of our truest desire as a will. And this will is therefore godly because it is a desire that can only return to the source of its making; it can have no other intention: as it is of God, so necessarily it is for God. That desire can "never consent to sin."[39] But we also face the other way: *we* can consent to sin—for our desire, taken as a whole, is also "bestely," and in our day-to-day historical existence our actual desires can become disconnected from our godly will. For even if God is always within us however much and however often we fail, then our experienced desire, our desires as we know them in time, have through sin been ripped up from their roots in what is most truly wanted so that we are not "within ourselves." And desire thus experienced, thus indulged, is, as Julian puts it, a "bestely wille" that can will no good at all.

Julian tells us in terms that match Augustine's that the source of the godly will in us is our creation. She says quite generally, and without exception of anyone, "And thus is the kinde [created nature] made rightfully oned to the maker, which is substantial kinde unmade, that is God. And therfore it is that ther may ne shall be right noughte betwene God and mannis soule."⁴⁰ Nothing, not even sin, can unmake our making. Therefore, nothing, not even sin, can break apart our fundamental oneness with God. How, then, are we to respond to a Calvinist objection that we are "wholly corrupted" by sin, or to Cranmer's objection in the General Confession of the *Book of Common Prayer* that there is "no health in us"?

Much of the difficulty in defending Julian's theological anthropology, whether for internal consistency or theological orthodoxy, would appear to derive from anachronistic interpretations of her Middle English word "wille," as if it meant much what we might mean by the modern English word "will." No doubt, in view of Julian's description of "wille" as being that which is "in" us, unbreakably "oned" with God, and in view of the likelihood that we, inheritors of more than six hundred years of subsequent philosophies of mind, should understand her word "will" in terms of a faculty or power defined in distinction against "desire," it is all too easy to read her in terms according to which her "godly will" contrasts with her "animal will," as "will" in our terms contrasts with the discrepant desire it succeeds or fails to control. It can seem that way, as we saw: for when in the first introduction of her teaching concerning the godly will in chapter 37 of the Long Text she tells us that it can never consent to sin, she immediately contrasts it with a "bestely wille in the lower party that may wille no good,"⁴¹ as if to say that the two forms of inclination within different parts of human nature (one fallen, the other not) are actually distinct powers of the soul, battling one another as do uncorrupted good and corrupted evil. Such a reading of her teaching would, were it in fact true to Julian's thought, reduce her theological anthropology to a form of interiorized Manichean dualism. In fact, that is exactly how David Aers does interpret it, noting a "link between [Julian's] doctrine and one that emerges in Augustine's Confessions. When he was in Rome Augustine still associated with those 'false and deceiving saints,' the Manichees. Following their teaching, he confesses, 'I still thought it is not we who sin, but some alien nature which sins in us' [5.10]. The consequences of Julian's teaching on the unfallen will of the one who sins is congruent with the Manichean belief that Augustine recalls . . . whatever Julian's intentions may have been, her teaching about a will that is untouched by the sin performed by the sinner takes her toward the position Augustine had held as a Manichee."⁴² But such a reading seems at odds with the plainer sense of what Julian says.

It seems a universal truth that all the terms available to us in which to describe human spiritual and moral conflict are problematic. All conflict supposes opposition. We can experience ourselves as torn apart, split in two by a rift, as Julian puts it, between a "higher" and a "lower party" of the self. It is almost impossible to find terms for the description of those conflicts of soul that do not appear to carry with them dualistic implications. But the metaphor of "parts," if perhaps inevitable, is almost certainly further unhelpful and misleading. It would seem better to think through Julian's understanding of the struggle with sin in the Janus-like terms in which it seems right to think through Augustine's. Rarely does any desire of ours face just one way, unambiguously toward good or toward evil. Nor do we have to think of moral conflict as necessarily occurring between two distinct desires or forms of desire, but as ambiguity within one and the same structure of desire. As a fallen human being, all my desire is conflicted—*I* am conflicted—for all my desire is characterized in three aspects. First, that of its orientation toward the God who made us for himself; second, and pulling against that orientation to God, its fallen orientation toward creatures who can never satisfy human desire; and third, the conjunction of the two that is the concrete reality of my selfhood, the experience of desire thus conflicted. The language of "parts" is no help at all in explaining how this could be so. Better is to return to the language of chapter 3: there we saw that for Julian the meaning of sin lies in our failure to know, and in our failure to live within the knowledge of, our true being, our truest desire. We are fallen beings, we are indeed "as a whole corrupt": I as a whole am corrupted by sin, not some part of me. For the whole "I," as we put it in chapter 3, lives within the boundaries of time, and within our fallen temporality is misaligned with its selfhood. And now we can add that I, as fallen, live in and through a selfhood constituted by the conflict between a desiring self which is beastly and that same desiring self which is also godly. And in consequence, our self-understanding is constituted by that same orectic conflict replicated cognitively: how we perceive ourselves is misaligned with how we really are in the same way as my experienced desire is out of true alignment with what I really want. And yet, in another sense of "real," what we really are is constituted in either case by the conflicted conjunction. That is what I am: conflicted as a whole, in self-knowledge and in desire.

In such terms, then, there is less difficulty in seeing how Julian can say with consistency that I am as a whole corrupted by sin and that there is "in" me a godly will that in no way consents to that corruption. As Denise Baker says, I sin because my selfhood has fallen apart. Conversely, my selfhood's falling apart is the consequence of sin. It seems to me, then, that Julian is right: it cannot be in consequence of my creation as such that I am fallen, unless one is to say that I am fallen exactly insofar as I am made by God ex nihilo. And not even Calvin says that.[43] Therefore it seems to be the logic of Julian's position as regards the relation between Creation and the Fall that that reduplicative "insofar as I am created I do not consent to sin" remains true within our fallenness. We are indeed fallen as a whole. But it is not insofar as we are created that we are fallen, just as it is not insofar as he is a policeman, but rather as a husband, that Peter who is unfaithful to his wife is an adulterer. You do not need the language of parts to analyze such complexities—indeed, such language unhelpfully obscures them. For Peter is not partly adulterer, partly policeman: Peter is both wholly a policeman and not thus far adulterer, and wholly a husband who thus far is one. In the same way it seems perfectly consistent for Julian to say that just insofar as I am created I am indefeasibly "oned" with God, and at the same time insofar as I am fallen my selfhood has become fractured and ambiguous because my desires, my will, have been torn away from their moorings in the will endowed to me as created being. All my desires are caught within that conflict. I therefore need salvation as a whole because I am fallen as a whole, albeit that by virtue of my creation, my will remains firmly anchored in God. On this account it is the view of neither Julian nor Calvin that there is "*no* health in us," even if for both it is "as a whole" that we are corrupted by sin. If I have cancer it is *I* who am sick—as a whole. But it does not follow, indeed it could not follow, that my body lacks healthy cells: for cancer is a parasitical disease that can flourish only on the condition that I am alive. Dead people do not have cancer, not anymore.[44]

Issues of Orthodoxy III: Is Julian a Dualist?

This clarification ought to facilitate the answer to our third question concerning the orthodoxy of Julian's teachings—it is in fact a cluster of different, if related, questions. The question is whether it is the case that in her account of the relationship between the godly and beastly wills, and correspondingly between substance and "sensualite," Julian's theological anthropology is in one form or more dualistic.

For it may seem so. As there are dualisms of different sorts—moral dualisms between good and evil, psycho-physical dualisms between body and soul, ascetical dualisms between flesh and spirit—so there are different inferences for making out the relationships between these different pairs dualistically. Not all distinctions are dualistic, if dualism consists in setting terms in mutual and exclusive opposition to one another; to distinguish and to oppose are not always the same. If we may take it that by our "substance" Julian refers to our being as created and eternally held in the knowledge and love of God, and by "sensualite" as our being in time and history, then by no means does she imagine that this distinction entails any opposition between them as such. Nonetheless, Julian also thinks that on account of the Fall our sensualite has *become* disjoined from our substance in God, that our fallen selfhood is made up of that misalignment between the two, and that—as we saw in chapter 3—to get ourselves thus wrong is to get God correspondingly wrong, and vice versa.

And here Julian certainly does seem to be distinguishing between substance and sensualite in terms of opposition between them: that is what the Fall does to our created nature. Likewise, as we have seen, when in chapter 37 Julian says emphatically that while our godly wills can never consent to sin, our beastly wills can will no good, she is describing a relation of moral and psychological conflict between them. This conflict entails, on the assumption of equivalence between the distinctions separating godly from beastly will and substance from sensualite, an equivalently oppositional form of contrast in the case of the latter. But how are we to understand that misaligned relationship between our substance, which is our selfhood insofar as it is in God, and our sensualite, which is our selfhood insofar as it is inserted into history and time and worldly experience?

There are more places than one in Julian's text where it might seem that she is treading a dualistic path. The appearance of moral dualism in the account of the godly/beastly wills distinction in chapter 37 is reinforced, in similarly disjunctive terms, by what Julian says in chapter 57 about the substance/sensualite distinction: "And anemptes [as regards] our substance, he made us nobil and so rich that evermore we werke his wille and his worshippe. There [I] say 'we,' it menith man that shall be saved. For sothly I saw that we be that he loveth and do that he liketh lastingly withoute ony stinting. And of this grete richesse and of this high noble, virtues by mesure come to our soule, what time it is knit to our body; in which knitting we be made sensual. *And thus in oure substance we be full, and in our sensualite we faile.*"[45]

Were we to interpret Julian only on the basis of the chapter 37 distinction between godly and beastly wills and ignore reference to the many other texts on the godly will, and if we were to deduce that the contrast between substance and sensualite corresponds with that between godly will and beastly will, based on the assumption that godly will and substance refer to the same human reality; and if, finally, we were to take all these inferences together with the statement that "in oure substance we be full, and in our sensualite we faile," then indeed we would get a picture of our true selfhood consisting of our godly will/substance, with all and only failure and falsehood proceeding out of our animal will/sensualite. Therefore, we have to revisit the substance/sensualite distinction, asking whether it is truly as dualist as Julian sometimes makes it sound. For if it is, then Aers's attribution to Julian of an unintended Manicheism might well be justified.

For if we were forced to concede in any absolute way this dualistic and oppositional construction of the relation between our substance and our sensualite, then we would have to track that same dualism back through the whole nexus out of which her theology is constructed. Nothing I have tried to explain concerning the structure of that theology could remain in place as I have explained it—indeed, that interpretation of her theology would be turned completely inside out, the relations between its elements reversed like an image in a mirror.

For if we had to say that what is fallen due to sin is our sensualite, and that what is innocent is our substance (hence that sensualite is in itself sinful), then the account of prayer that I attributed to Julian in chapter 5 is nonsense. For on no such construction of sensualite could prayer be represented as the means by which the *interpretation* of experienced desire leads to our truest desire. We would also have to rewrite our account in chapter 4 of all that Julian has to say about salvation history. And further: if the sense we can make of the core governing theological category of "the behovely" depends upon understanding it in terms of the narratively fitting, then, with the undermining of the narrative, this core notion would in turn be undermined and unintelligible. Everything in my account of Julian's theology depends, therefore, on the substance/sensualite distinction not being understood dualistically.

We should not underestimate the difficulties of interpretation here. Apart from the psychologically dualistic-sounding passages that contrast "godly" with "bestely" wills along lines parallel with "substance" and "sensualite," there is a further passage constructed out of an alarmingly dualistic image, this time of a body-soul kind, but overlaid with a corresponding morally dualistic depreciation of the body:

> And in this time I saw a body lyeng on the erth, which body shewde hevy and feerfulle, withoute shape and forme, as it were a swilge stinking mire [as if it were a bog of stinking mud[46]]. And sodeynly oute of this body sprong a fulle fair creature, a little child, full shapen and formed, swift [energetic] and lifly [lively], whiter then the lilye, which sharpely glided [quickly glided] uppe into heven. And the swilge [bulkiness] of the body betokenith grette wretchednesse of our dedely flesh, and the littlehede of the child betokeneth the clennes and the puernesse of oure soule. And [I] thought: "With this body bliveth no fairhede of this childe [no beauty of this child survives], ne of this childe dwelleth no foulhede of the body."[47]

And there is an earlier passage that, if the tone is less moralizing, is equally provocative of a dualistic reading in psychological terms of "inner" and "outer":

Repenting and willful choyse be two contrarites, which I felt both in
one at that time. And tho be two partes: that on outward, that other
inwarde. The outewarde party is oure dedely flesh, which is now in
paine and now in wo, and shalle be in this life, whereof I felte moch
in this time. And that party was that repented. The inward party
is a high, blisseful life which is alle in peece and in love, and this is
more prively felte. And this party is in which mightly, wisely and
willfully, I chose Jhesu to my heven. And in this, I saw sothly that
the inward party is master and sovereyne to the outward, nought
charging [taking responsibility for] nor taking hede to the willes of
that [i.e., of the "outewarde party"]. But alle the intent and the wille
is sett endlessly to be oned to our lorde Jhesu. That the outward
part sholde drawe the inward to assent was not shewde to me. But
that the inwarde party draweth the outwarde party, by grace, and
both shalle be oned in blisse without ende by the virtue of Criste,
this was shewde.[48]

It is tempting to discount such passages, conceding their presence
in Julian's text as indicating no more than the terminological flotsam of
a conventional, and relatively innocent, dualistic Christian vocabulary,
and as entailing no substantive theological departure from an otherwise
explicitly nondualist reading of Julian. There are two reasons why one
might yield to that temptation. The first is not far from being merely ideo-
logical: Julian is for our times an iconic theological nondualist. And how
many want to see their nondualist icons smashed, when in Christian
theological circles there are few enough of them to call upon in aid of
contemporary antidualist theological preferences? This might seem to be
a reason—or rather, a motivation—unworthy of consideration by true
scholars. I mention it, though, because I suspect that it is an operative
motive sustaining much of the enthusiasm with which her theology is
welcomed today: we want Julian, we need her, in our antidualist camps.

But there is a second reason for simply ignoring the few passages that would seem to indicate at least residually dualistic elements in her thought, and to those who are less ideologically motivated and simply puzzled by Julian's text, it is the worthier reason; it arises from an inability to see how those few passages can be made consistent with the vast preponderance of the evidence explicitly and emphatically supporting a nondualist theology. It is tedious to quote all such plainly nondualist texts when the simplest reading of chapters 53–59 shows very precisely where Julian's theology leads.[49] Tedious as it is, though, it is enough for the purposes of quashing a dualistic reading of Julian if we observe the centrality of the simple proposition linking together the substance/ sensualite distinction with the inner dynamic of the Trinity, that Christ is our "moder sensual": "Our substance is in our fader, God almighty, and our substance is in oure moder, God al wisdom, and our substance is in our lorde God the holy gost, all goodness. For oure substance is hole in ech [each] person of the trinite, which is one God. And our sensualite is only in the seconde person, Crist Jhesu, in whom is the fader and the holy gost."[50] And again, Julian tells us: "The seconde person of the trinite is oure moder in kind [nature] in our substantial making, in whome we be grounded and roted [rooted], and he is our moder of mercy in our sensualite taking."[51]

What are we to say, then, if no sustained evidence is provided in her theology for ascribing to Julian the dualism found in a few passages in her Long Text? Are we to say that Julian's theology as it stands in that text is a poorly edited incoherent mess, since in the end she comes out with what would seem to be plainly dualistic formulas? Hardly. For if anything else is as clear as the overall antidualist instinct of *Revelation*, it is that hers is a text that has been revised with supreme care.

Theology in Double Focus

Over and over again we have seen how Julian's theology has a bifocal character, how she is minded to keep constantly in play two angles of vision. One is the perspective seen from within her own personal experience of sin, the other that to which she is drawn by her shewings. That first perspective, when taken on its own, issues in what I have called the "story that sin tells." That story is indeed riddled with dualisms of all sorts, although that is not so surprising, since, as a result of our fallen condition, we inevitably see everything dualistically, including the world, ourselves, and God. For Julian, I dare to say, as for Luther, we are *simul iustus et peccator:* being saved does not somehow magically put an end either to our sinning or to the perspective in which we see things from the standpoint of our sinfulness.

We see things as we are; and as we are, so we see things. Therefore, because by reason of sin we are divided selves who have fallen apart, so it is that we see ourselves, God, and our fellow human beings in dualistic terms. We could say, then, that dualism is the natural and spontaneous mode of thought corresponding with our fallen condition, reflected by that condition, and sustaining what it reflects. Dualism makes a world. Dualism makes a "god." Dualism experiences a self. Indeed, dualism makes what John the Evangelist in his Gospel calls "*the* world," together with its corresponding natural and spontaneous theologies and theological anthropologies.

And so it is that we can run through the whole gamut of connections of thought that structure Julian's theology, but now only from the standpoint opposed to what she sees in her shewings, turning that theology inside out. Insofar as within this mode of thought we see ourselves as sinful, we see an angry punishing God, like the elder brother of the prodigal son, whose expectations of his father's anger are the dialectical counterpart to his own resentment. From this standpoint we see prayer and providence as opposed, and so, looking at prayer in a pagan way as action standing outside and independently of the causality of providence, we suppose ourselves to be praying in the hope of modifying it. On these distorted terms, prayer becomes a matter of our seeking to deflect the divine will from its expected course rather than, as in Julian's terms, something that the divine will providentially effects in and through us. And we see things that way because out of our own dividedness of self we have turned the inner and outer worlds against one another, no longer able to see our acts of prayer as the activity of God in us working with and within our free desire. Collectively, then, all of this is part of the dualistic story that sin tells: the dualisms interact with, generate, and reinforce one another. Nor are they just autobiographical narratives, matrixes of individual self-perception. They are whole theologies and worldviews. And they are all the natural and spontaneous modes of thought and feeling and self-perception of a sinful self, of *homo peccator.*

It is no use supposing that the sources of dualistic consciousness, embedded so deeply in our experience, can be swept away with merely philosophical arguments against them—you cannot *philosophize* the Fall away, or primly occupy a merely attitudinizing antidualist higher moral ground. For, in taking note of the roots of divided selfhood created by such forms of oppositional consciousness, and of their correlates in phenomena of personal self-perception and theology, one is but acknowledging within them a certain truth, or at least a certain *kind* of truth. If such dualisms are the natural and spontaneous modes of thought of a fallen, and thus divided, selfhood, it is because in a certain way they genuinely reflect the way things are. There is a certain sense in which, as things stand in our fallen condition, the dualism that Julian notes between "oure substance," which is "ful," and "oure sensualite," in which we "faile," reflects a truthful perspective. It is not in any simple way a false consciousness, for it reflects how things are with us insofar as we are fallen. As fallen beings, we are conflicted. As conflicted beings, necessarily we construe the world, ourselves, God, and the relationships between all in conflicted, fractured, and dualistic terms.

Julian as "Antidualist" Dualist

And yet, while it is true to say, as Julian does, that "in our sensualite we faile," whereas in "substance" we are "ful," this is not because in any absolute way our sensualite is the source of sin. Rather, it is the opposite. It is because we are fallen, because our substance and our sensualite are as a consequence divided from one another, that we can sin in our sensualite. In this connection, Denise Baker is once again right in distinguishing Julian's account of our fallen condition from one that she attributes, rightly or wrongly, to Augustine. "For Augustine," she says, "sin causes separation from God; for Julian, sin ensues from such separation."[52] It does not seem to be Julian's view that we sin because there are, naturally, two parts to our selfhood, namely, our substance and our sensualite, but because of our separation from God, substance and sensualite have unnaturally come apart—and being two parts only because they have come apart, they can be at war with one another, can suffer conflictual relations. Or we can put it in other terms, closer to those that have dominated my account of Julian's theology: it is because we are fallen beings that our sensualite no longer narrates our substance. Because of sin, time misnarrates the eternal providence that sustains it, and all because our sensuality has been torn away from our substance.

And so a vicious circle of historical conditions and corresponding consciousness loops backward and forward. As I said in chapter 2, Julian's central preoccupation in *A Revelation of Love*, insofar as it concerns the consequences of sin, is with the way in which sin miscalls its own nature. Sin fundamentally does not know itself. And that is true enough. It is a strange but pervasive assumption, and itself a symptom of the grip that a sinful condition has upon how we perceive our own natures, to suppose that we sin because we are human. And it belongs with the same assumption to imagine that because we are weak, fallible, and sinful creatures, we can understand one another better than we would were we sinless. For we think sinners alone know what sin is like from the inside. And I have to confess to having shared a doubt of that kind upon reading the words of the Letter to the Hebrews, which state that we have a High Priest who shares with us every weakness consequent upon our human condition *except* sin (Hebrews 4:15)—for that exception can seem like a very drastic limitation upon Christ's solidarity with us. How, we wonder, can Christ really know what it is like to be us if he does not experience sin?

It is just such thoughts that, as I understand her, Julian wishes to tear us away from. The point about the exception made in the Letter to the Hebrews is that "solidarity in sin," like "infinite degree," is in fact an oxymoron. There is, as Plato points out in a similar connection, little honor among thieves.[53] The point about sin is precisely that it either is, or results from—but in any case inevitably causes—division and enmity, everything subversive of solidarity. The "except" in the Letter to the Hebrews is therefore, if I may say so, a weasel word. It is because there is no sin in Christ that his solidarity with us can be without any limitation, because it is sin itself that limits solidarity. Indeed, you might more forcefully say, and most certainly would on the evidence of Dante's *Inferno,* that it is in hell's parody of social order that is revealed what "solidarity in sin" truly looks like—it looks like Ugolino's perpetually gnawing away at Archbishop Ruggieri's skull.

Only sin divides, and sin *only* divides. Equally, it is only out of our dividedness that sin can arise. And so we need to say both things at the same time: that dualism truly reflects our actual fallen experience, and that, true as it is to that experience, the experience is itself false. But false in relation to what?

There is only one answer to that question for Julian. Our divided, fallen selfhood is false in relation to a wholly integrated human self, a self in whom the lineaments of sensualite and substance coincide in focus, and in whom, therefore, existence in time and contingency perfectly narrates the self's eternal being in God, hence one in whom "bestely" and "godly" wills perfectly coincide. In short, our false selfhood is false in relation to the selfhood of Christ alone. And so it is, Julian says, that "I saw that our kind [nature] is in God hole, in which he makyth diverssetis flowand out of him to werkyn his will, whom kind kepith [which nature he preserves], and mercy and grace restorith and fulfillith; and of these non shall perishen; for our kind which is the heyer part is knitt to God in the making; and God is knitt to our kinde which is the lower partie in our flesh taking; and thus in Christ our ii kinds are onyd."[54] And as for suspicions that Julian counts on any sort of generalized psychological dualism—at any rate, any such as might be intended to undergird the substance/sensualite distinction by means of a body-soul dualism—Julian explicitly allays them: "And as anempts [as regards] our substance and sensualite, it may rytely be clepid [called] our soule; and that is the onyng that it hath in God."[55]

"In Him We Are Beclosed and He in Us"

In much the same way is Julian's apparently dualistic vocabulary of "inner" and "outer" to be understood. We have seen how she is capable of casting the distinction between godly and beastly wills in terms of "two parties: that one outward, that other inward." Here, as so often elsewhere, Julian's vocabulary tracks back historically to sources in Augustine. The metaphor of "inwardness" may be crucial as structuring the narrative of Augustine's discovery of God. But it is within the narrative of his life, not within any purely introspective gaze, that Augustine discovers God as the depth and breadth and height of significance within which that narrative is situated.[56] God, therefore, is indeed within Augustine. But it is just as true to say—and Augustine just as frequently says it—that Augustine is within God. For, he says, it is only within God that we know ourselves and thus know the God within us.[57] Hence, for Augustine, the language of interiority is set within paradox. The God we can find only within us is the God within whom alone we can find ourselves.

But the paradoxes of interiority in Augustine further intensify. For the trope of within and without, being a metaphor derived from material relations of spatial position, itself belongs to the vocabulary of exteriority. Necessarily this is so. We do not possess any language in which to describe the world of the spirit other than that of our natural and spontaneous modes of designating the material world of our experience. The interior is known only by means of exterior. And therein lies the wonder of Augustine's paradoxes of interiority and exteriority. The more interior we become, the more we thereby become engaged with the world of spirit, the more we transcend the materialistic vocabulary of within and without, in which, perforce, we necessarily describe that engagement. And that complexity of paradox is concentrated in a fused density in that most typical of Augustinianisms: "You were within me, and I was outside myself."[58] Augustine's discovery of the God within is in fact the recovery of his exteriority from the contraposition in which it had stood with his inwardness. His conversion is the reintegration of his selfhood: the restoration of unity between inner and outer, between the spiritual and the carnal, between the eternal, unchangeable providence of God and his own changeable, contingent historical being. So much for Augustine's supposed dualism.

What for Augustine is the language of interiority is transposed in Julian into the anchoritic metaphor of "beclosure." And other than a simple substitution of synonyms, nothing more is needed to get a more or less exact parallel between Augustine's play with the dialectics of the interior and the exterior and Julian's play with beclosed. For Augustine,

God is to be sought within and not in some exterior object, and yet, when found, he is discovered to transcend and also to draw into harmony all relations of within and without. In just this same manner, Julian perceives herself to beclose what she is beclosed by—to enter a universe, to beclose it, precisely by means of her being beclosed within the smallness of her anchorhold. The linguistic strategy is subtle, complex, and recognizably Augustinian. It is a strategy of self-subversion, that of deploying the resources of a metaphor with a view to drawing the mind beyond its immediate resonances. For just as Augustine's pervasive metaphor of interiority stands in initial dualistic contrast to exteriority but is deployed so as to draw the mind beyond the very dualism on which it relies, so also Julian's play with the oppositional active and passive voices of beclosed does its work to force the sensuous image to disclose the theological truth that lies beyond the opposition it draws upon.

And it is certainly not irrelevant to note how this same dialectical strategy is deployed in connection with Julian's motif of Jesus as mother. As Baker says, "Julian of Norwich's characterization of Jesus as Mother both reflects and refracts her socially constituted identity as woman. As a reaction against the contradictory attitudes towards women expressed by the Church, Julian of Norwich's androgynous deity provides both an index to the stereotypes associated with each gender in Christianity and a paradigm for transcending the theology of sexual difference."[59] Here too, then, the same strategy of self-subversion is deployed, in that by characterizing the Creator Word and the incarnate Word in terms of conventional maternal imagery of birth and nutrition, she transgenders the traditionally male representations of the Trinity and the incarnate Christ. In consequence, her sexual imagery, intentionally or otherwise, revises the traditionally masculine understanding of the *imago Dei* that derives from Augustine's *De Trinitate,* and in consequence revises, indeed resists, the conventional medieval representation of women as in some way falling further short of the image of God than do men. For if

Julian can safely represent Christ, who is the perfect imago Dei, in female terms, then nothing can stand in the way of women's appropriating as fully as men may the right to be regarded as *ad imaginem Dei*, to be in the image of God. That point being confidently and firmly established in chapters 60 and following—Julian is remarkably unemphatic about it— she has thereby set in place alongside the purely conventional representations in chapter 51 of Christ as male and of the soul as female an inverse representation of Christ as female. By such means Julian effectively cuts across traditional gender stereotyping, especially the Augustinian gender stereotyping of the *De Trinitate*, which contrasts the masculine *animus*—the highest, most spiritual part of the human person—with the feminine *anima*, the most enfleshed and bodily part of the human person. The effect, then, is once again "dialectical." For by deploying the conventional typings of gender characteristics while at the same time assigning them to their conventional opposites, Julian achieves, as Baker says, a transcendence of "the theology of sexual difference."

It should be noted that the deployment in these ways of that truly dialectical strategy that I referred to at the end of the first chapter is pervasive across Julian's *Revelation*. Indeed, it could with justification be described as a, even perhaps the, distinctive feature of her theological method in general. It is a strategy that moves from opposition and difference toward the achievement of a transcendent inclusiveness. We need the vocabulary of within and without—they cannot simply be collapsed into one another on the grounds of some prejudicial preference for an antidualist inclusiveness. For our experience is so divided into either/ or. And yet this disjunctive either/or is not itself to be set in an exclusive relationship of either/or with the both/and that draws inner and outer together. You do not have to choose between dualism and antidualism, between disjunction and conjunction—indeed, you ought not to, because that simply prioritizes disjunction over conjunction, exclusiveness over inclusiveness at a second-order level. It is as Wittgenstein describes it in another connection: we need to climb the ladder of a dualistic inner and outer only in order to throw it antidualistically away, so as to achieve an inclusiveness that does not exclude exclusion.[60]

Distinctive as it is in Julian, this dialectical strategy of conjunctive disjunction is by no means unique to Julian in her own times. Her contemporary the anonymous author of the *Cloud of Unknowing* makes an identical play with Augustine's interiority. Moreover, unlike Julian, the *Cloud* author explicitly articulates its dialectical lineaments as a cataphatic-apophatic theological epistemology. There are some, he tells us, who would have us seek God within ourselves, and while that seems to him all well and good, he himself does not advise it.[61] For all too easily is the metaphor of inwardness understood materialistically, thus to provoke all sorts of psychologically introspective contortions, as disciples of the "inner life," misled by the metaphor, attempt to turn their minds within themselves. And the upshot of their mind-bending strains, which are the price of such effortfulness, are distortions of piety found in the pursuit of a misguidedly introspective inwardness.[62] And so, the *Cloud* author tells us, he would have us neither within nor without, neither above nor below, neither to this side nor to that; indeed, he would have us nowhere, in a nowhere that is an everywhere, because it is only if we are nowhere materially that we can be everywhere spiritually.[63] Thus is the *Cloud*'s epigrammatical paraphrase of the whole meaning of Augustine's *Confessions:* true inwardness is the transcendence of the opposition between the within and the without.

Julian does concretely, by means of dense concentrations of conflicting tropes, what the *Cloud* author does by means of a formally articulated epistemic strategy. But it is this very same strategy of metaphoric self-transcendence that is deployed, though in her by the most sensuously metaphoric of means. Julian sweeps away the dichotomies of enclosing and being-enclosed through their oxymoronic juxtaposition. On the one hand, the Lord's "homely loving . . . is oure clothing, that for love wrappeth us and windeth us, halseth [embraces] us and all becloseth us."[64] More graphically still, she is beclosed in the wound in Jesus's side, invited into it: "With a glad chere oure good lorde loked into his side and behelde, enjoyenge. And with his swete loking he led forth the understanding of his creature by the same wound into his sid, within."[65]

But that enclosure of Julian's understanding within the side of Jesus is no constriction of her selfhood within the confines of an individualistic, pious moralism. On the contrary, Julian's confinement within the narrow wound in the side of Christ is an opening out of Julian's own selfhood to a universal consciousness so vast as to enclose her evencristen, the whole Church, "alle mankinde that shalle be saved," without a relation to which she cannot conceive of her own self. But more profoundly even than that, her being "wrapped" and "winded" within the Lord's "homely love"—the domestic overtones of the adjective "homely" emphasize its familiar particularity, its smallness of scale—draws Julian immediately into the vision of the hazelnut, that tiny object, teetering on the edge of the abyss of nothingness, which nonetheless includes within it the whole of Creation, Fall, and Redemption—that is to say, the whole of reality. For there is nothing to all there is but that hazelnut and the divine love that holds it securely in existence.[66] They are within Julian, as she is within that cosmic reality. Here is the theology of the anchoress: the reflection in terms of a Christocentric soteriology, and the dialectic of place in which the confinement of her cell is precisely the means by which she gains access to a universe—to *the* universe. And once again, the theme is overtly Augustinian. Where he says that God is "more within me than I am to myself," Julian says, "God is more nerer to us than oure owne soule."[67] And in the same way, in a second implicit citation, now of Augustine's *De Trinitate*,[68] Julian adds that because God is "nerer to us than oure owne soule" it is "redier to us and more esy to come to the knowing of God then to know oure owne soule."[69] Naturally this is so, for God is pure, transparent, knowable light, whereas we are but a tangled and opaquely unknowable mess. But in neither Augustine nor in Julian are the knowledge of God and the knowledge of ourselves set in opposition with one another, for, as both say, to attempt to know ourselves in some light of our own making must fail. We can know ourselves only insofar as we know ourselves as beclosed in God. But that is the same as knowing how God is enclosed in us, for Julian says, "by the gracious leding of the holy gost, we shall know them both in one."[70] And so it is that, as Julian puts it summatively: "We are beclosed in the fader, and we are beclosed in the son, and we are beclosed in the holy gost. And the fader is beclosed in us, the son is beclosed in us, and the holy gost is beclosed in us: all mighty, alle wisdom, and alle goodnesse; one God, one lorde."[71] And so also it is that to know oneself in God is the same as knowing God in oneself, the God who is present within us, within the mess that we are. And that which we see in ourselves when we see ourselves in God, Julian says, is our godly will, and what she calls our beastly will is the mess we are in.

Conclusion

I asked at the beginning of this chapter how we might characterize Julian's "spirituality," and the answer to that question seemed to depend on how we are to understand her theological anthropology. But in that matter we encountered a number of difficulties, both of interpretation and of theology. Drawing together such solutions to these difficulties as we have been able to derive, the overall picture looks like this: we are to characterize Julian's spirituality in the same terms in which we described her account of prayer. For just as in the previous chapter we saw that for Julian it is through prayer that eternity and time meet in the contingency of human desire, so now in her doctrine of the godly and beastly wills we can see on what theological anthropology her account of prayer rests. Our origin as created beings in the eternal knowledge and love of God is not just a past fact about us as we once were prenatally, but rather a present reality, historically existent in the form of our truest desire: it is a will, a true desire, which is no more separable from God than is our being as created. Hence, Julian told us, she could see no distinction between God and our substance. But our desiring being is inserted into contingency and time, into a historicity fraught with misalignments, both cognitive and orectic: we do not square with ourselves. In short, we are, as far as our desires go, a conflicted mess; and as far as our self-knowledge goes, an opaque tangle of self-misperceptions.

It is *as a whole* that we are in this predicament. We do not simply do sin, as the Pelagians thought. We are in it. It is for this reason that as fallen beings, there is no strategy of retrieval from our predicaments available to us from within our own resources. There can be no strategy of self-help where it is the very self that is helpless, struggling in a ditch, unable to rise.[72] And yet it is indeed from within this predicament that the desire arises that causes us to pray, a desire and a beseeching that is therefore ours, a seeking and a wanting that arise from within our contingency. But as that prayer is ours, so also is it of God: it arises from what it seeks, from the presence of God within us existing as our godly will, always there, always had, and therefore always there to be seen, beheld. Julian's spirituality as a whole has the same structure of self-discovery as has prayer itself, nor is there anything complacent or quietistic about it. For that meeting of eternity and time in the contingency of desire is a transformative intersection, it is eternity seeking itself out in the medium of time. And in terms of our human agency it is at once a hermeneutical strategy, a sort of interpretation of our wills, as Thomas put it, and an ascetical practice, for there is a necessary practice of realigning our sensual being with our substantial, of overcoming the practical dualisms that, on account of our fallen condition, overdetermine our perceptions of self, of God, and of the world. Prayer is therefore a strategy of self-retrieval or, more simply, it is the strategy of discovering what is really wanted. For what we most truly want is what we most really are, a seeking for what we already—from eternity—have, the God at once given and had, at once the source and goal of all our desiring. And so it is that Julian says: "I saw him and sought him, and I had him and wanted him."

CONCLUSION

Julian's Soteriology

"SINNE IS BEHOVELY." Having cleared away some philosophical and
theological obstacles blocking the route to understanding what Julian
means in this statement, I have opened the path to a more positively
theological account of the context of Julian's teaching about sin. I argued in chapter 2 that the logical force of the Middle English adjective
"behovely" lay somewhere between that of the necessary and the contingent, and that sense is made of this theological term of art within the
more informal logic of narrative. But as to the substantive truth-claim
that in our fallen world sin is behovely—the statement remained counterintuitive on whatever ground, including on Julian's own.

But whenever a statement is said to be "counterintuitive," it is important to ask what intuitive expectations it counters. For intuitions do
not inhabit unchallengeable epistemic space free of the need for justification: to get to a conclusion without argument is not the same as getting
to one without good reason. And in the course of setting out in a more
positive spirit the justification for Julian's claim, it seemed necessary
to distinguish two narratives of sin. I called them the story that love
tells of sin, and the story that sin tells of itself. Both stories tell of God,
both are allied with some kind of soteriology, both contain a subplot of
punishment for sin and reward for virtue, both tell of eternal damnation.
But within only one of them, the meta-story that love tells of sin, does
it make sense to envisage, or to maintain to be true, that sin is behovely.

The prodigal son and the elder brother tell of the same facts of failure, betrayal, and forgiveness. But their narratives of those facts differ entirely. For the father, the prodigal son's sin is behovely, and so too (as he learns to his amazement and joy) for the prodigal son. For the elder son, his brother's sin is nothing but betrayal deserving punishment. The two accounts exclude one another. They cannot both be true.

They cannot both be true, and yet both have real force and agency in the world that human beings inhabit. Or, to put it in another way, more often than not we attempt to live within and think through our lives' meaning in terms of both stories together, now one, now the other—torn between hope and despair. And so, trying to have it both ways and yet neither way exclusively, we attempt to live impossibly neither in the pure light of the one nor in the pure darkness of the other. Like the prisoners in Plato's cave, we prefer the dim half-light of their conjunction;[1] like the women of Canterbury in T. S. Eliot's *Murder in the Cathedral*, "We do not wish anything to happen," for we have "succeeded in avoiding notice / living and partly living."[2] Julian thinks of this fraught human condition as intellectual, spiritual, and emotional two-sidedness, the experiential by-product of a fundamental fracture in the human condition. For our sensualite has broken away from that unity with our substance into which we were first created, our experience in time having broken free from its ground in the eternal will and love of God. Because of sin we are fractured selves. So to speak, in our substance we inhabit the story that love tells and in our sensualite we inhabit the story that sin tells—or, more precisely, in our fallen condition we inhabit the impossible story that is neither because it attempts to tell both stories at once.

Irrupting into this charged condition is the truly counterintuitive image of Christ on the Cross. There are no antecedent expectations to make sense of it, and yet it makes sense of everything before and after. It was only as one among other requests that Julian had prayed for "minde of the passion." She tells us that she had "sumdeele [some measure of] feeling in the passion of Christ, but yet I desired to have more, by the grace of God."[3] More, of course, she is given, as the following shewings attest, but by the time we reach the end of the Long Text it is clear that "minde of the passion" is not just one among other items on the list of gifts that Julian had prayed for, alongside her desire to "have Gods gifte a [of] bodily sicknes" and the three "woundes" of contrition, compassion, and "wilful longing to God."[4] What Julian quickly realizes in that first shewing is that the gift of "minde of the passion" contains the whole of what she had prayed for. At the very outset of her work, when providing a chapter-by-chapter précis of her *Revelation,* she tells us that in the first shewing "of [Christ's] precious crowning of thornes" was "comprehended and specified the blessed trinity, with the incarnation and the oning betweene God and mans soule, with many fair shewinges and techings of endlesse wisdom and love, *in which all the shewings that foloweth be groundide and oned.*"[5] That first shewing is itself a précis of the whole work because in the Cross is contained the whole meaning of all sixteen shewings. And it is in her "minde of the passion," entered into through her bodily sickness, that she is given all the gifts of contrition, compassion, and longing for God.

After two days and nights of illness during which she and those around her believed that she was about to die, her curate was brought to her bedside to administer the last rites. Setting an image of the Crucifixion before her, he asked her to look at it, which at first she was reluctant to do. For her "eyen [were] set uprighteward into heaven, where I trusted to come by the mercy of God." At that moment Julian was tempted too quickly to bypass the image of the Cross and to remain in her contemplation of heaven. But soon enough she resisted the temptation and "ascented to set my eyen in the face of the crucifixe, if I might, and so I dide," and she did so because she understood that by turning her mind away from heaven to the Cross she would extend the experience of bodily sickness and death and thereby allow the dying she had prayed for to complete its work. The result was immediate, for thereupon Julian was swiftly drawn into a deep darkness that obscured everything but that image of the Cross, all else "beside the crosse [being] oglye and ferful to me, as if it had been mekille [fully] occupied with fiends."[6]

The narrative detail contains a clear general lesson. The Cross is all. The Cross is not only what she sees in her shewings. The cross of her deathbed is the condition of her seeing them. The Cross explains everything, insofar as we have an explanation of anything. As I said in chapter 2, inasmuch as the word is a term of theological explanation and answers the question "Why?"—where neither the answer "It was necessary" nor the answer "It was contingent" would seem to meet the case—the description of the Incarnation as behovely is by Julian's time a common topos of Western Christian theology. Moreover, although the emphasis in Julian is particularly dramatic, and above all is crucial to the structuring of her work as a whole, there is nothing unusual for her times in her insistence in this same first shewing that, throughout her work—"it was shewed in the first sight and in all. . . . wher Jhesu appireth the blessed trinity is understand"[7]—though, alas, the connection of Incarnation and Trinity is sometimes missing in ours, where theologies, and more particularly devotional and homiletic practices, can seem to be characterized by what Philip McCosker describes as a "Christo-monism."[8] For Julian, everything about the Incarnation draws us into the inner life of the Trinity, and our only way into the Trinitarian meaning of the Incarnation is through the Cross, and that through the presence of death, in one way or another, in our own lives.

It is just here that a subtle though important distinction emerged between the soteriologies of Julian and Duns Scotus. Scotus envisaged a different answer to the Anselmian question "Why did God become man?" maintaining, even if only as a counterfactual conditional, that the Father would have sent his Son to be born of the Virgin Mary had there been no sin, for the love of God for his human creatures is so intense that no other motive for the Incarnation was needed than the joy itself of dwelling among them. Julian agrees that the counterfactual—free human beings might not have sinned—may legitimately be entertained, for she knows that a world of free, sinless human beings was creatable. But she appears to be unable to make any sense of the Incarnation, that is to say, of the Incarnation's being behovely, except as a response of the divine love and compassion for the predicament of fallen humanity. It is for this reason that, as I said in chapter 1, Julian finds herself boxed into an exceptionally tight conceptual and theological corner. For if God created the world, willing it despite knowing that it would be a sinful world when it might not have been; and if the Incarnation is the "fitting" divine response to that sin; and if, beyond the mere fact of the Incarnation, it is because of Christ's dying on the Cross that the love and compassion of the Trinity for Creation is revealed to us; and if it is just because of sin that the Incarnation is behovely—then the whole interlocked theological structure—of Creation, Fall, and Redemption—collapses *unless* some sense can be given to the proposition that sin itself is behovely.

And so it is that we are brought back to the problem with which we started, that is, to Julian's conviction that sin is behovely. Because unless it is, all of the connecting links that make of these Christian teachings a narrative of love are broken, and they undermine all claims to that narrative's systematic character. It is for this reason that Julian's questions about sin—"Why sin?" "What is sin?"—trouble her so. What, then, as we conclude, is her answer?

"How shoulde anything be amisse?" Nothing can be amiss because from all eternity all of it was intended by a God who can only love and cannot will sin, but can, out of pure love, will a world in which there is sin. Julian believes this because she is shown how the solution is willed all at once with the problem, so that while in one sense it is true that everything went wrong with Creation, in another she has overriding reasons for believing that nothing has gone wrong at all. Everything went wrong because the Fall excluded all human beings from the destiny for which they were created: they can no longer enjoy the beatitude of the vision of God because they repeatedly choose for themselves, through sin, the blindness of mind and soul into which, as the result of the Fall, they are born. Their predicament is real; they can do nothing whatever about it. And yet nothing has gone wrong, because that same divine act that willed the world as it is, thus fallen, willed also the remedy—which is not a "remedy" at all, because it goes far beyond the measure that any remedy would require. The compassionate gaze enclosed, *fore*closed, the falling itself. And Julian is sure that it is a better world in which the problem is solved than any world would be in which, because there had been no problem in the first place, there was no need for the solution. But Julian has to win through to that conviction, for at first she doubts it, and it does not come easily; it takes time and much reflection to reach. It is in those terms, however, that at last in chapter 59 she finds the answer to the question she had put to the Lord in chapter 27. In that earlier chapter she tells us that at one time she had been thinking "in [her] foly" that "if sinne had not be, we shulde alle have be clene and like to our lorde as he made us" and, wondering why sin had not been prevented, all she is told in response at this earlier point in the Long Text is, less than helpfully, that sin notwithstanding, nothing's being amiss is "an high, mervelous private [secret] hid in God, which private he shalle openly make knowen to us in heven."[9]

But Julian has already learned to tear her eyes away from the ultimate solution in heaven and to turn them toward the here and now of the suffering Christ, and it is all of a piece with this shift of theological perspective that rather than simply leave the question "Why sin?" to be solved in the eschaton, in chapter 59 Julian is ready to say more about that "Why?"—almost certainly because of what her reflections over twenty years on the example of the Lord and the Servant have allowed her to see. Now she can say that we have bliss in our salvation "be mercy and grace; which manner of bliss we myte never had ne knowen but if that [had it not been that the] propertes of goodness which is God had ben contraried, wherby we have this bliss; for wickednes hath ben suffrid to risen contrarye to the goodnes, and the goodnes of mercy and grace contraried ageyn the wickidnes, and turnyd al to goodness and to worship to al these that shal be savid; for it is the properte in God which doith good agen evil."[10]

It is all too easy to misinterpret what Julian is saying here, and the misreading comes all the more easily to those who cannot think beyond the moral limitations of a utilitarian consequentialism. Julian does not suppose that "the ways of God" might be justified on the grounds that, by the cruel device of visiting disaster on the human condition, God is the better able to show forth his mercy and compassion to the end of self-glorification, inflating thereby the value of his salvation—as if in the manner of the manipulative therapist who exaggerates his diagnoses thus to inflate the charge for his therapies. The soteriological solution indeed comes at a higher price than any that could be paid by those who are to be saved. But it is God's Son who pays the whole price himself, exacting no charge at all from those thus saved. Jesus bears all the burdens of the problem himself, for only if he bears them all can he lift them all.

Of such a kind is the divine economy of salvation: that is, simply, it is not an "economy" at all. It is a *convenientia*, a deed done out of no compulsion but out of the divine love, revealed spontaneously not as a solution equal to the problem but as an infinite surplus to it. Julian's God no more acts to save us in view of some gain of his own than does Thomas's; he says of God that "ille est maxime liberalis," "he is absolutely free-handed," and he goes on to explain that God does nothing as if answering to any sort of divine need, *propter suam utilitatem.*[11] Correspondingly, Julian's soteriology supposes no means of consequentialist manipulation of evil devised to self-serving divine ends, and this is for the reason that the divine action cannot be construed in terms of means-to-an-end. Julian's soteriology rather supposes a God who wills in a single act of love, a single unbroken narrative of solidarity with Creation so intimate as to have been unachievable in any other way than one: by sharing not in the sin but in its interim price, which is sin's "sharpe pain" in life, and then in its final down payment, which is death. So striking is Julian's refusal of an economic conception of God's willing, of its motivation, that, although they have already been cited, I nonetheless repeat her words in full: "Then saide oure good lorde, asking: 'Arte thou well apaid [satisfied] that I suffered for thee?' I saide; 'Ye, good lorde, gramercy [great thanks]. Ye, good lorde, blessed mot [may] thow be.' Then saide Jhesu, our good lord: 'If thou arte apaide, I am apaide. It is a joy, a blisse, and endlesse liking to me that ever I sufferd passion for the[e]. And if I might suffer more, I woulde suffer more.'"[12] Julian adds that she has noted exactly what the Lord had told her: "He saide not, 'if it were nedfulle to suffer more' but, 'if I might suffer more.' For though it were not nedful, and if he might suffer more, he wolde."[13]

Julian's refusal of a soteriology on any model of an economic trans-action is all the more striking in view of the prevalence in her own times of just such soteriological models. As we have seen in chapter 4, there is no suggestion in Julian's soteriology of quid pro quo, though we are told of the prodigal son's mistaken expectation that he will have to strike a deal with his father. On the contrary, the father's response to his wayward son is entirely gratuitous. For that reason nowhere in Julian is there any suggestion of a soteriology according to which by his suffering and death the Son pays back on their behalf the debt to the Father that, through sin, human beings owe.[14] The Father exacts no price from anyone, directly or vicariously, for nothing is owed.[15] In the work of our Redemption, the relationship of the Father to the Son is conceived and imagined quite differently in Julian. Upon being told

"If I might suffer more, I woulde suffer more," Julian tells us that her understanding was "lefted uppe into heven." And there

> Crist shewed me his father, in no bodily liknesse but in his properte and in his working: that is to sey, I saw in Crist that the father is. The werking of the father is this: that he gaveth mede [reward] to his sonne Jhesu Crist. This gift and this mede is so blissful to Jhesu that his father might have geven him no mede that might have liked him better. . . . the first heven, that is the plesing of the father, shewed to me as an heven, and it was fulle blisseful. For he is fulle plesede with alle the dedes that Jhesu hath done about our salvation, wherefor we be not only his by his buying, but also by the curteyse gifte of his father. We be his blisse, we be his mede, we be his wurshipe, we be his crowne.[16]

It is perhaps in this chapter, and most especially in this passage, that Julian most explicitly integrates her teaching of the Incarnation with her soteriology, and both with her Trinitarian theology—as we have seen, a Dantean theological move through and through. Just as in *Paradiso* 33 Dante sees the Trinity transformed into our human form, so Julian sees all the Father's "beyng" and "werkyng" in "the blissid manhode of Criste";[17] and the Father's "werkyng" is to reward the Son with a gift than with which there is none that the Son could be more pleased. And the Son's reward? It is us, humanity redeemed: "wherefor we be not only his by his buying, but also by the curteyse gifte of his father. We be his blisse, we be his mede, we be his wurshipe, we be his crowne." The delight of the Son, in short, is to be with the sons of men (Proverbs 8:31).

The motive of our Redemption, then, is described by Julian in that least economic of all terms: our Redemption is a work of pure delight, a Trinitarian delight, the delight of the Father in giving the perfect gift, and the delight of the Son in the perfect gift that the Father gives him.

Before all else, the Cross is a Trinitarian transaction of love, a transaction of that love that *is* the Trinity. There is no reason for this outside the Trinity's own being as Trinity. Here there is no fair exchange, no utility, nothing lost that is due, nothing gained that can be demanded. Everything is pure gratuitous surplus, that is to say, everything God does has to do with just how God is, with the behovely in God, and not for any further reason. For God has nothing to gain, nothing to lose, and can act only out of pure joy; and we have everything to gain, for in us too, our salvation is entirely gratuitous—it has only to do with grace, so that as so many medieval theologians were wont to say, by that grace we become what God is by nature and so *unus spiritus*, "one spirit" with God, or "one in the Spirit," as William of St. Thierry says.[18] All that there is exists just because that is how God lives, in delight shared. Hence, the Father's "blisse" and the Son's "blisse" and our "blisse" are all one "blisse," one life, one sharing, one giving, and one receiving.

And sin? Sin is a *felix culpa*, sin too is behovely. It fits, if anywhere, within that delight that the Father has in his Creation, within the Father's delight in the Son, and in the Son's delight in the Father's gift to him, which is humanity redeemed—that much Julian knows. And she knows that on this account "alle is wele"; and it is on the same account that she can see that the greater gift of the Father to the Son is the gift of humanity fallen and redeemed than that of a humanity which, not having fallen, had no need of Redemption. She sees that somehow, laid out over all time, and therefore in successive events, one occurring after the other, one event giving rise to another, one anticipation being met by its fulfillment, Creation followed by the Fall, the Fall followed by the Incarnation and the Cross, the resurrection meeting its fulfillment in the coming of the Spirit and in the life of the Church—in these events, stretched in sequences across time, are to be found a historical map of the Trinitarian life itself, of the Trinity's very constitution as God. For salvation history is, as I put it in chapter 4, the Trinity observed in the only way human beings can observe it—in time, in succession, in history; and our individual histories, our narratives (the narratives of those, at any rate, "who are to be saved") are, too, the Trinity narrated. For, Julian says, "thus was my understanding led of God to se in him, and to wit, to understonde, and to know, that oure soule is made trinite like to the unmade blessed trinite, knowen and loved fro without beginning, and in the making one to the maker."[19]

We could know none of this, Julian avers, were it not that we sin. Could we not know that life and love, we could not share it. But know it we do and share it we can, for we can *live* by the Trinitarian life, that is to say, we can allow our sinful lives to be rewritten by the story that the Trinitarian love tells. And that rewriting is sorely needed, for if we have fallen, it is as having fallen out of the story that love tells and into the hybrid, compromised and compromising story that sin tells, and what is required is no mere adjustment to the way we see things. For, as I put it in chapter 6, if our sensualite under sin has fallen out of focus with our substance, it is out of focus that we live. For we live as we see, out of focus—beings in whom the failure of sensualite and substance to coincide is the failure of two realities in us to line up with one another, a failure that, as we saw in chapter 2, results in a third reality, which is our being constituted through sin by the mismatch itself. And so it is that we do the terrible evils that we do. Our doing them can be—has been—redeemed. But the evil of them can never be erased, never forgiven, except by a love that is infinite.

Thus it follows that the realignment of our sensual being with our substance, of our being in history with our being in God, is no matter simply of a shift of mental perspective, as if we could set things right simply by deciding to change our point of view on the facts—like deciding at will to read out loud in Cantonese rather than Mandarin or the other way round from the same Chinese ideograms. We are body and soul out of line with ourselves, and this is a predicament so radical that, fallen as a whole, it is only by our transformation as a whole that we can be retrieved from it—that is to say, by our entering through "minde of the passion" into death itself.

It is because the price of love cannot be less than death that the Cross is the central image of Julian's theology. It is because the price of love is death that Julian herself is an anchoress, living her death within a life conceived of as an *ars moriendi,* and it is for the same reason that Julian's theology may truly be described as "anchoritic." Its being anchoritic, however, doesn't confine that theology to exclusive relevance. On the contrary, we saw that Julian's anchoritic specialization is privileged only because from the vantage point of her enclosure she can see with uncluttered vision that which all Christians—that is to say, "all that shalle be savid," *whoever* they may be—could see for themselves, on the same vision-clearing condition of living death. For they too are enclosed in the embrace of the divine love, the embrace of divine compassion, and the human longing for that embrace that is contrition.

It is not easy to write about Julian's theology in the accepted styles of the academic theologian. Everything in Julian links up with everything else synthetically, more in the manner of the condensed image than in the analytic manner of the extrusions of multiple inferences. Julian's centering image of the Cross fuses onto the particularity of a contingent historical event a profusion of theological resonance more in the manner of a musical piece than in the logical style of the schoolman's treatise. But who would be so obtuse as to suggest that, for want of being a treatise on composition, Beethoven's C# minor quartet fails to be systematic? If, as I have wanted to say in this essay, Julian's theology is truly systematic, it has been a proposition worth arguing, as it has seemed to me, for reasons both negative and positive. Negatively, I have wanted to eradicate the impression that Julian's *Revelation* may be read as a work of spirituality *rather than* as a work of theology proper, because, as I hope has become evident from all I have thus written, her work allows no place for any such polarization. If in any sense Julian's is a work of spirituality, it is a spirituality that is distinctly contestable theologically, and contested she insists it be. Julian becomes a theologian because her shewings leave her with no alternative. Positively, then, I have insisted on describing Julian's theology as systematic because that conjunction of a sinewy and taut inner coherence with which Julian constructs a defense of her spirituality of hope with the rondo-like repetitiveness of her meditative practice on the themes of sin and love may play some role in revising and expanding our current notions of the systematic, rather than because she conforms to some stereotype of the systematic typified by the formal theological treatise, whether of her own times or of ours. In our times, wherein we experience so many forms of theological fragmentation consequent upon our school-based divisions of labor, we may have something to learn from a fourteenth-century "unletterde" anchoress who resists those fragmentations because she knows nothing of them, and, had she known of them, would have seen no good reason why they might be justified. And right enough she is.

NOTES

Preface

1. I prefer Watson and Jenkins's title for the Long Text: *A Revelation of Love: The Writings of Julian of Norwich*, ed. Nicholas Watson and Jacqueline Jenkins (University Park: Pennsylvania State University Press, 2006), as also Glasscoe's *Julian of Norwich: A Revelation of Love*, ed. Marion Glasscoe (Exeter: Exeter University Press, 2003) to the more common *Revelations of Divine Love*. Though Julian herself divides her revelation into sixteen distinct episodes, so closely interconnected are they and so importantly do they interpret one another as to all have the same meaning—as she says in chapter 86, the "mening" of love. As to the "divine," this qualification is as unnecessary for Julian as for Dante's *Commedia*. All love is divine for Julian, just as for Dante there is only one possible comedy, and that is divine.

2. One of the most useful discussions of Julian's texts in relation to contemporary models of literary composition is to be found in Elisabeth Dutton, *Julian of Norwich: The Influence of Late-Medieval Devotional Compilations* (Cambridge: D. S. Brewer, 2008).

3. "*A Revelation* is a work with no real precedent: a speculative vernacular theology, not modelled on earlier texts but structured as a prolonged investigation into the divine, whose prophetic goal is to birth a new understanding of human living in the world and the nature of God in his interactions with

the world, not just for theologians but for everyone" (Watson and Jenkins, *A Revelation of Love*, 3).

4. *LT*, 86:379.

5. Ibid., 3:129.

6. Ibid., 2:125–27.

7. See *The Mirrour of the Blessed Lyf of Jesu Christ* by her contemporary, the Carthusian Nicholas Love, ed. James Hogg and Lawrence F. Powell, 2 vols., Analecta Cartusiana 91 (Salzburg: Institut für Anglistik und Amerikanistik, 1989).

8. *Paradise Lost*, ed. Scott Elledge, 3rd ed. (New York: Norton, 2004), 1.1.

Chapter 1. Julian the Theologian

1. As my colleague at Yale Alastair Minnis has suggested to me.

2. It might be asked, is Julian a "biblical" theologian? Among the many books that need to be written about Julian (and this is not it) is a study of the explicit and implied biblical references scattered through the text, resonating constantly but so integrated into her vocabulary and speech forms as to be imperceptible to the scripturally unalert. I give but one example where this is too obvious to be missed, in chapter 4, but, as Bernard McGinn has suggested to me—and as readers can tell for themselves once alerted—her chief scriptural source must be the Pauline letters. The edition of Colledge and Walsh is an indispensable source for Julian's implicit scriptural references (Julian of Norwich, *A Book of Showings to the Anchoress Julian of Norwich*, ed. Edmund Colledge and James Walsh, 2 vols. [Toronto: Pontifical Institute of Medieval Studies, 1978]). But see also Annie Sutherland, "'Oure Feyth Is Groundyd in Goddes Worde'—Julian of Norwich and the Bible," in *The Medieval Mystical Tradition in England: Exeter Symposium 7*, ed. E. A. Jones (Cambridge: D. S. Brewer, 2004), 1–20.

3. Pseudo-Denys, *Divine Names*, 4.9, 705A-B, in *The Complete Works of Pseudo-Dionysius*, trans. Colm Luibheid (New York: Paulist, 1987), 78.

4. Thomas Aquinas, *Summa theologiae: Prologus:* "[In structuring this work] we have taken into account how those new to this teaching are in so many ways held back by the writings of various authors, partly because of the prolifera-

tion of pointless questions, articles and arguments, partly because what such newcomers need in order to progress in knowledge is set out not in obedience to the structure of the discipline itself, but in accordance with the exigencies of textual commentary or of set-piece disputations; but also because repetitiousness has bred boredom of spirit in the students." Mark Jordan argues that Thomas never actually taught the *Summa* as disputed questions. The *Summa* represents "an ideal curriculum for Dominican education . . . a pattern for an ideal pedagogy for middle learners in a vowed community of preachers": "The *Summa's* Reform of Moral Teaching—and Its Failures," in *Contemplating Aquinas*, ed. Fergus Kerr (London: SCM, 2003), 45.

5. Jean Leclerq, *The Love of Learning and the Desire for God*, trans. C. Misrahi (London: SPCK, 1978), 107, for a clear, if somewhat oversimplified, account of the differences between monastic and scholastic styles of biblical commentary.

6. In Western Christian theology the distinction is most frequently made out in terms of that between the Martha and Mary in Luke 10:38–42. Martha, who is busy about many things, has chosen an active role of engagement with tasks that have no future beyond the present times: her achievements will be "taken away from her" by death. Mary, who sits in contemplative conversation at the feet of Jesus, has "chosen the better part which will not be taken away from her" (Luke 10: 42). See, for example, Augustine, *De Trinitate (On the Trinity)*, ed. Gareth Matthews, trans. Stephen McKenna (Cambridge: Cambridge University Press, 2002), 1.10, for a classic exposition along these lines.

7. See *Sic et Non: A Critical Edition*, ed. B. Boyer and R. McKeon, 3 vols. (Chicago: Chicago University Press, 1976–77).

8. Though it should be noted that the purpose of Abelard's work was to show that with dialectical intervention the internal consistency of the tradition could always in fact be demonstrated.

9. Thomas Aquinas, *Summa theologiae*, 1a q1 a8 *corp*.

10. Ibid., 1a q1 a6 ad 3.

11. There is here, of course, only a matter of emphasis, not of exclusive disjunction. No reader of the first quaestio of Thomas's *Summa theologiae* could possibly be misled into thinking that for him the study of theology had any other source than that it derives from, or any other purpose than to serve the holiness

of the theologian and more broadly that of the Church. While Thomas does say that a person of unworthy life may very well be able to engage effectively in the dialectical techniques of the theologian, he explicitly affirms that theology is a *sacra doctrina*, a "holy teaching." Considered not merely as a dialectical art, what the theologian teaches is what the divine Word teaches the theologian, and the knowledge of the divine Word is a form of wisdom, possession of which is determined ultimately by the degree of charity in the soul. See *Summa theologiae*, 1a q1 a6 ad3.

12. Guigo II, *Scala claustralium*, in *Guigo II: The Ladder of Monks and Twelve Meditations*, trans. Edmund Colledge and James Walsh (Garden City, NJ: Doubleday, 1978).

13. See Aelred of Rievaulx, *The Rule of Life for a Recluse*, book 3, trans. Mary Paul Macpherson, in *Aelred of Rievaulx: Treatises and Pastoral Prayer*, ed. David Knowles, Cistercian Fathers Series 2 (Kalamazoo, MI: Cistercian, 1982), 80. And, for an example of monastic meditatio on the Passion of Christ, see Nicholas Love, *The Mirrour of the Blessed Lyf of Jesu Christ*, ed. James Hogg and Lawrence F. Powell, 2 vols., Analecta Cartusiana 91 (Salzburg: Institut für Anglistik und Amerikanistik, 1989), 2:216–61.

14. Henri de Lubac, *Exegèse medieval: Les quatres sens de L'ecriture*, 3 vols. (Paris: Aubier-Montaigne, 1959–61). See also my *Eros and Allegory* (Kalamazoo, MI: Cistercian, 1995), 294–307. On the four senses of scripture in medieval exegesis, see 83–125.

15. Alain of Lille, *Elucidatio in cantica canticorum*, Migne, *Patrologia Latina*, 210, of which a partial translation is contained in my *Eros and Allegory*, 299–300.

16. Oliver Davies, "Transformational Processes in the Work of Julian of Norwich and Mechtild of Magdeburg," in *The Medieval Mystical Tradition in England* (Cambridge: D. S. Brewer, 1992), 39–52.

17. *LT*, 86:379.

18. See Leclerq's partially accurate summary of the distinction between monastic and scholastic styles of theology in the High and later Middle Ages: "Scholastic commentary is almost always complete; it explains the entire 'letter' of the sacred text. Monastic commentary is often incomplete. . . . When the spiritual man has told what he feels, what he thinks of the love of God—and

he may be able to do so in a few verses—he has the right to lay down his pen." *The Love of Learning*, 107.

19. For a discussion of the nature of this experience, see Jean-Pierre Torrell, *St. Thomas Aquinas*, vol. I, *The Person and His Work*, trans. Robert Royal (Washington, DC: Catholic University of America Press, 1996), 294–95.

20. *On First Principles*, IV.2.9, in *Origen: An Exhortation to Martyrdom, Prayer and Selected Works*, trans. Rowan Greer, Classics of Western Spirituality (New York: Paulist, 1979), 180–88.

21. See, e.g., Gregory's *Commentary on the Song of Songs*, translated in my *Eros and Allegory*, 217–47.

22. John Cassian, *Conferences*, trans. Colm Lubheid (Mahwah, NJ: Paulist, 1985), VI.viii.

23. It is possible, but there is no evidence that she ever was.

24. Augustine, *On Christian Doctrine*, I.35–36, trans. D. W. Robertson (New York: Macmillan, 1958). "Whoever, therefore, thinks that he understands the divine Scriptures or any part of them so that it does not build the double love of God and of our neighbour does not understand it at all" (30).

25. See the continuing dialogue between Julian and the Lord, beginning in *LT* 27 with Julian asking the Lord why he had not "letted sinne" and ending in *LT* 31 with Julian conceding that "thus oure good lorde answered to alle the questions and doutes that I might make" (217). Also, *LT*, 86:379.

26. Ibid., 9:157. For though, as she says, the faith of the Church "stode continually in my sighte" and though she "beheld the shewing" too "with all my diligence" and held both "as one in Gods mening," she could not show that meaning "as openly ne as fully as I would."

27. Virtually all the dates of composition, whether of the Short or the Long Text, are controversial, as is the date of Julian's entry into the anchorhold at Norwich. It seems that Julian was already an anchoress not later than 1394, and if, as Watson and Jenkins say, *A Revelation* "may not have been begun until the middle of the 1390s and may have been finished any time between then and Julian's death, after 1416" (*A Revelation of Love: The Writings of Julian of Norwich*, ed. Nicholas Watson and Jacqueline Jenkins [University Park: Pennsylvania State University Press, 2006], 2), then it would seem that Julian

wrote the whole of the Long Text in her cell in Norwich. This is especially likely if, as Watson and Jenkins believe, the Short Text was composed perhaps as late as 1385. In much of what follows in the next few paragraphs I am much indebted to conversations with Laura Miles, PhD student in the English department at Yale University.

28. As to what medieval female religious read, see David N. Bell, "What Nuns Read: The State of the Question," in *The Culture of Medieval English Monasticism*, ed. James G. Clark (Woodbridge, UK: Boydell, 2007), 113–33.

29. See *Approaching Medieval English Anchoritic and Mystical Texts*, ed. Dee Dyas, Valerie Edden, and Roger Ellis (Cambridge: Boydell and Brewer, 2005).

30. That is, insofar as the thirteenth century *Ancrene Wisse* may be called a "rule," though it is more concerned with the interior dispositions and virtues, or otherwise with the temptations, of the anchoress than it is with an external set of regulations for daily living.

31. "What can be a clearer sign of [the soul's] heavenly origin than that she retains a natural likeness to it in the land of unlikeness [*in regione dissimilitudinis*], than that as an exile on earth she enjoys the glory of the celibate life, than that she lives like an angel in an animal body?" Bernard of Clairvaux, sermon 27.6, in *Bernard of Clairvaux: On the Song of Songs II*, trans. Kilian Walsh (Kalamazoo, MI: Cistercian, 1976), 79. But the phrase is a commonplace of twelfth-century Cistercian writing; see also Aelred of Rievaulx, *A Commentary of the Venerable Aelred, Abbot of Rievaulx, on the Passage of the Gospel "When Jesus Was Twelve Years Old,"* trans. Theodore Berkeley, in *Aelred of Rievaulx, Treatises and Pastoral Prayer*, Cistercian Fathers Series 2 (Kalamazoo, MI: Cistercian, 1971), 6.

32. In any case, the character of Julian's ME prose as "vernacular" ought not to be overemphasized. As Watson and Jenkins say, Julian's language has theological Latin as its "reference point" to such a degree that *A Revelation* would have been hard work for a contemporary readership not acquainted with Latin—see Watson and Jenkins, *A Revelation of Love*, 26–27.

33. This is so even if a colophon inserted at the end of the Sloane MS of the Long Text (almost certainly by another's hand) prays "almyty God that this booke com not but to the hands of the[m] that will be his faithfull lovers." *LT,*

86:135 (Glasscoe edition: *Julian of Norwich: A Revelation of Love*, ed. Marion Glasscoe [Exeter: Exeter University Press, 2003]).

34. In this positive sense one could say, as Laura Miles does in an illuminating parallel, that Julian's anchorhold serves for her theological writing that which "a room of one's own" serves for Virginia Woolf's fiction. See Laura Saetveit Miles, "Space and Enclosure in Julian of Norwich's *A Revelation of Divine Love*," in *A Companion to Julian of Norwich*, ed. Liz Herbert McAvoy (Cambridge: D. S. Brewer, 2008), 154–65, esp. 162–63.

35. See Carolyn Walker Bynum, *Jesus as Mother: Studies in the Spirituality of the High Middle Ages* (Berkeley: University of California Press, 1982), esp. 170–262.

36. *LT*, 3, for Julian's description of the progress of her illness.

37. The theme of the enclosed life as an imitation of the burial of Christ in the tomb is, of course, generic for monastics and not exclusively applied to anchoresses. But from the earliest English rule for anchoritic women, Aelred of Rievaulx's *De inSTitutione inclusarum*, it is a common theme addressed to reclusive women: "But now, whoever you may be who have given up the world to choose this life of solitude, desiring to be hidden and unseen, to be dead as it were to the world and buried with Christ in the tomb." *The Rule of Life for a Recluse*, 62.

38. For the Old French text (supplemented by Latin and Middle English translations), see Romana Guarnieri and Paul Verdeyen, eds., *Corpus ChriStianorum, continuatio medievalis*, 69 (Turnhout, Belgium: Brepols, 1986). For a modern English translation, see *The Mirror of Simple Souls*, ed. and trans. Edmund Colledge, J. C. Marler, and Judith Grant, Notre Dame Texts in Medieval Culture 6 (South Bend, IN: University of Notre Dame Press, 1999), lxxxvii, 209.

39. Rebecca Stephens, "Orthodoxy and Liminality in Marguerite Porete's *Mirror of Simple Souls*," doctoral thesis, University of Birmingham, 1999.

40. *Mirror of Simple Souls*, ch. 96, p. 170. Porete's "thought about [God] told her to seek Him . . . at the depth of the core of the intellect of the purity of her sublime thought," and she desires that "her neighbors might find God in her, through writings and words."

41. Scholars debate Julian's orthodoxy, frequently in arguing that Julian's views were proto-feminist and meant to challenge the structures of male-dominated

Church and male-centric doctrines. As Frances Beer writes, "The fact that Julian may have been brought up to equate womanliness and motherhood with gentleness, and may herself have had a particularly close bond with her own mother, cannot in itself have given rise to her understanding of Jesus as Mother, which was (and still is) in direct contradiction to the orthodox view of the Trinity." *Women and Mystical Experience in the Middle Ages* (Rochester, NY: Boydell, 1992), 7–8. And, as we will see in chapter 6, there are those who question Julian's orthodoxy on more than one account, but most especially as regards the consistency of her teaching about the "godly wille" with the Christian doctrine of the Fall.

42. Though the Long Text was preserved in the library of the recusant women's Benedictine community in exile in Cambrai, it was not until the early decades of the twentieth century that the work began to achieve any significant readership in the wider Church.

43. What a pity it is, therefore, that so little contemporary theology has the demotic character of Julian's *Revelation;* so much theology today is written within an exclusive and excluding patois of impenetrability and jargon quite foreign to Julian's style. Much contemporary theology is marginal because it is self-marginalizing.

44. *LT*, 32:223.

45. Ibid.

46. Ibid., 5:139.

47. Ibid., 32:223.

48. Ibid., 33:225.

49. Ibid., 16–17:179–85.

50. Ibid., 32:223.

51. Ibid., 33:227.

52. Ibid., 3:131–33.

53. See ibid., 10:161: "And this vision was a lerning to my understanding that the continual seeking of the soule pleseth God full mekille."

54. Ibid., 11:165.

55. Ibid., 33:225–27.

56. Ibid., 6–7:143–49 on the "homelyhede" of God, meaning not only "familiar-

ity" but also "intimacy," "closeness"—and as of God, so of Julian's language about God.

57. See *The Cloud of Unknowing*, ch. 37, in *The Cloud of Unknowing and Related Treatises*, ed. Phyllis Hodgson (Salzburg: Institut für Anglistik und Amerikanistik, Universität Salzburg, 1982), 40–41.

58. *LT*, 58:307.

59. Ibid., 59:311.

60. Ibid., 58:307.

61. Ibid.

62. Ibid., 59:311.

63. Ibid., 58:307.

64. Ibid., 31:219. It should be noted—by way of authorial comment on my part—that there is no theological justification for substituting any of Julian's triadic nomenclatures for the traditional "Father, Son, and Holy Spirit"—nor in fact does Julian show any inclination to do so. None of Julian's additional names for the persons of the Trinity do the apophatic work of the traditional names, for none of them embody the intrinsically and internally relational character of the Trinitarian persons, and some of them (e.g., "Father," "Mother," "Love") simply muddle those relationalities. Julian's "alternates" can do their work only on the basis of the traditional names, and no good Trinitarian theology can be constructed except on that basis. Conceivably, if one must move away from the male-gendered resonances of the traditional formula, "Mother," "Daughter," "Spirit" would meet the case just as well, but such is not to be found anywhere in Julian.

65. *The Darkness of God* (Cambridge: Cambridge University Press, 1995).

66. There is a long tradition of apophatically prescribing the maximization, not the minimization, of theological vocabulary, even of plainly "inappropriate" language, which stretches back to the Pseudo-Denys. In his *Mystical Theology* he describes a hierarchy of denials of the name of God, as it were a ladder of metaphors reaching from the most purely perceptual to the most purely conceptual, leading finally to the silence of the apophatic. See Pseudo-Denys, *Mystical Theology*, 1033B, in *Complete Works*, 139.

67. Sermon no. 53, "German Works," in *Meister Eckhart: The Essential Sermons*,

Commentaries, Treatises, and Defense, ed. Edmund Colledge and Bernard McGinn, Classics of Western Spirituality (New York: Paulist, 1981), 204–5.

68. For this distinction, see Bernard McGinn, *"Vere tu es Deus absconditus:* The Hidden God in Luther and Some Mystics," in *Silence and the Word,* ed. Oliver Davies and Denys Turner (Cambridge: Cambridge University Press, 2002), 94–114.

69. See Bonaventure, *Bonaventure: "The Soul's Journey into God," "The Tree of Life," "The Life of St. Francis,"* trans. Ewert Cousins (New York: Paulist, 1978), ch. 7. See also my *Faith, Reason, and the Existence of God* (Cambridge: Cambridge University Press, 2004).

70. Turner, *The Darkness of God,* 270.

71. *LT,* 36:231.

72. Ibid., 36:234.

73. In *The Darkness of God.*

74. Bernard McGinn, *The Foundations of Mysticism,* vol. 1 of *The Presence of God: A History of Western Christian Mysticism* (New York: Crossroad, 2005), xvi.

75. William James, *The Varieties of Religious Experience: A Study in Human Nature; Being the Gifford Lectures on Natural Religion Delivered at Edinburgh in 1901–1902* (London: Longman's, Green, 1902).

76. Kevin Magill, *Julian of Norwich: Mystic or Visionary?* Routledge Studies in Medieval Religion and Culture (Abingdon, UK: Routledge, 2006). Incidentally, Magill suspects that in that work I was trying "to represent the neo-Platonic tradition of mystical writing as normative" (5). I was not. I made it clear (Turner, *The Darkness of God,* 7–8) that I was restricting myself to those forms of medieval mystical theology that lay under significant Neoplatonic influence. It was for this reason that in that work I made only a few perfunctory remarks about Julian of Norwich, for I do not think of her as thus influenced, and none at all about Thomas Aquinas, on the same grounds. Subsequently I published another monograph devoted to Thomas Aquinas as mystical theologian (*Faith, Reason, and the Existence of God*) as I now do about Julian under the same description, precisely with a view to demonstrating that Neoplatonism has no normative role within medieval forms of mystical theology.

77. In the argot of the academic theologians, they are *gratiae gratis datae*, free gifts that do not in themselves sanctify their recipient, for they are meant for the building up of the Church—as Julian puts it, they are meant for her evencristens. In this both Julian and her "school" contemporaries say no more than Paul does when he insists that without charity (which alone sanctifies), the other "charismatic" gifts are but clanging cymbals, empty noise (1 Corinthians 15).

78. Someone once said to me that Protestant theology is characterized by the spirit of the disjunctive "either/or," Catholic theology by the spirit of the conjunctive "both/and." I guess that a test of a truly "Catholic" theology is its organization around the conjunction of both. I am much indebted to the work of Philip McCosker, whose doctoral thesis on Christology and paradox for the University of Cambridge has greatly assisted me in coming to appreciate how the meta-theological doctrine of the apophatic nature of language about God generally is rooted in the paradoxes of Christology. See "Ephrem the Syrian (c. 306–73)," in vol. 1 of *The Blackwell Companion to the Theologians*, 2 vols., ed. Ian Markham (Malden, MA: Wiley-Blackwell, 2009).

Chapter 2. Clearing the Conceptual Space

1. For a comprehensive explanation of the free-will defense, see Alvin Plantinga's *God, Freedom, and Evil* (Grand Rapids, MI: W. B. Eerdmans, 1977), 29. For the argument concerning theodicy, see John Hick, *Evil and the God of Love* (New York: Harper and Row, 1966).

2. See Herbert McCabe, *God Matters* (London: Geoffrey Chapman, 1987), 2–53.

3. Ibid., 14–15.

4. Gödel's famous second "incompleteness" theorem shows that, on the condition of the consistency of a number theoretic formal system, that consistency cannot be proved within the formal system. "On Formally Undecidable Propositions of *Principia Mathematica* and Related Systems," in *A Source Book in Mathematical Logic, 1879–1931*, ed. Jean van Heijenoort (Cambridge, MA: Harvard University Press, 1967), 596–616.

5. *LT*, 27:209. Julian's ME word in Sloane is "behovabil," which Glasscoe glosses

as "expedient" or "appropriate"—*Julian of Norwich: A Revelation of Love*, ed. Marion Glasscoe (Exeter: Exeter University Press, 2003), 144.

6. *Rights, Representation, and Reform: Nonsense upon Stilts and Other Writings on the French Revolution*, ed. Philip Schofield, Catherine Pease-Watkin, and Cyprian Blamires (Oxford: Clarendon, 2002), 330. Bentham, of course, was referring to the theoretical and rhetorical bombast, as he thought of it, of "natural law" theories of morality.

7. *LT*, 27:209.

8. Ibid., 30:217.

9. Ibid., 2:125.

10. Julian of Norwich, *A Book of Showings to the Anchoress Julian of Norwich*, ed. Edmund Colledge and James Walsh, 2 vols. (Toronto: Pontifical Institute of Medieval Studies, 1978).

11. See Elisabeth Dutton, *Julian of Norwich: The Influence of Late-Medieval Devotional Compilations* (Cambridge: D. S. Brewer, 2008).

12. In fact, on the only evidence we have of Julian's knowledge of Latin, it may have been poor enough that she could unwittingly make elementary grammatical errors. In Watson and Jenkins's edition (*A Revelation of Love: The Writings of Julian of Norwich*, ed. Nicholas Watson and Jacqueline Jenkins [University Park: Pennsylvania State University Press, 2006]) she exclaims *Benedicite Dominus!* (*LT*, 4:135), evidently confusing the nominative *Dominus* with the vocative *Domine*, or else the imperative *Benedicite* with the subjunctive *Benedicat*. Colledge and Walsh, *A Book of Showings* (whose modernization follows the Paris Bibliothèque nationale MS Fonds anglais 40) simply translate "Blessed be the Lord," which is curious, for that would translate a third Latin phrase, *Benedicatur Dominus*, not found in any MS. Glasscoe's edition, *A Revelation of Love* (following British Library Sloane 2499) has a grammatically correct *Benedicite Domine*, which would translate as "Lord bless!"

13. *Julian of Norwich: Showings*, trans. Edmund Colledge and James Walsh (New York: Paulist, 1978), 177.

14. Watson and Jenkins, *A Revelation of Love*, x.

15. *LT*, 27, in Clifton Wolters, trans. and ed., *Revelations of Divine Love* (Harmondsworth, UK: Penguin, 1962), 103.

16. Colledge and Walsh, *Showings*, 225.
17. *Revelations of Divine Love (Short and Long Text)*, ed. Elizabeth Spearing (New York: Penguin, 1998).
18. Glasscoe, *A Revelation of Love*, 144.
19. W. V. O. Quine, "Two Dogmas of Empiricism," in *From a Logical Point of View* (New York: Harper Torchbooks, 1961), 20.
20. See Anselm of Canterbury, *Cur Deus homo?* in *Anselm of Canterbury: The Major Works*, ed. Brian Davies and G. R. Evans (Oxford: Oxford University Press, 1998); Aquinas, *Summa theologiae*, 3a q1 a1; Bonaventure, *The Soul's Journey into God*, in *Bonaventure: "The Soul's Journey into God," "The Tree of Life," "The Life of St. Francis,"* trans. Ewert Cousins (New York: Paulist, 1978).
21. Wittgenstein gets nearer to this open-minded medieval laxity about the scope and character of the necessary and the contingent when he points out that contrary to the empiricist dogma, not all statements that are necessarily true are exceptionless, analytical statements. "Most chess moves are valid" is, Wittgenstein says, a necessary truth, though it is not, of course, an exceptionless universal. Nor is that proposition's necessity de dicto and analytic, for it is a truth about what actually happens; after all, as a matter of fact some inexpert chess players actually break the rules. If, manifestly, not every actual chess move is a valid move, nonetheless it could not be the case that none are, nor even that most are not. For there could be no chess moves at all if there were no game of chess. And if most chess moves were invalid, there would be no chess game, and hence no invalid chess moves. Necessarily, then, *most* chess moves are valid. But empiricists have no way of allowing that proposition space between the Scylla of their de dicto necessity and the Charybdis of their de re contingency.

And for the other part, Thomas Aquinas is better than the Platonists on the score of knowledge and necessity. We can of course "know" the contingent. If you know that "Socrates is sitting" is now true, then, necessarily, Socrates is now sitting, he says. But that is just a de dicto necessity, from which it does not follow, as the Platonists would have it, that Socrates' sitting is necessary. After all, Socrates just has to stand up and walk away to make "Socrates is sitting" false. (See *Summa theologiae*, 1a q14 a13 ad3.) What

Wittgenstein and Thomas both do is unbind the chains that tie necessity and contingency to exclusive disjunction, and so they allow room for yet other kinds of nonlogical and nonnatural necessity—hence, correspondingly, of nonarbitrary contingency.

22. *Faith, Reason, and the Existence of God* (Cambridge: Cambridge University Press, 2004), 243–45.

23. Of course it *could* have mattered that at the age of eighteen I was 5 feet 8 1/2 inches tall and not 5 feet 7. Had I at that age wished to become a policeman in the United Kingdom and been but 5 feet 7 inches tall my ambition would have been frustrated, since at that time UK police forces required a minimum height of 5 feet 8 as a condition of entry into the service. But that is the point. Individual and contingent stories generate their own internal differentiations between the necessary and the contingent.

24. If the logic of the behovely is that of the structure of meaningful narrative, one important consequence follows: you could not say that Creation *as such* is behovely. Consider a question that goes finally beyond any possible answer in terms of story: "What if nothing at all existed?" The answer to that question has to be that the world—everything that exists—is in every possible respect and mind-defeatingly contingent, absolutely so. It follows that there is no story the coming into existence of everything belongs to, because there could not be a *story* of everything's coming to be ex nihilo. The existence of all that exists *is* the story, and outside of it, *ex hypothesi*, there is nothing. And we see this on account of the completely unreasonable (because completely unanswerable) nature of that question. There simply cannot be an answer to the question "What if nothing at all existed?" because the "What if?" part of it means: "What state of affairs would obtain if nothing at all existed?" and obviously, no state of affairs of whatever kind would obtain if nothing existed. As between there being something of any kind and there being nothing at all, we are no longer looking at construable alternatives, as if they were different stories. Something would be missing from the story of the universe, though not very much, had I never existed. But nothing at all would be missing had nothing at all ever existed, because to be missed there has to be something that what is missing is missing from. So the question itself seems entirely off

the scale of what can be envisaged, or, as you might say, the question is now properly theological, because to entertain it at all is already to have raised the question of God.

But if that is so, it would seem that the logic of the behovely, as heretofore explained, precludes any possible answer to the question "Why is there anything at all?" in terms of its convenientia. For there is nothing at all that there being *just anything* fits with. But we do need an account of why we have got just *this* world, especially if, as because of sin we do, there might seem to be reasons to challenge the wisdom of bringing into existence a work of art so easily thought to be flawed.

25. In this respect, too, narratival explanations differ from scientific. For the whole point of science is to eliminate surprise entirely.

26. I am indebted to Dr. Férdia Stone-Davis for alerting me to a parallel in Kant, for whom what he calls "pure aesthetic judgment" lies in the logical space between theoretical judgments of science governed by the a priori categories of understanding that determine relations of causal necessity, and empirical judgments of taste that are purely arbitrary. As with my "narratives," so with Kant's aesthetic judgments: they possess a universality that is not that of the necessary, and a particularity that is not that of the purely contingent. See Dr. Stone-Davis's PhD thesis for the University of Cambridge, "The Resonance of Beauty," 2005.

27. In chapter 5 I develop more fully the proposition that for Julian, theology of necessity can work only from such incomplete narratival fragments, and in the absence of the full story.

28. Note that Julian does not say only that however awful things are in the meantime, all *will* turn out well in the end. What happens "in the end" is that we will *see* how everything was all right at the time; and that is what we must *believe* now at the time of its awfulness. As Julian says: "For in the thirde shewing, whan I saw that God doeth all that is done, I saw not sin. And than saw I that alle is welle. But whan God shewede me for sin, than said he: 'Alle shalle be wele.'" *LT*, 34:229.

29. I paraphrase Professor Philip Alexander at the graduate seminar of the Depart-

ment of Religions and Theology at the University of Manchester, October 2002.

30. Presumably this is a truism of historical explanation, though one hears historians pretending to believe that the entertaining of counterfactual conditionals is an unhistorical thing to do. This seems strange, since one also hears the same historians talk confidently of this or that event occurring *because of* the other. And it is hard to know what the meaning of this "because" could be if not that without "the other" there would have been no "this or that."

31. Alvin Plantinga, *The Nature of Necessity* (Oxford: Clarendon, 1974), 186.

32. "I should ask this: if God has made men such that in their free choices they sometimes prefer what is good and sometimes what is evil, why could he not have made men such that they always freely choose the good? If there is no logical impossibility in a man's freely choosing the good on one, or on several, occasions, there cannot be a logical impossibility in his freely choosing the good on every occasion. God was not, then, faced with a choice between making innocent automata and making beings who, in acting freely, would sometimes go wrong: there was open to him the obviously better possibility of making beings who would act freely but always go right. Clearly, his failure to avail himself of this possibility is inconsistent with his being both omnipotent and wholly good." J. L. Mackie, "Evil and Omnipotence," *Mind* 64, no. 254 (1955): 209.

33. *LT,* 27:207–8. By "prevented it" I (and I think Julian too) do not mean, "knowing that sin would have happened unless God intervened to stop it, God intervened to stop it." I mean (and I think Julian does too) that, knowing what worlds were possible, God could have brought about just that world in which no sin was actually committed. No freedom to sin is blocked in the latter case, as it is in the former. In the former case, I would have freely sinned had God not prevented me from doing so. In the latter case, everyone freely chooses the good because that is what God brought about.

34. Ibid., 27:209.

35. I used to wonder whether Jesus was not an exception. Was Jesus the best possible human being? In one sense the answer is yes, since no sin was found in him, and so no diminution of his humanity by sin; and in us there is plenty.

And, as Thomas Aquinas says, you could not do better, as human beings go, than to be hypostatically united to the second person of the Trinity (*Summa theologiae*, 1a q25 a6 ad4). But in every other sense he was not. In the first place, de facto there were possibilities of human "realization" that Jesus could have achieved as a man, and did not—for example, he was not a father: I am, and to that extent I am a more "perfect" human being than Jesus was. Second, being male excluded his achieving possibilities of human realization available only to women—thus he was not a mother, to which extent my wife is a more perfect human being than Jesus was. Moreover, much as there is to be made of the human wisdom and knowledge of Jesus, as a man of his times there are things of which Jesus knew nothing that you and I know as a matter of course—e.g., Einstein's theory of relativity or that there is no square root of −1, and so on. Whatever *perfectus homo* does mean, it cannot mean "perfect human being." There isn't anything that "perfect human being" means.

36. The inevitability that there be sin does not require that any sinful act be inevitable, and so not freely done. "Necessarily there will be sin" does not entail that any particular sin is necessary.

37. Thomas agrees. While this world may not be the best possible world, its governance is the best possible governance—see *Summa theologiae*, 1a q103 a3 *corp: necesse est quod mundi gubernatio sit optima.*

38. *LT*, 11:165.

39. Ibid., 11:163. And: "He wille we witte that not onely he taketh heed to nobille thinges and to gret, but also to litille and small, to lowe and to simple, and to one and to other. And so meneth he in that he seyeth: 'Alle maner of thing shal be welle.'" Ibid., 32:109.

40. *Summa theologiae*, 1a q103 a6 *corp.*

41. On this distinction between how you know what I am doing ("by observation") and how I know what I am doing ("without observation"), see Elizabeth Anscombe's still unrivaled discussion in G. E. M. Anscombe, *Intention* (Oxford: Basil Blackwell, 1957), ch. 8.

42. *Summa theologiae*, 1a q103 a6 *corp.*

43. See the development of this point in connection with prayer in chapter 5.

44. See my discussion of the meaning of Thomas's *esse* and its relation to Creation in *Faith, Reason, and the Existence of God*, 177–87.

45. Of course, Thomas has no knowledge of any theory of the evolution of species. His account of the diversity of species is borrowed from Aristotle, for whom the origin of species is the effect of what he calls the "equivocal" cause, namely, the sun. There is nothing of which I am aware in Thomas's cosmology, however, that would have caused him to reject in principle Darwin's account, and as one who was temperamentally open to any well-founded scientific explanation of the natural order, much to suggest that he would have welcomed it. In which connection, Thomas by no means agrees with those of a so-called creationist persuasion in supposing that, if God governs all things, then nothing can happen "by chance." This is because for Thomas chance effects are simply de facto outcomes of interacting chains of causality; and while those interactions themselves could not be predicted as the outcome of any *single* causal process, the outcomes that "just so happen" can be predicted as being the outcomes you would expect *given* the interactions of those causal processes that "just so happen." It is chance that I meet Peter on my way to the station as he is on the way to work. But my being on the way to the station and Peter's being on the way to work at just that time are not "chance." From a combination of general causal laws in conjunction with statements about particulars you can retrodict our meeting just then, even if no causal law determined that we would. For Thomas, then, there is no reason why God should not bring about some effects by means of chance. See *Summa theologiae*, I. q25 a5 *corp*.

46. This does not, of course, mean that there is no narrative of a free act. All sorts of processes of deliberation, calculation, judgment, decision, and choice are involved in my freely acting in this way rather than that. But the structure of that narrative is governed by *reasons* for acting internal to the action itself, not by *causal* sequences antecedently determining them. On this distinction, see, for example, Peter Winch, *The Idea of a Social Science* (London: Routledge and Kegan Paul, 1958), 80–83; and McCabe in *Faith within Reason*, ed. Brian Davies (London: Continuum, 2007).

47. Augustine, *Confessions*, trans. Henry Chadwick (New York: Oxford University Press, 2009), 3:6.

48. *Summa theologiae*, Ia q45 a5 *corp.*

49. *LT*, 40:245.

50. Ibid., 32:221.

51. Ibid., 86:379.

52. "For as alle that hath being in kinde is of Gods making, so is alle thing that is done in properte of Gods doing. For it is esy to understand that the beste dede is done wele. And so wele as the best dede is done and the highest, so wele is the leest dede done, and all in the properte and in the order that our lord hath it ordained to fro withoute beginning. *For ther is no doer but he*" (my emphasis). Ibid., 11:165.

53. Ibid., 11:163.

54. Ibid., 27:209–11.

55. *ST*, 8:77.

56. It is in his failure to see this that consists Ockham's error in maintaining that God *could* will what is now evil, because in any case it is only God's willing that makes an action good.

57. *LT*, 11:163.

58. Ibid., 23:113.

59. *Faith within Reason*, 92.

60. *LT*, 33:226–27.

Chapter 3. Two Stories of Sin

1. *LT*, 45:261.

2. Ibid., 49:269.

3. Ibid.

4. Ibid., 32:223.

5. In spite of the fact that in her thirteenth revelation "on which was made litille mention of eville, yet I was not drawen therby from ony point of the faith that holy church techeth me to beleve." Ibid., 33:225.

6. Ibid., 50:271–73.

7. See Wolter's introduction to his translation of *Revelation* (New York: Penguin, 1966).

8. Gerald Downing, "Theological Breadth, Interconnection, Tradition, and Gender: Hildegard, Hadewijch, and Julian Today," *Anglican Theological Review* (Summer 2004); Frances Beer, *Women and Mystical Experience in the Middle Ages* (Rochester, NY: Boydell, 1992), 7–8.

9. "God shewde full gret pleasance that he hath in alle men and women that mightly and meekly and wisely take the preching and teching of holy church. For he it is, holy church." *LT*, 34:227.

10. Ibid., 7:149.

11. Ibid., 8:153.

12. Ibid., 9:153–55.

13. Ibid., 7:149.

14. For historical background on Lollardy and the Wyclif heresy, see Richard Rex, *The Lollards*, Social History in Perspective Series (New York: Palgrave, 2002).

15. *Summa theologiae*, 2–2ae q177 a1 *corp*. Note, alas, that in article 2 of this question Thomas denies to women the role that Julian confidently undertakes in the Long Text, namely, that of a teacher of the Church. Thomas rules out any prophetic role for women, especially that of teaching before the Church as such. For Thomas, the prophetic role of women is confined to "familiar conversation with one or a few" ("privatim ad unum aut paucos familiariter colloquendo"). I am grateful to Katie Bugyis for drawing my attention to this passage.

16. See Kevin Magill's excellent discussion of this aspect of Julian's writing in *Julian of Norwich: Mystic or Visionary?* Routledge Studies in Medieval Religion and Culture (Abingdon, UK: Routledge, 2006), ch. 3.

17. *LT*, 8:151–53.

18. Ibid., 9:153.

19. Ibid.

20. Ibid., 70:345.

21. Ibid., 61:317.

22. See *The Varieties of Religious Experience: A Study in Human Nature; Being*

the *Gifford Lectures on Natural Religion Delivered at Edinburgh in 1901–1902* (London: Longmans, Green, 1902), lectures 16 and 17, 379–429.

23. See Nicholas Lash, *The Beginning and End of "Religion"* (Cambridge: Cambridge University Press, 1996).

24. James, *Varieties*, 381–82. Though James does not deny—on the contrary, he insists—that such experiences, "ineffable" in themselves, can be retained in the memory of their effect on the life and consciousness of their recipients.

25. Ibid., 380.

26. For instance, Zaehner in *Mysticism Sacred and Profane: An Enquiry into Some Varieties of Praeter-natural Experience* (Oxford: Clarendon, 1957); W. Stace, *Mysticism and Philosophy* (London: Macmillan, 1961); N. Smart, "Interpretation and Mystical Experience," *Religious Studies* 1 (1965): 75–87.

27. "I saw" is ubiquitous throughout the text.

28. Jenkins and Watson tend to distinguish them rather too sharply, in my view. See introduction to *A Revelation of Love: The Writings of Julian of Norwich*, ed. Nicholas Watson and Jacqueline Jenkins (University Park: Pennsylvania State University Press, 2006), 33.

29. *LT*, 8:151: "And alle this our lorde shewde in the furst sight, and gave me space and time to beholde it. And the bodily sight stinted, and the gostely sighte dwelled in my understonding."

30. Ibid., 5:139.

31. Ibid.

32. Ibid.

33. And if Watson and Jenkins's speculation is right that the Long Text was composed any time after the middle 1390s and before her death after 1416, then we could be talking of over forty years of reflection on the original revelations of 1373.

34. *LT*, 6:143.

35. Oliver Davies, "Transformational Processes in the Work of Julian of Norwich and Mechtild of Magdeburg," in *The Medieval Mystical Tradition in England* (Cambridge: D. S. Brewer, 1992), 39–52.

36. In any case, most contemporary medieval accounts of the "analogy of the senses" stress not the directness of the sense of seeing (and hearing) but, on

the contrary, its mediated character by contrast with the immediacy of touch, taste, and smell, for seeing encounters its objects across the medium of space, whereas touch, taste, and smell are in immediate contact with their objects. For this reason, Denys the Carthusian notes that there are some (e.g., Hugh of Balma) who interpret the Psalm's instruction "taste and see that the Lord is good" as indicating the priority of love over knowledge, because love's immediacy "tastes" God, whereas intellect's mediated knowledge merely "sees" God. See Denys the Carthusian, *De contemplatione*, III.15, in *Opera omnia divi Dionysii Cartusiensis*, vol. 9, ed. M. Leone (Montreuil-sur-mer: Tournai Parkminster, 1912), 272; Hugh of Balma, *Viae sion lugent*, in *Carthusian Spirituality: The Writings of Hugh of Balma and Guigo de Ponte*, trans. Dennis Martin, Classics of Western Spirituality 88 (Mahwah, NJ: Paulist, 1993); see also Giles of Rome's *Commentary on the Song of Songs*, trans. Denys Turner, in Turner, *Eros and Allegory* (Kalamazoo, MI: Cistercian, 2005), 363–65.

37. I have found but few occurrences of any cognate of the word "mystical" in her *Revelation*, and most of them in chapter 51. The opening sentence of that chapter reads: "And then oure curteyse lorde answered in shewing, full mistily" (273).

38. Origen, *On First Principles*, IV, in *Origen: An Exhortation to Martyrdom, Prayer and Selected Works*, trans. Rowan Greer, Classics of Western Spirituality (New York: Paulist, 1979).

39. Andrew Louth, *Denys the Areopagite* (London: Chapman, 2002), 101–9.

40. *LT*, 30:217.

41. Some people seem just to *say* this, as if it were too obviously invulnerable to challenge, presumably because it sounds "realistic." All the same, it is very hard to know on what principle of calculation one is supposed reliably to draw such a conclusion.

42. Which is, of course, not the same thing as saying that *what makes* an action evil is that it causes suffering. Some actions cause no suffering at all and yet are evil. Some good actions do cause suffering and are not the less good for doing so.

43. David Aers, *Salvation and Sin: Augustine, Langland and Fourteenth Century Theology* (Notre Dame, IN: University of Notre Dame Press, 2009), 164.

44. *LT*, 40:245.
45. Ibid., 32:221.
46. "ne it might not be knowen but by the paine that it is cause of." Ibid., 27:211.
47. Ibid., 39:239.
48. Ibid., 67:333.
49. Ibid., 39:243.
50. Ibid., 52:289.
51. Ibid., 15:177.
52. Ibid., 52:289.
53. Though there is more to it than that; see chapter 6.
54. *Inferno*, 12:38–45, trans. Robin Kirkpatrick (London: Penguin Classics, 2006), 101.
55. Dante Alighieri, *The Divine Comedy*, vol. 1, *Inferno*, trans. Robin Kirkpatrick (London: Penguin Classics, 2006), 360.
56. Dante Alighieri, *Paradiso*, trans. John Sinclair (New York: Oxford University Press, 1961), 33:145.
57. Ibid.
58. It is important to note that this is not inconsistent with saying, as in the previous chapter I argued Julian to be saying, that God could have created a world in which everyone freely chose the good. McCabe is quite right to say that "there is no question of God *having* to permit me to sin in order to leave me with my freedom." "Evil," in *God Matters* (New York: Continuum, 2005), 37. The fact is that God did not create a world without sin. And in this world in which there is sin, among the choices I can freely make is the choice to sin without repentance. And if this is the sort of world in which I can freely sin, then in creating such a world, God necessarily created a world in which I could reject the love that created it. For it goes with *such* a world, the world God has actually created, that choosing hell is possible.
59. In fact, if only negatively, the very ordering of hell's regime does reveal the love that made it. For Dante's carefully constructed gradations of descent down the circles of hell each reveal with progressive clarity the nature of the love that is rejected and the nature of the effects of that rejection. In the end, you come to know about love in hell best from the evidence of its total loss,

from the total, sullen, inarticulate, frozen silence of Satan—not, then, from Francesca and Paolo's tragic near miss.

60. *Inferno*, 3:1–6; emphasis mine.

61. Milton, *Paradise Lost*, ed. Scott Elledge, 3rd ed. (New York: Norton, 2004), 4.109–11.

62. *Inferno*, 5.

63. Ibid., 32.

64. As Courtney Palmbush asked it.

Chapter 4. The Lord and the Servant

1. *LT*, 73:353.

2. Ibid., 76:363. See *The Cloud of Unknowing and Related Treatises*, ed. Phyllis Hodgson (Salzburg: Institut für Anglistik unf und Amerikanistik, Universität Salzburg, 1982).

3. *LT*, 36:231.

4. Ibid., 33:225.

5. J-P Sartre, *Huis-Clos (No Exit)*, in *No Exit and Three Other Plays*, trans. Stuart Gilbert (New York: Vintage, 1989).

6. J-P Sartre, *Existentialism Is a Humanism*, trans. Carol Macomber (New Haven: Yale University Press, 2007); and *Huis-Clos*.

7. Friedrich Nietzsche, *On the Genealogy of Morals*, trans. Walter Kaufmann and R. J. Hollingdale (New York: Vintage, 1989).

8. Clifton Wolters believes that Julian's soteriology "trembles on the brink" of universalist heresy—see his introduction to *Julian of Norwich: Revelation of Divine Love*, trans. and ed. Clifton Wolters (London: Penguin, 1966), 36. But also Elizabeth Spearing: "A God who cannot be angry without self-contradiction, and who will ultimately make all things well, surely leaves no place for damnation," *Revelations of Divine Love (Short and Long Text)* (New York: Penguin, 1998), xxv; and "Julian clearly entertains [universalism] as a possibility," xxvi. Also, Watson and Jenkins: "This promise [that all shall be well] tantalizingly suggests that all humanity will gain salvation," *A Revelation of Love: The Writings of Julian of Norwich*, ed. Nicholas Watson and Jacqueline Jenkins (University Park: Pennsylvania State University Press,

2006), 2. There are two further possibilities, both consistent with some texts in the Long Text but not with others: the Barthian, namely, that hell exists but is entirely unpopulated; the other, suggested to me by Andrew Kraebel of Yale University, that all and only Christians are to be saved.

9. *LT*, 32:223.

10. Watson and Jenkins (*A Revelation of Love*, 222) suggest that here Julian is immediately citing Walter Hilton's *Scale of Perfection*, 2.3. Hilton in turn is drawing on a tradition extending through Hugh of St. Victor and Anselm of Canterbury back to Augustine's *Enchiridion*. The doctrine that "outside the Church there is no salvation," interpreted as meaning that none who are unbaptized can be saved, was formally stated at the IV Lateran Council, entailing that the majority of human beings are damned to hell, and some unspecified number of Christians with them.

11. Watson and Jenkins, *A Revelation of Love*, 222.

12. E.g., *LT*, 27:211.

13. Watson and Jenkins, *A Revelation of Love*, 2.

14. *LT*, 32:223.

15. After, of course, the Gospels themselves, Augustine's *Confessions* must be the paradigm for all narrative theologies.

16. *Hamlet*, act 2, scene 2.

17. Robin Kirkpatrick, "Dante," in *Purgatorio*, trans. Robin Kirkpatrick (London: Penguin, 2007), xxvi–xxxviii.

18. Dante Alighieri, *Paradiso*, trans. John Sinclair (New York: Oxford University Press, 1961), 9:103–7.

19. In a private comment.

20. In fact, Dante makes the comparison himself when he protests to Virgil at the beginning of *Inferno* that the proposed journey through hell, purgatory, and paradise is too much for him, for he is not made of the stuff of Aeneas and of Paul. *Inferno*, trans. John Sinclair (New York: Oxford University Press, 1961), 2:32.

21. There is a long tradition of theological discussion of this topos, extending in the Western tradition from Augustine's *De videndo Deo* through Thomas Aquinas's discussion in his *Commentary on 2 Corinthians* to Nicholas of Cusa's

De visione Dei, in all of which the wholly exceptional character of Paul's rapture into the third heaven is emphasized.

22. For example, as Bernard McGinn has pointed out to me, Catherine of Siena in her *Dialogue*, ch. 83.

23. For this emphasis on the striking combination in Dante of the centrality of the ethical with the apophatic I am much indebted to the work of Vittorio Montemaggi—see his 2006 PhD thesis at the University of Cambridge, "*Nulla vedere e amor me coſtrinse:* On Reading Dante's *Commedia* as a Theological Poem."

24. *LT*, 4:135.

25. *Paradiso*, 33:143.

26. Ibid., 33:146.

27. *Inferno*, 32:1.

28. Ibid., 5:73–142.

29. Ibid., 26:48–122.

30. Ibid., 33:1–78.

31. Ibid., 34:22–69.

32. Dante Alighieri, *Purgatorio*, trans. John Sinclair (New York: Oxford University Press, 1961), 30.

33. *Paradiso*, 24–26.

34. "And to alle this I ne had no other answere but a marvelous example of a lorde and a servant, as I shall sey after, and that full mistily shewed." *LT*, 45:261.

35. Ibid., 50:273.

36. Ibid., 51:274–75.

37. Ibid., 51:277. Though it is clear that this shewing was given to Julian at the same time as the others, no mention of it is made in the Short Text. Evidently it took Julian those twenty years of reflection to make any sense of it at all.

38. Although it should be said that Julian warns the reader not to neglect the detailed significances, for example, of the servant's clothing, for they and the significance of the "example" taken as a whole are, she says, "so unified, as I understand it, that I cannot and may not separate them." Ibid., 51:269.

39. Ibid., 51:274–75.

40. David Aers, *Salvation and Sin: Augustine, Langland and Fourteenth Century Theology* (Notre Dame, IN: University of Notre Dame Press, 2009), 164.

41. *LT,* 11:163.

42. Ibid., 27:209.

43. Ibid., 49:269.

44. "Oure lorde God as aneynst himselfe [in regard to himself], may not forgeve, for he may not be wroth. It were unpossible." Ibid., 49:269.

45. Watson and Jenkins, *A Revelation of Love,* 7.

46. *LT,* 73:162.

47. Ibid., 86:179.

48. In this way, there is more than autobiographical significance in Julian's precise dating of her shewings on May 8, 1373. The eventlessness of eternity is what she sees. But her seeing it is very much an event in time.

49. See *The Darkness of God* (Cambridge: Cambridge University Press, 1995).

50. For a discussion of this medieval hermeneutic, see my *Eros and Allegory* (Kalamazoo, MI: Cistercian, 1995), ch. 4.

51. Denise Baker, *Julian of Norwich's Showings* (Princeton: Princeton University Press, 1994), 99.

52. Aers, *Salvation and Sin,* 164.

53. Baker, *Julian of Norwich's Showings,* 100.

54. See Herbert McCabe's very beautiful sermon on the parable in *Faith within Reason,* ed. Brian Davies (London: Continuum, 2007), 155–59.

55. *LT,* 22:197.

56. J. P. H. Clark, "Time and Eternity in Julian of Norwich," *Downside Review* 109, no. 377 (1991): 272.

57. Ibid.

58. John Duns Scotus, *Ordinatio: Opera omnia III* (Vatican City: Typis Polyglottis Vaticanis, 1950), d.9, q.un., n.6.

59. *LT,* 22:193, 195.

60. "[Deus] preordinavit sive praevidit [incarnationem] de remedio . . . ut medicina contra lapsum." *Ordinatio,* III, d.9, q.un., n.6.

61. Clark, "Time and Eternity," 273.

62. *LT,* 4:135.

63. Watson and Jenkins, *A Revelation of Love*, 134, col. 2.

64. This follows because the man Christ was God, though, of course, it is not *insofar as* Christ was God that God died on the Cross, but only *insofar as* Christ was human. That Julian knew of this principle, and knew how to employ it, is clear from *LT* 51:283 and 285, where she distinguishes between what Jesus knew as God and what Jesus knew as man about his Passion. Her Christological employment of the so-called *in quantum* ("insofar as") principle is precise.

65. *Inferno*, 34:55–69.

66. *LT*, 13:169.

Chapter 5. Prayer and Providence

1. In private correspondence.

2. Simon Tugwell, *Ways of Imperfection* (London: Templegate, 1985).

3. *The Darkness of God* (Cambridge: Cambridge University Press, 1995), 252–73.

4. *Viae sion lugent;* for a translation, see *Carthusian Spirituality: The Writings of Hugh of Balma and Guigo de Ponte*, trans. and ed. Dennis D. Martin (New York: Paulist, 1997).

5. William of St. Thierry, *The Golden Epistle*, trans. Theodore Berkeley (Kalamazoo, MI: Cistercian, 1995).

6. Bernard of Clairvaux, *Sermons on the Song of Songs*, vol. 1, trans. Kilian Walsh and Irene Edmonds (Kalamazoo, MI: Cistercian, 1989).

7. *Itinerarium mentis in Deum*, rev. ed., trans. Zachary Hayes, in *Works of St Bonaventure* 2 (Saint Bonaventure, NY: Franciscan Institute, Saint Bonaventure University, 2002).

8. *LT*, 66:331.

9. Ibid., 68:339.

10. *Darkness of God*, ch. 3.

11. Augustine, *Confessions*, trans. and ed. Henry Chadwick (New York: Oxford University Press, 2009), 1.1.

12. Ibid., 3.4.

13. Ibid., 10.27.

14. *LT*, 10:157–59.

15. Ibid., 10:159.

16. Ibid.

17. Ibid.

18. Ibid. Colledge and Walsh have "lacked" for Watson and Jenkins's and Spearing's "wanted." *A Revelation of Love: The Writings of Julian of Norwich*, ed. Nicholas Watson and Jacqueline Jenkins (University Park: Pennsylvania State University Press, 2006); *Revelations of Divine Love (Short and Long Text)*, ed. Elizabeth Spearing (New York: Penguin, 1998).

19. *LT*, 10:161.

20. Ibid.

21. Ibid., 10:159.

22. Ibid., 10:161.

23. Ibid.

24. Ibid.

25. Ibid., 46:261–63.

26. Ibid., 10:161.

27. Ibid.

28. I use the rather vague term "dispositions" here by way of including two distinct but closely related medieval discussions: those that concern the "contemplative" and "active" ways of life, and those that concern "contemplative" and "active" activities. Some medieval theologians (most of whom are monks) suppose that because contemplative activity is the higher of the two, so it follows that the contemplative life is the higher form of life. But not all, especially not all friars, agree. Thomas Aquinas maintains that though contemplative activity is the highest in which a person can engage, the best form of life is the "mixed" life, which includes both—see *Summa theologiae*, 2a–2ae, q188 a6 *corp*. Meister Eckhart goes further when he notes that all Jesus says to Martha is that Mary's is the better part; the best of all, he says, following Thomas, is the mixed life, and adds that it is Martha, not Mary, who is better disposed to achieve the synthesis of the two—see sermon 9, *Intravit Jesus*, in *Meister Eckhart, Sermons and Treatises*, vol. 1, trans. and ed. M. O'C. Walshe (Shaftesbury, UK: Element Books, 1979), 79–90. For the standard study of the Martha/Mary theme in medieval theology, see Giles Constable, "The

Interpretation of Martha and Mary," in *Three Studies in Medieval Religious and Social Thought* (Cambridge: Cambridge University Press, 1998), 1–93.

29. Augustine, *City of God*, ed. R. W. Dyson (Cambridge: Cambridge University Press, 1998), 19.

30. Gregory the Great, *Homilies on Ezekiel*, trans. Theodosia Tomkinson (Etna, CA: Center for Traditionalist Orthodox Studies, 2008), 2.2, pp. 279–92.

31. Nicholas Love, *The Mirrour of the Blessed Lyf of Jesu Christ*, ed. James Hogg and Lawrence F. Powell, 2 vols., Analecta Cartusiana 91 (Salzburg: Institut für Anglistik und Amerikanistik, 1989), 2:174.

32. *Summa theologiae*, 2–2ae, q181 a 4 *corp.*

33. E. Ann Matter comments, "the profusion of manuscripts [of the Song of Songs] suggests that it enjoyed the sort of popularity that turns serious textual study into a punishing task." *The Voice of My Beloved: The Song of Songs in Western Medieval Christianity* (Philadelphia: University of Pennsylvania Press, 1990).

34. Bernard of Clairvaux, sermon 27.6, in *Bernard of Clairvaux: On the Song of Songs II*, trans. Kilian Walsh (Kalamazoo, MI: Cistercian, 1976), 79. Baker distinguishes between Bernard's own employment of this theme of the regio dissimilitudinis, in which our "exile" is associated with the dangers of embodiment as such and its burdens of sensuality and earthly cares, and Julian's. For Julian our exile, represented by the servant fallen in the dell, is chiefly experienced as separation from God and consequent loneliness. See Denise Baker, *Julian of Norwich's Showings* (Princeton: Princeton University Press, 1994), 96–97.

35. See my *Eros and Allegory* (Kalamazoo, MI: Cistercian, 1995), 83–89.

36. Gregory was foundational in the tradition in which the contemplative life involves rest from external action. See, for example, his *Morals on the Book of Job*, trans. J. H. Parker (London: F. and J. Rivington, 1844), 6.38.60, pp. 360–61.

37. Simon Tugwell, "Prayer, Humpty Dumpty, and Thomas Aquinas," in *Language, Meaning and God: Essays in Honor of Herbert McCabe*, ed. Brian Davies (London: Geoffrey Chapman, 1988).

38. Guigo II, *Scala claustralium*, in *Guigo II: The Ladder of Monks and Twelve*

Meditations, trans. Edmund Colledge and James Walsh (Garden City, NY: Doubleday, 1978).

39. Not, of course, that Christians today do not "read" and "meditate." But if they do, it is in severely truncated forms of *otium* (contemplative rest), as activities fitted in as time permits in a day filled with much *negotium* (business). For the monks it was the other way around.

40. *The Ladder of Monks*, 83.

41. Oliver Davies, "Transformational Processes in the Work of Julian of Norwich and Mechtild of Magdeburg," in *The Medieval Mystical Tradition in England* (Cambridge: D. S. Brewer, 1992).

42. See *ST*, 19:104, "For whate time that mannes saule es hamelye with God, him nedes nought to praye, botte behalde reverentlye whate he says . . . when we see God we hafe that we desire, and than nedes us noght to praye. Botte when we se nought God, than nedes us to pray for failinge and for habelinge of ourselfe to Jhesu"; and ibid., 78:367–69.

43. See the contemporary *Cloud of Unknowing*, ch. 25 in *Classics of Western Spirituality*, ed. James Walsh (Mahwah, NJ: Paulist, 1981), almost certainly written by a Carthusian monk in the decade of Julian's revelations.

44. *LT*, 41:249.

45. *Confessions*, 10.

46. "Sero te amavi, o pulchritudo tam antiqua, tam nova, sero te amavi," "Late have I loved you, o beauty every ancient, ever new, late have I loved you," *Confessions*, 10.27.

47. Plato, *Phaedo*, trans. D. Gallop (New York: Oxford University Press, 1975), 72e3–78b3, and *Meno*, 80d–86c, in *Meno and Other Dialogues*, trans. Robin Waterfield (New York: Oxford University Press, 2005).

48. Marguerite Porete gets very close to this Augustinian instinct when she speaks of the "loing-pres" of God, God's "far-nearness"—see *Le mirouer des ames simples*, in Romana Guarnieri and Paul Verdeyen, eds., *Corpus Christianorum, continuatio medievalis*, 69 (Turnhout, Belgium: Brepols, 1986). For a modern English translation, *Marguerite Porete: The Mirror of Simple Souls*, trans. Ellen Babinsky (New York: Paulist, 1993).

49. Bonaventure, *The Soul's Journey into God*, in *Bonaventure: "The Soul's Journey*

3

2

into God," "The Tree of Life," "The Life of St. Francis," trans. Ewert Cousins (New York: Paulist, 1978), ch. 5.

50. *Confessions,* 11.18.

51. Henry Vaughan, "The World," in *The Oxford Book of English Mystical Verse,* ed. D. H. S. Nicholson and A. H. Lee (Whitefish, MT: Kessinger, 2007).

52. See, for example, Jürgen Moltmann's *Theology of Hope: On the Ground and Implications of a Christian Eschatology* (London: SCM, 1967), in which "eschatology" is set *against* the understanding of God as "timeless."

53. *City of God,* 10.7.

54. Bonaventure, *Soul's Journey into God.*

55. John of the Cross, *Dark Night of the Soul,* trans. K. Kavanaugh and Otilio Rodriguez, in *Collected Works* (Washington, DC: Institute of Carmelite Studies, 1979).

56. For obviously the end of time cannot be in the future.

57. George Herbert, "Prayer," in *George Herbert, Verse and Prose,* ed. Wendy Cope (London: SPCK, 2002), 30.

58. *LT,* 11:163.

59. Aquinas, *Compendium theologiae,* II, 4, in *Compendium of Theology,* trans. Cyril Vollert (London: B. Herder, 1947).

60. *LT,* 42:253.

61. Ibid.

62. Ibid., 43:257.

63. Gerard Manley Hopkins, "I Wake and Feel the Fell of Dark, Not Day," in *Poems* (London: Humphrey Milford, 1918), 45.

64. *LT,* 41:247.

65. *Summa contra gentiles,* XCV–XCVI, pp. 187–88, in *Basic Writings of Saint Thomas Aquinas: Man and the Conduct of Life,* vol. 2, trans. Anton Pegis (Indianapolis: Hackett, 1997).

66. Ibid., 86.

67. *LT,* 41:249.

68. Ibid.

69. Ibid., 43:255.

70. Ibid., 43:257; emphasis mine.

71. *Summa theologiae,* 1a q19 a 5 *corp.*

72. *LT,* 6:143.

73. *Summa theologiae,* 3a q21 a2 *corp.*

74. Augustine, *Enarrationes in Psalmis,* 32.1, sermon 1, in *Patrologia Latina,* 36, 277.

75. *LT,* 19:249.

76. "Prayer."

Chapter 6. Substance and Sensuality

1. *LT,* 53:293.

2. Ibid., 37:237.

3. Ibid., 53:293.

4. Ibid., 53:293, 295.

5. Grace Jantzen makes this connection in *Julian of Norwich: Mystic and Theologian* (London: SPCK, 2000), 167: "If our substance, our essential self, is continually united with God and there is in each of us a godly will, how is it that we so regularly and by our own hand get ourselves, individually and collectively, into such disastrous situations?" Elizabeth Spearing says in her introduction, "God's judgment expresses justice, but (contrary to normal medieval assumptions) is not harsher but less harsh than men's judgments, because human beings see only the 'animal will' corrupted by the Fall, while God sees the 'godly will' that reflects his own purity and remains uncorrupt." *Revelations of Divine Love (Short and Long Text)* (New York: Penguin, 1998), xxvii.

6. *LT,* 53:295.

7. *A Revelation of Love: The Writings of Julian of Norwich,* ed. Nicholas Watson and Jacqueline Jenkins (University Park: Pennsylvania State University Press, 2006), 294.

8. Biographer Lyndall Gordon notes, "During Eliot's last years at Harvard he made a study of the lives of saints and mystics, St. Teresa, Dame Julian of Norwich, Mme Guyon, Walter Hilton, St. John of the Cross, Jacob Böhme, and St. Bernard." *T. S. Eliot: An Imperfect Life* (New York: Norton, 1999), 89. "What we call the beginning is often the end / And to make an end is to

make a beginning. / The end is where we start from." Part 5 of "Little Gid-
ding," in *Four Quartets* (Orlando, FL: Houghton-Mifflin Harcourt, 1971), 58.

9. Watson and Jenkins, *A Revelation of Love*, 294.

10. It is an unfortunate assumption of much so-called kenotic theology of our times
to misunderstand the "self-emptying" of God, referred to by Paul in Philip-
pians, 2:6–11, as entailing some diminution on both sides—that is to say,
both on the side of God as self-emptying, and on the side of the creature into
which God self-empties. In the classical Christologies of the medieval period
no such "zero-sum" dualism is ever envisaged as would entail either any self-
diminution or any self-realization consequent upon the kenotic self-emptying
of the Godhead in Christ. Likewise for Julian, the divine in the human is
no less fully God than is the divine in the Trinitarian source of kenosis. See
Philip McCosker, in chapter 5 of his doctoral dissertation for the University
of Cambridge, "Parsing Paradox, Analysing 'And': Christological Configu-
rations of Theological Paradox in Some Mystical Theologies," 2008, for an
effective critique of the misuse of Paul's *kenosis* in much modern theology.

11. *LT*, 54:297; emphasis mine.

12. Watson and Jenkins, *A Revelation of Love*, 296.

13. Robert Lerner, *The Heresy of the Free Spirit in the Later Middle Ages* (South
Bend, IN: University of Notre Dame Press, 1991).

14. On the heresy of the Free Spirit, see also Malcolm Lambert's *Medieval Heresy: Popular Movements from the Gregorian Reform to the Reformation*, 3rd ed.
(Oxford: Wiley-Blackwell, 2002).

15. In 1306, the bishop of Cambrai condemned Marguerite Porete's book. She
was accused of continuing to circulate it after the condemnation, and was
executed after regent masters at the University of Paris confirmed that her
writings were heretical. She was burned at the stake in Paris on June 1, 1310.
See Marguerite Porete, *The Mirror of Simple Souls*, ed. and trans. Edmund
Colledge, J. C. Marler, and Judith Grant, Notre Dame Texts in Medieval
Culture 6 (South Bend, IN: University of Notre Dame Press, 1999).

16. Eckhart died sometime shortly after his trial before the papal commissioners
at Avignon. The papal commission upheld the ruling against Eckhart made
by the Archbishop Henry of Virneburg's commissioners in Cologne in 1326,

but modified the condemnation in the papal bull *In agro dominico* issued by Pope John XXII in 1329. *The Essential Sermons, Commentaries, Treatises and Defense*, trans. and ed. Edmund Colledge and Bernard McGinn (Mahwah, NJ: Paulist, 1981), 12.

17. Gerson thought Ruusbroec's teaching on the contemplative experience of union with God in *The Spiritual Espousals* was indebted to and indistinguishable from the heresy of the Free Spirit. *John Ruusbroec: The Spiritual Espousals and Other Works*, trans. James Wiseman (Mahwah, NJ: Paulist, 1985), 20–21.

18. Respected Paris theologian Godfrey of Fontaines defended Porete to no avail, as did the cleric Guiard de Cressonessart. *Mirror of Simple Souls*, 20–27. For the documents of the trial of Porete and de Cressonessart, see "Le procès d'inquisition contre Marguerite Porete et Guiard de Cressonessart (1309–1310)," ed. Paul Verdeyen, *Revue d'histoire ecclésiastique* 81 (1986): 47–94.

19. Throughout his inquisition, Eckhart maintained that he was not guilty because heresy is a matter of the will, and his will was to remain faithful to the Church. In his *Defense* against the accusations of heresy put to him in Cologne in 1326 he argued against the competence of his inquisitors and appealed to the papal court at Avignon. See *The Essential Sermons*, 11.

20. Denys van Rykel, or "Denys the Carthusian," drew on Ruusbroec's works in his own prolific body of writings and considered him a "second Dionysius the Areopagite." See *De contemplatione*, III.25, in *Opera omnia divi Dionysii Cartusiensis*, vol. 9, ed. M. Leone (Montreuil-sur-mer: Tournai-Parkminster, 1912). See also *John Ruusbroec: The Spiritual Espousals*, 33.

21. See Plato's *Phaedrus*, trans. R. Hackforth (Cambridge: Cambridge University Press, 1972).

22. See Plotinus's *Enneads*, trans. A. H. Armstrong (Cambridge, MA: Harvard University Press, Loeb Classical Library, 1966), esp. 6.7.31, 6.7.33, 6.9.4.18.

23. Proclus, *Commentary on Plato's Parmenides*, trans. Glen R. Morrow and John M. Dillon (Princeton: Princeton University Press, 1992), book I, p. 65.

24. Pseudo-Denys, *Divine Names*, 709A–713B, in *The Complete Works of Pseudo-Dionysius*, trans. Colm Luibheid (New York: Paulist, 1987).

25. Aristotle, *Nicomachean Ethics, Books VIII and IX*, trans. Michael Palakuk (New York: Oxford University Press, 1998), IX.8.

26. Augustine, *Confessions*, trans. and ed. Henry Chadwick (New York: Oxford University Press, 2009), 7.17.

27. Bonaventure, *Bonaventure: "The Soul's Journey into God," "The Tree of Life," "The Life of St. Francis,"* trans. Ewert Cousins (New York: Paulist, 1978), 3.3, p. 82. "But since our mind itself is changeable, it can see such a truth shining forth unchangeably only by means of some light which shines in an absolutely unchangeable way; and it is impossible for this light to be a changeable creature."

28. The full text of the bull *In agro dominico* is to be found in *The Essential Sermons*, 77–81.

29. *The Essential Sermons*, sermon 48, "Ein Meister Sprichet," 198.

30. Watson and Jenkins, *A Revelation of Love*, 296.

31. *LT*, 54:297; my emphasis.

32. *The Darkness of God* (Cambridge: Cambridge University Press, 1995), 159–62.

33. Pseudo-Denys, *Mystical Theology*, ch. 9, p. 118, in *The Complete Works*.

34. But then, in my view, neither is Eckhart. That, however, is another story.

35. See Bernard McGinn, *The Mystical Thought of Meister Eckhart: The Man from Whom God Hid Nothing* (New York: Herder and Herder, 2001).

36. *LT*, 53:293–95.

37. *Confessions*, 1.1.

38. Ibid., 10.27.

39. This Augustinian teaching passes into medieval theology in the West in a variety of forms, one of which, as Bernard McGinn has reminded me, is the doctrine of *synderesis*, the doctrine that the Fall notwithstanding, there remains unextinguished within human nature the capacity to judge of good and evil at least at a level of general propositions. As one might say, a person who cannot see the difference in point of morality, but only in the quality of the entertainment, between kicking a paper bag down the street and kicking a human being on the sidewalk is, as we would say, a psychopath because, lacking all capacity to discriminate between moral and nonmoral considerations, he or she cannot even begin to engage in moral discourse. That capacity the medievals called synderesis, which, short of psychopathic illness (as we would say) a person cannot lack.

40. *LT,* 53:295.

41. Ibid., 37:237.

42. David Aers, *Salvation and Sin: Augustine, Langland and Fourteenth Century Theology* (Notre Dame, IN: University of Notre Dame Press, 2009), 164.

43. Calvin doesn't say that I am fallen inasmuch as I am created ex nihilo, *Institutes* II.VI, p. 292: "The whole human race having been undone in the person of Adam, the excellence and dignity of our origin, as already described, is so far from availing us, that it rather turns to our greater disgrace, until God, who does not acknowledge man when defiled and corrupted by sin as his own work, appear as a Redeemer in the person of his only begotten son." *Institutes of the Christian Religion,* trans. Henry Beveridge (Grand Rapids, MI: Eerdmanns, 1989).

44. Erinn Staley, graduate student in the Department of Religious Studies at Yale, reminds me of the common analogy for Calvin's doctrine, which may be better than mine: a glass of water infused with a drop of ink retains all the properties of water even if it is tinctured with black "as a whole." Just so Julian.

45. *LT,* 57:303; my emphasis.

46. Watson and Jenkins's translation, *A Revelation of Love,* 324.

47. *LT,* 64:325.

48. Ibid., 19:189.

49. See Grace Jantzen, *Julian of Norwich: Mystic and Theologian* (Mahwah, NJ: Paulist, 2000), esp. "Part Three: Julian's Theology of Integration," 89–166. Also F. C. Bauerschmidt, *Julian of Norwich and the Mystical Body Politic of Christ* (South Bend, IN: University of Notre Dame Press, 2008).

50. *LT,* 58:309.

51. Ibid.

52. Denise Baker, *Julian of Norwich's Showings* (Princeton: Princeton University Press, 1994), 104.

53. Plato, *Republic,* trans. G. M. A. Grube (Indianapolis: Hackett, 1992), I, 351c–352a.

54. *LT,* 57:305.

55. Ibid., 56:301. I have taken this text from Glasscoe's edition (*Julian of Norwich: A Revelation of Love,* ed. Marion Glasscoe [Exeter: Exeter University Press,

2003]). Watson and Jenkins, *A Revelation of Love*, have: "As anemptis our substance: it may rightly be called our soule. And as anemptis our sensualite: it may rightly be called our soule, and that is by the oning it hath in God."

56. And it should be noted, not incidentally, that Augustine's narrative, that is to say, the *Confessions*, is no work of mere personal self-communing. It is a public text, written by a bishop for his own community of Christians, perhaps by way of an apologia for his life—his credentials for episcopal office perhaps being in some doubt among those who had known only his dubious reputation in his pre-Italian, North African days and knew nothing of his conversion in Milan. There is a sense, then, that Augustine addressed his *Confessions* to his "evencristen," just as Julian addressed *A Revelation* to the wider Church of her own times.

57. Augustine, *De Trinitate* (*On the Trinity*), trans. Stephen McKenna, ed. Gareth Matthews (Cambridge: Cambridge University Press, 2002), XIV.4.

58. *Confessions*, 10.27.

59. Baker, *Julian of Norwich's Showings*, 108.

60. See Ludwig Wittgenstein, *Tractatus logico-philosophicus*, trans. David Pears and Brian McGuinness (New York: Routledge, 2001), 89.

61. *Cloud of Unknowing*, ed. James Walsh (New York: Paulist, 1981), ch. 68, p. 251.

62. Ibid., chs. 51–53, pp. 218–23.

63. Ibid., ch. 68, p. 251.

64. *LT*, 5:139.

65. Ibid., 24:201.

66. Ibid., 5:139–40.

67. Ibid., 56:301.

68. Augustine, *De Trinitate*, X.2.

69. *LT*, 56:301.

70. Ibid.

71. Ibid., 54:297.

72. Ibid., 51:275.

Conclusion

1. Plato, *Republic*, trans. G. M. A. Grube (Indianapolis: Hackett, 1992), VII, 514a–17e.

2. T. S. Eliot, *Murder in the Cathedral* (London: Faber and Faber, 1935), act 1.

3. *LT*, 2:125.

4. Ibid., 2:127–29.

5. Ibid., 1:123; my emphasis.

6. Ibid., 3:131–33.

7. Ibid., 4:135.

8. Philip McCosker, formerly a PhD student at the University of Cambridge, now deputy master at St. Benet's Hall, Oxford.

9. *LT*, 7:211.

10. Ibid., 59:309.

11. Thomas Aquinas, *Summa theologiae*, 1a q44 a4 ad1.

12. *LT*, 22:195.

13. Ibid., 22:197.

14. Anselm of Canterbury, *Cur Deus homo?* in *Anselm of Canterbury: The Major Works*, ed. Brian Davies and G. R. Evans (Oxford: Oxford University Press, 1998).

15. Or even if from time to time Julian does use words derived from an "economic" vocabulary—for example, her ME "aseeth" ("reparation" in modern English)—this "reparation" is still no quid pro quo: "for this aseeth-making is more plesing to the blessed godhed . . . without comparison, than ever was the sinne of Adam harmfulle." *LT*, 29:215.

16. Ibid., 22:195.

17. Ibid.

18. William of St. Thierry, *The Golden Epistle* (Kalamazoo, MI: Cistercian, 1976), 97–98.

19. *LT*, 55:299.

INDEX